T0066561

CHEF ON FIRE

CHEF ON FIRE

*The Five Techniques
for Using Heat
Like a Pro*

~

JOSEPH CAREY

TAYLOR TRADE PUBLISHING
Lanham • New York • Boulder • Toronto • Oxford

Published by Taylor Trade Publishing
An imprint of The Rowman & Littlefield Publishing Group, Inc.
4501 Forbes Boulevard, Suite 200
Lanham, Maryland 20706

Distributed by National Book Network

Library of Congress Cataloging-in-Publication Data

Carey, Joseph, 1942-
    Chef on fire : the five techniques for using heat like a pro / Joseph Carey.—
1st Taylor trade publishing ed.
      p.   cm.
    ISBN-10: 1-58979-306-4 (cloth : alk. paper)
    ISBN-13: 978-1-58979-306-4
    1. Cookery. I. Title: Five techniques. II. Title.
TX714.C373154 2006
641.5—dc22   2005003421

Contents

vii
~

PART IV
The Fourth Technique
Braising—Cooking with Fat and Liquid Combined
251

PART V
The Fifth Technique
Extraction—Stocks, the Five Mother Sauces,
Additional and Derivative Sauces, and Soups
283

Acknowledgments

FIRST, I MUST thank the two gentlemen who put me on the path to understanding technique in the culinary arts. I have an old battered, taped copy of *Le Guide Culinaire* by Auguste Escoffier that has traveled with me as a valuable companion for about 35 years. The book is an amazing compilation of over 500 recipes sorted, more or less, by technique. He was very organized.

Kenneth Wolfe was in charge of the culinary arts department at Contra Costa Community College when I met him. In 1976 he published a book called *Cooking for the Professional Chef.* This book, too, is organized by technique. Ken Wolfe is the person who recommended that I teach evening classes as well as my professional classes during the day. He was absolutely right. I have learned much from my evening students about what serious home cooks want to know. I have tried to put that knowledge in this book. He also taught me the "Turkey Trick" I feature in "The Three-Hour Thanksgiving." The highest compliment I can pay to Chef Wolfe is the fact that I hired every single graduate of his who made an appearance at the door of the kitchens I ran in the San Francisco Bay area.

I religiously watched Julia Child when I was a young man. She is missed. I have a photo of Simone Beck and myself as we stood talking at a convention of The International Association of Cooking Professionals in Washington, D.C. She, too, is missed. Too many are gone too soon.

My professional students have given much back to me. I am very happy to have lived to see many of them achieve great success.

I have had many assistants over the years. I don't think I ever thanked any of them enough. I could not have done it without them. You all know who you are. Thank you.

Last, I'd like to thank all my evening students over the years who asked the question, "When are you going to write a damn book?!"

Here's the damn book.

Introduction

THE FIVE TECHNIQUES: AN OVERVIEW

I know of no more appropriate usage of the old saw "You can't see the forest for the trees" than in culinary arts. There are *so* many cookbooks—*so* many theories! This book is not in the least theoretical. I have no theories. All I have is nearly forty years of practical experience cooking food professionally and teaching culinary arts. My cooks and students—and myself—have cooked these recipes hundreds and often thousands of times. Guess what? They work every time. Why? Because we are never guessing. Even when we try a new dish we know the technique and the steps required to achieve the desired results. This book will not teach you creativity. Nor does it contain the latest trendy dishes. There are no tricks and no secrets. If you pay attention to the tenets at the beginning of the chapters, you will see in them all the basics you need to cook terrific food.

Chef on Fire is a cookbook, not just a recipe book. It guides you in learning what you need to know to cook like a professional chef. You will improve your culinary skills for familiar dishes and discover what went wrong when you have not achieved perfection. You will see how all cooking breaks down into five distinct, unwavering, predictable procedures that all good intuitive cooks know how to apply and that you can learn.

What if you could look at a recipe and instantly grasp which one of the five techniques will help you prepare the dish, the time needed, and the equipment required? What if, by recognizing the technique and having full confidence that you could execute it, you could frequently cut your cooking time by half or more because you know which steps in the dish are essential, which are unnecessary, and which can be prepared in advance? What if you could approach a new recipe you have never made before and make it with complete confidence for a dinner party that evening? After you prepare 10 or 12 recipes in this book using the five-technique method, you will be on your way to cooking better than you ever imagined. After 20 or 30, you'll be able to look at any recipe completely confident that you can instantly recognize which technique the recipe employs and unflinchingly execute it.

Every cook who is a culinary artist first becomes a master craftsman. *Chef on Fire* is organized to take you step by step through what you need to know to perfect your craft like the great chefs. Parts I through V define and illustrate the techniques with recipes, tips from professionals, and tricks of the trade: Cooking with Dry Heat, Boiling, Cooking with Fat, Cooking with Fat and Liquid Combined, and Extraction.

For example, what every professional chef knows is that there are only five things you can do to food with heat. What do *Boeuf a la Bourguinonne*, *Sauerbraten*, *Grillades*, *Swiss Steak*, *Coq au Vin*, *Braised Lamb Shanks*, and *Ossobucco* have in common? They are all made with the same technique. They are all braised dishes. Once you know how to make one of them, you can make them all. How about dishes as diverse as *Saltimbocca*, *Scampi*, *Shrimp Creole*, *Veal Marsala*, *Poulet Sauté*, *Stir-Fry*, and *Entrecote au Poivre*? They are all made with the same technique. They are all sautés. Within each of the five techniques, the rules *never* vary.

READ THE RECIPE, KNOW THE TECHNIQUE

Without doubt, the very first thing you want to do is identify which of the five techniques a recipe employs. How do you spot the technique? Check the preparation time in the instructions or *method*. Sautés and grilled items will have a very short cooking time. So will some poached items, which leads us to the second thing to check.

The cooking *medium*. Is it the oven? A pot? A pan? Is there fat involved? Water? Is there a piece of tough meat involved?

Third, look at the *ingredient* list. These will be your clue as to how many may be fed with a given recipe even where you have not been provided with a yield. For example, 3 quarts of liquid = 96 fluid ounces. If you have a soup recipe calling for 3 quarts of liquid, you will know immediately you have 12 8-ounce portions. You will also know that once the solid ingredients are added, you will probably have a little soup left for tomorrow's lunch.

Do you have access to all the ingredients? If you get down to Brown Stock in the middle of your ingredient list and you do not already have it on hand, you have just embarked on a minimum 6- to 8-hour hiatus in the middle of making your dish, for that's how long it will take you to make the brown stock.

So, look at method, medium, and ingredients. You're already on your way to being a better cook.

The First Technique: Cooking with Dry Heat

When chefs use dry heat to cook large pieces of meat or poultry or game, we call this *roasting*. As a general rule, the "roast" will contain more than one portion of food. One of the basic characteristics of the roast is cooking before portioning. A roast may be done in an oven, over an open fire or coals, or on a rotisserie, but whichever heat source is used, the roast will be *surrounded* by heat. No liquids are added, and the roast is never cooked in a closed container.

When we portion the food before we cook it and then cook it on a grill or broiler of some sort, we call this application of dry heat *grilling* or *broiling*. The two terms mean the same thing. The difference in usage is mostly regional. The same cuts of meat or poultry may be roasted or grilled.

If we cook vegetable substances with this dry technique, we call it *baking*. The difference between roasting and baking is dependent on the type of food being cooked. The one exception to this general rule is the fact that we may grill and roast vegetables as well. When we cook any *vegetable* substance in an oven, we are baking, although common parlance now has us "roasting" vegetables. I never argue with common parlance.

The Second Technique: Boiling

This technique involves no caramelization or *browning*. The food is either submerged or partially submerged in boiling or simmering liquid or surrounded by steam in a steamer. This technique is used with both individual portions and much larger pieces of food containing several portions.

The Third Technique: Cooking with Fat

Here we have only two terms: *frying* and *sautéing*. When we fry, we either partially, in the case of pan frying, or completely, with deep frying, submerge the food in hot fat. Once the food is cooked, we remove as much fat as possible from the outside of the food. *Sautéing* involves the use of a small quantity of high-quality fat, such as clarified butter or olive oil. The fat, almost invariably, is incorporated as part of the sauce in the finished dish.

The Fourth Technique: Braising—Cooking with Fat and Liquid Combined

In English, the terms we use are stewing, braising, and *pot roasting*. The French have many terms for this technique—*Estouffade* and *Étouffée*, for instance. This technique is characterized by first caramelizing the food in hot fat, adding a liquid to the pot, and cooking the food until it is done. For the most part, this technique is reserved for tougher pieces of food.

The Fifth Technique: Extraction

The four techniques I have already discussed share a common goal: they are intended to keep the maximum amount of flavor and nutrition in the solid food. The last of the five techniques performs an entirely different job. We are making liquid food here. Stocks, soups, and sauces fall within this method.

Are you ready to be the best cook you can possibly be? By giving you not just another book for your shelf of recipe books but rather a step-by-step introduction to the five techniques, I am freeing you from being a slave to recipes. It will not take you very long to run through these techniques. And when you come out the other side, I think you will be astounded at how things come together for you in the kitchen. Let's cook!

WHY TECHNIQUES, NOT RECIPES?

No matter how creative you happen to be, your creativity will be wasted if you can't predict precisely what is going to happen every time you go into the kitchen. There is, in fact, very little creativity involved in learning how to cook food to obtain maximum flavor, nutrition, and eye appeal, but there is a very definite series of steps that need to be followed to have success. Your creativity will blossom as never before once you master the five techniques.

The drawback to the traditional manner of cookbook structure is that it tends to overshadow the similarity of technique involved in all aspects of preparing a meal. While that book might be a great *recipe* book, it is not a *cook* book. To cook *any* dish, you merely have to understand and apply the five techniques.

Chefs have historically looked at cooking from a slightly different perspective from the home cook. No chef collects recipes; there is no need because there are no "secrets" in recipes. A chef knows he can look at any recipe, immediately recognize the technique, and prepare the dish. Chefs think in terms of "dishes," not recipes. The word "recipe" has a certain rote-learning feel to it. "Dish" implies an aura. As a general rule, all we are looking for in a recipe is how many people it will feed and what ingredients we will need. The method with which we apply heat—the technique—is instantly recognizable. You will soon be cooking from this perspective.

Know these five things and know them well, and there is nothing you cannot cook. You will learn the techniques in a logical order of difficulty and, in all likelihood, the order in which they developed organically over the centuries.

Note to the Reader

ALTHOUGH MOST of these recipes were conceived and tested in the restaurant—and bakery—setting, they have been tested hundreds of times for the smaller serving numbers appropriate to the home cook. In doing so, I have converted the typical restaurant and bakery measurements—pounds and ounces—into measuring equivalents you are likely to have in your kitchen, such as tablespoons and cups.

There are a few exceptions to this, however, mostly notably measurements for flour. Good baking requires exact measurements of flour, and this is notoriously difficult to achieve with measuring cups because different amounts of flour can fit in a cup depending on how densely it is packed. And *everybody* packs a cup differently.

The best way to measure flour is by weight. A small kitchen scale is an invaluable tool for the serious home cook: it's inexpensive, handy, and easy to use. With this in mind, I have kept the flour in ounces in this book in the recipes for baked goods to help you achieve the very best results. Likewise yeast is presented in ounces: ¼ ounce of yeast is equal to 2¼ teaspoon—the amount of yeast in most commercial yeast packages. Water measurements are given in liquid ounces, as most home cooks have liquid measuring cups that clearly show ounces. Again, this is the best measurement to use for accuracy.

Now that I've said all that, bear in mind that the weight of flour will vary according to moisture content. So this is my last caveat: look always for texture in a bread. Unless you are making the same recipe in the same environment over and over again under the same climactic conditions, the amount of flour relative to liquid will change.

A Note about Ingredients

Good ingredients are the cornerstone of good cooking. I've used a shorthand for some of the ingredients listed in the recipes, listing, for example, "black pepper" when I really mean "black pepper, freshly ground." Here are a list of key ingredients and what I really mean when I list them:

black pepper black pepper, freshly ground

butter unsalted, always

dry yeast active dry yeast

eggs whole eggs unless other indicated

flour unbleached, all-purpose white flour unless otherwise indicated

herbs assume dried herbs unless "fresh" is specified

milk whole milk unless otherwise indicated

minced onion refers to very finely chopped onion, not the dried onion flakes sold in the spice section

minced parsley refers to fresh parsley, not the dried herb

parmesan parmesan cheese (Parmigiano-Reggiano if possible), freshly grated

spices freshly ground from whole spices whenever possible

sugar plain white granulated sugar

PART I

The First Technique
Cooking with Dry Heat— Roasting, Grilling, and Baking

❶ Roasting
The Rules of the Roast
Barbecuing or "Slow Roasting"
Roasting Poultry
Roasting Vegetables

❷ Grilling
The Canon of the Grill
The Steak
Grilling Poultry
Grilling Fish and Shellfish
Grilling Vegetables
Grilling Bread

❸ Baking
Seafood
Meats and Poultry
Cheeses, Eggs, Vegetables, and Starches
Breads

F OR NOW, remember this: this technique is reserved, as are sautéing and frying, for foods that are *naturally tender*. Either the cooking time is not long enough or the heat is not high enough to permit penetration far enough into the food to tenderize tougher connective tissues. You will notice as we go along that the same foods are appropriate for roasting, grilling, and sautéing, only tender pieces of food. On a steer, for instance, these would be the "middle" meats, from the *rib* and *loin*. The tougher portions, again using the example of the steer, the *round* and *chuck*, are suitable for braising or boiling. These four sections of a steer are called primal cuts. Smaller divisions from each are called subprimals.

Unquestionably, the first cooking technique known to man was roasting. It requires no cooking equipment. I seriously doubt we came up with this idea of cooked food intentionally. A man or woman stumbled one day over a mammoth or caribou that had been caught in a forest fire or some natural conflagration. Or maybe someone dropped a bloody haunch in the fire and couldn't retrieve it immediately. I think the guy or gal was hungry and said, "Hey, this is not the raw meat I know and love, but I am starving to death, so I'll risk it." Thus, history was made. Next thing you know, we had convection ovens and expensive pots and pans. Well, maybe not the next thing. But, at the very least, we went back to the cave and put a piece of meat in the fire.

Over the centuries, we have developed a palate for caramelized meats and poultry and nearly always prefer browned meats to boiled meats. We use three words to describe what we do with this technique—roasting, baking, and grilling (or broiling). Originally, the term "roasting" was reserved *exclusively* for meats, poultry, and game. When we apply dry heat in an oven or on a spit to meat or poultry, we call it roasting. We roast meat. We roast poultry. What is the difference between roasting and baking? When we apply dry heat to vegetable or grain substances in an oven or when we combine sauces and/or vegetable substances with meat, seafood, or poultry, we call it baking. We bake breads. We bake casseroles. In today's modern culinary terminology, we also "roast" vegetables and starches. What is the difference? It seems to me that when vegetables or starches are peeled or processed in some way and then cooked over a fire or in an oven with dry heat, we are now calling this "roasting." If we leave the peel, for instance, on an Idaho potato and cook it in an oven, it is a "baked" potato. Peel that same potato and cook it in that same oven, and it becomes a "roasted" potato.

When we place food—any food—on an open grid and cook it over coals, wood, gas, or electricity, we call it grilling or broiling. Those are the three dry-heat applications that make up this technique.

If you wish to have consistent success roasting, there are certain "rules" that apply invariably. There is no guesswork involved.

Roasting

THE RULES OF THE ROAST

1. Forget the timetables you have seen for pork, beef, or poultry in nearly every home cookbook ever written. They don't work. They are meant to be very loose guidelines. In a few pages, I'll show you what I mean.

2. The roasting time for anything will depend on these four factors:

    a. The density of the food

    b. The size of the food

    c. The shape and configuration of the food

    d. The temperature of the heat source

3. As with grilling, if you wish to caramelize the outside of the meat, dry it thoroughly.

4. Use a lower temperature for large roasts and a higher temperature for smaller ones.

5. Season the roast, after drying, while still raw.

6. Always allow a time for the *retained heat* to continue cooking the roast after it is removed from the heat source. A large roast will retain heat for a much

3

longer period than a small one. This period of time allows the juices in the roast to redistribute evenly.

7. Don't use too large or too deep a roasting pan. If the pan is much wider than the roast, whatever juices are expelled in the bottom of the pan will burn and consequently prove useless in any *deglazing* sauce you may wish to make. If your pan is too tall, it will tend to hold a certain amount of the water you are attempting to drive off; it will hinder caramelization and partially "steam" the roast. You will achieve the unattractive grayish coloration instead of a nicely browned roast.

8. Buy an oven thermometer. Unless you have had your oven professionally calibrated in the past few months, you are probably not roasting at the temperature you think you are. Roasting mistakes for which you have been blaming yourself may be attributable to a miscreant oven.

9. Buy and use a meat thermometer.

What You Need to Know

If you attempt to carve a roast as soon as it is removed from the oven, you will notice its juices will literally spurt from the roast and onto your board, counter, plate, or platter. This will provide you with a quantity of lovely juice and a nice dry roast. You will also notice the roast will appear more well done toward the outside and less well done toward the middle. If, on the other hand, you permit the roast to "rest" for a time, you will notice the juices will have retreated into the tissues, redistributed themselves, and produced a more uniform degree of doneness throughout. It will be more succulent and tasty.

ROASTING MEAT

Beef roasts are by far the most common roasts in this country. The beef carcass is broken into four "primal" cuts—the chuck, the rib, the loin, and the round. The best roasts come from what we call the "middle meats"—the rib and loin. These are the muscles the animal uses most infrequently. The more the muscle is exercised, the tougher it becomes. The chuck (shoulder) and round (rump) of the steer—the muscles of locomotion—are the toughest.

The following three beef roast techniques are from the middle meats. You may also roast the beef brisket and portions of the chuck and round.

Roast Ribs of Beef

You probably know this as "prime rib." Most likely, it ain't—"prime," that is. *Prime* is a *grade* designation and has nothing to do with the name of a cut of

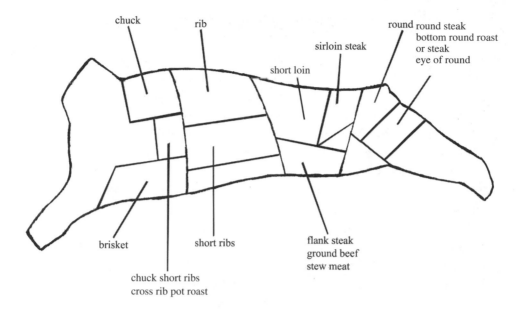

beef. The three top grades of beef in the United States, in descending order of quality, are *Prime*, *Choice*, and *Select*. These are the only three grades commonly available in the marketplace. Since only about 6 percent of the beef graded in this country is Prime, I really don't think there is quite enough to go around for all the restaurants serving prime rib. Choice is an excellent cut, though.

Remember one of the general roasting guidelines; always dry the meat completely before placing it in the oven. You may use a rib with the bones still in place, or you may use a boneless one. The ribs with the bones will actually roast a little faster since the bones transmit heat better than the flesh.

A trimmed 8- to 9-pound roast with the bones will serve about 6 people (1½ pounds per person). For a boneless roast, allow 10 to 12 ounces per person.

Method

1. Preheat oven to 450°.
2. Dry roast completely.
3. Salt and pepper roast.
4. If you are roasting a standing rib with the bones, place the roast in the roasting pan with the bones down. For a boneless roast, place the fattier side up so that the roast will baste itself.
5. Roast 25 to 30 minutes at 450°.
6. Reduce heat to 350° and continue to roast until an internal temperature of 135° is attained.
7. Allow the roast to rest for at least 15 to 20 minutes before carving so that the juices recirculate.

What You Need to Know

You'll notice I didn't indicate a "per-pound" roasting schedule. The roasting time will vary considerably, not only with the weight of the roast but also in its geometric shape. A very small (3–4 pounds) roast may roast in as little 1½ hours, but a large one (8–10 pounds) may take as long as 2¼ hours.

These per-pound schedules can be quite misleading. Let's say you are roasting the boneless rib eye roll that weighs 3 to 4 pounds. Roasting this cut of beef to medium rare—all our beef cooking times are to medium rare—will take you between 1½ and 1¾ hours. If you follow per-pound timetables, you would then double this for an 8-pound roast. No, don't do it. Not unless you are trying to take an excellent cut of meat and turn it into beef jerky.

Here the importance of geometric shape enters the picture. Whatever the weight, the rib eye maintains the same basic shape and configuration. In effect, the only change you are making when you move from the smaller to the larger is the length of the roast. The heat does not penetrate only from the ends of the roast; consequently, the length is of much less importance than the shape. In essence, the only reason the larger roast will take longer to roast is that the sheer bulk requires a little longer to warm. The larger roast will not take 3 to 3½ hours as the timetables would suggest. I would be very surprised if it took longer than 2 hours.

Although 145° is the temperature of a medium-rare beef roast, you will notice we removed the roast from the oven at 135°. The roast will continue to cook after you remove it from the oven. Should you remove it at the "right" temperature for medium rare, the roast will continue to cook, and your roast will be medium.

Roast Tenderloin of Beef

(Filet de Boeuf Roti)

Chock full of superlatives, this roast is, by far, the quickest, the simplest, and the most expensive. Lying along either side of the spine, these are the muscles the steer uses least. And that is the main determinant of tenderness.

You will be likely to find the "peeled" tenderloin we mentioned at your local meat counter. If not, the butcher will be happy to trim it for you. The average peeled tenderloin will weigh in at about 5 pounds and should sate about 10 carnivores. Thoroughly dry the meat and salt and pepper it. In Europe, traditionally, this piece of meat has been "larded." This procedure is not necessary with the quality of marbled beef we have available in the United States. All the tenderloins graded "Choice" or better will be amply marbled.

You may roast the tenderloin either on a rack or, as we prefer, on a bed of mirepoix (diced carrots, onions, and celery). Whatever method you choose, elevate the roast. The roast will cook more evenly, and you lessen the likelihood of burning the bottom.

Roast in a 475° oven for approximately 35 minutes for a 3- to 4-pound roast and 50 to 60 minutes for a whole tenderloin of approximately 5 pounds. If you wish this roast to be rare, remove it when a thermometer plunged into the center of the thickest part of the roast reads 130°. The tenderloin may be served with any of the derivative brown sauces or, as I like it, with a variation on the Raspberry/Zinfandel Sauce (page 38). For a starch, try the Gratin Jurassein (page 80) or the Pommes de Terre Parisiennes (page 217) or just plain Pommes Frites (page 248).

Contre Filet Roti

I use the French name for this roast because I find it much more descriptive of this particular piece of meat than any English expression for this piece of meat, and there are several. The word *Contre* means "against" in French, and this roast lies against the tenderloin ("filet"), separated only by a thin bone. Perhaps the following will give you a better visual image of both the tenderloin and the Contre filet. The best English phrase for this cut would be "boneless strip sirloin." "New York strip" would be perfectly acceptable.

When you have purchased a T-bone or porterhouse steak, you have bought a cross-sectional segment of both the tenderloin and the strip sirloin, separated by a featherbone. The larger piece of meat is the strip sirloin, and the smaller piece, on the other side of the bone, is the tenderloin. The porterhouse has a

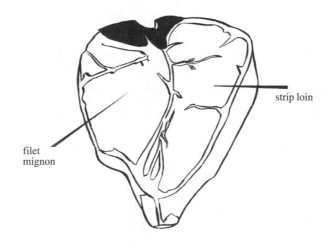

strip loin

filet
mignon

larger portion of tenderloin, the T-bone a smaller one. The T-bone will be a few cents per pound less expensive.

The Contre filet is my favorite beef roast. Although it may not be quite as tender as the filet, it has more flavor and is, in fact, much more tender roasted than grilled. When it is cut into individual portions, without the bone, and grilled, we know it as the "New York steak" or "Kansas City steak." Oddly enough, we decided to keep the French expression for the tenderloin when it is cut into individual portions and grilled—"*filet mignon.*" *Mignon* in French means "delicate" or "dainty." Thoroughly dry the Contre filet. You will probably be able to obtain a roast weighing between 8 and 10 pounds fairly handily. To achieve the internal 135° for medium rare, you will need to roast this cut for approximately 1 hour at 450°. Begin checking the temperature around 45 minutes into the roasting time.

Again, you may place the roast on a bed of mirepoix or a rack. With the Contre filet, try the béarnaise sauce (page 297), any of the potato dishes, and a sautéed green vegetable.

BARBECUING OR "SLOW ROASTING"

I've included this section in this chapter to get the notion out of your head that "barbecuing" is grilling because many Americans mean "grilling" when they say "barbecuing." Although the word "barbecue" has different meanings in different parts of the country, when you make barbecue, you are roasting. In a nutshell, barbecuing is smoky, slow roasting. The word definitely evolved from the wooden racks observed in the Caribbean. But that fact does not go far toward defining the meaning today. The two distinctly different meanings of the word appear to be largely regional, though all parts of the country recognize the only meaning in the border and southern states: meat, usually pork, sometimes beef or game, roasted slowly by either direct or indirect heat and served with a barbecue sauce.

Men, it seems, are particularly taken with this phenomenon called "barbecuing." Perhaps it's the rusticity of the event. This method of cooking is thought to be "manly." Maybe it's the vestigial Neanderthal or frontiersman in each of us. Maybe it's the stirring of genetic memory, the return from the successful hunt, the huddling around the fire discussing the hunt. American men do like to barbecue.

If you really want to get into barbecuing, or smoking, you will need to acquire a smoker. The type I have found works best has an offset firebox, and the main chamber is suitable for grilling, too. Although there are several other options, this is the one I have come to prefer over the years. Should you really want to pursue this, my good friend Denis Kelly has written a book called

Grilling and Barbecuing: Food and Fire in American Regional Cooking. I highly recommend it.

In Texas they "barbecue" whole steers. In Tennessee they "barbecue" pork shoulders and ribs. Since nearly all of us hearing the word "barbecued" expect it to be followed by the word "ribs," I think it wholly appropriate to barbecue some ribs. The best ribs are usually "marinated" for some hours before cooking in what is called a *dry rub*. Here is ours. I think you will find it merely exquisite!

Dry Rub

A dry rub is an integral part of barbecuing. This is one of several I utilize. I am including it here since I think it the best all-purpose rub.

INGREDIENTS

¼ c. cayenne pepper
¼ c. chili powder
¼ c. paprika
¼ c. black pepper, finely ground
¼ c. garlic powder
2 tbsp. cumin
1 tbsp. dry mustard
3 tbsp. celery salt

Barbecue Sauce

There are food writers out there who would have us believe the word "barbe-cue" comes to us from the French *barbe a queue*, which translates as "beard to tail." Far-fetched, I think. Several 18th- and 19th-century New World travel-ers and writers mentioned "barbacoa" or "borbecus," raised wooden frameworks used as beds or for smoking meats. This linguistic ancestry seems much more likely, given the "racks" or grids on which we "barbecue."

INGREDIENTS

2 c. minced yellow onions
12 finely minced cloves garlic
2 tbsp. finely minced fresh ginger
½ c. peanut oil
1 tbsp. cayenne pepper
4 tbsp. chili powder
6 c. catsup
3 tbsp. dry mustard
2 c. dry red wine
1 c. apple cider vinegar
1 c. apple juice
1 c. brown sugar
5 tbsp. paprika
½ c. soy sauce
Tabasco, to taste
1 tsp. black pepper

Method

1. Sweat onions, garlic, and ginger in the peanut oil in a sauce pan over medium heat until just soft.

2. Raise heat, add chile powder, and sauté about 60 seconds.
3. Dissolve dry mustard in 1 cup of the red wine.
4. Add all remaining ingredients to pan and thoroughly incorporate.
5. Bring to a boil, reduce to a simmer. Simmer about 15 minutes.

Note: For a marinade or a "basting" sauce, dilute 1 cup of the barbecue sauce with 3 cups of water. For chicken or fish, add ½ cup of lemon juice to the barbecue sauce.

Barbecued Baby Back Ribs

Item number 422 in the *National Association of Meat Purveyor's Meat Buyer's Guide* is "Pork Loin, Back Ribs." This is defined as "at least 8 ribs and related intercostal meat from a loin." If there can be said to be a "secret" to cooking pork ribs, that secret is this cut of pork. These are the "meaty" ribs that win barbecue contests, not spareribs. Ask your butcher for the "baby back ribs." The only other secrets are the slow cooking period, the sauce, and the rub. If you enjoy the flavor of various woods, add chips that have been soaked in cold water to your coals throughout the cooking process. Apple, pecan, mesquite, and hickory are popular choices.

Yield: This should satisfy 6 to 8 hungry folks.

INGREDIENTS
3 or 4 "slabs" pork loin, back ribs
dry rub (page 9)

Method

1. Prepare the coals from hardwood or hardwood briquettes. To properly cook the ribs, you will need an enclosed cooker of some kind. They may be done in a kettle-style grill or a smoker. The best ribs I ever had were cooked in one of these.
2. Whatever type of smoker you employ, you will not want to place the ribs directly over the charcoal. Set them off to the side. The idea is to create a draft so that the natural convection will pull the heat and smoke over the ribs.
3. Maintain a constant temperature of about 200° to 225°. Invest in an oven thermometer and keep it in the cooker. The ribs will take about 4 to 5 hours to cook at this temperature. Obviously, you will need to add coals periodically. You may add some soaked wood chips to the coals if you like. Hickory and apple are two popular choices.
4. Several options are now available to you, depending on your taste. You may choose to place the ribs directly over the coals at the end of the cooking period for a few minutes to "crisp" them. Mix 3 parts of water to 1 part of

sauce and use this mixture to baste the ribs occasionally, after the first 2 hours of cooking. Or you could baste the ribs with the undiluted sauce for the last 5 to 10 minutes of cooking.

I like to serve the ribs with one of the potato salads (pages 174–177), coleslaw (page 175), and onion rolls (page 98).

Both the beef brisket and the pork shoulder also make excellent barbecue and will barbecue in about the same time as the ribs. I use the same rub and sauce with chicken, too.

What You Need to Know

The ribs will have a thin membrane covering the back of them. If you can't see it, turn them over as you're looking at the front. Take a paring knife and slide it under the membrane so you can get a grip on it. Pull it off. Using a towel makes it easier to grasp. It doesn't taste bad and won't harm you, but removing it allows the dry rub and smoke to penetrate the ribs more completely. Rub the dry rub all over the ribs, front and back. Be generous.

ROASTING POULTRY

Here is a favorite Chinese "barbecued" dish. After the duckling has been smoked, it is fried to crisp the skin.

Tea-Smoked Duck

My friend Chinese chef Bernard Chang featured this dish at every one of the several restaurants he had over the years I knew him. I confess I am addicted to this dish.

Yield: 6 to 8 appetizer portions

INGREDIENTS

2 ducks, Pekin
¼ c. salt
¼ c. peppercorns
2 tbsp. saltpeter (optional)
1 lb. wood chips
2 c. black tea leaves
2 each orange peel and lemon peel
10 c. peanut oil

Method

1. Thoroughly dry the ducks. Prepare the smoker.
2. Cook salt and peppercorns in a skillet over high heat for a minute or so. Cool.
3. Rub duck inside and out with salt and peppercorns. You may rest ducks in refrigerator overnight.
4. Soak wood chips in water. Place ducks on rack in smoker. Prick the skin of the ducks with a fork to aid in rendering the fat from the ducks.
5. Place wet tea leaves mixed with peels in a stainless container in the smoker between the coals and the ducks. You may also put some of the mixture directly on the coals for a stronger flavor.
6. Place some of the wood chips on the coals and close the smoker. Replenish occasionally.
7. Smoke ducks for 3 to 4 hours, turning occasionally.
8. Heat peanut oil to 350°. You may either fry the duck whole or cut it into about 8 pieces before you fry it. Drain and pat dry.

～ The Three-Hour Thanksgiving ～

Roast Turkey

This dish is the core of the "Three-Hour Thanksgiving." Turkey and chicken consist of two different kinds of meat. They require different cooking times. White meat, the muscles less involved in locomotion, cooks more quickly than dark meat. This is the reason the turkey breast is nearly always overcooked in most American homes on Thanksgiving. By separating the turkey into one large white-meat roast and two, smaller, dark-meat roasts, you equalize the cooking time for the roasts. Both the breast and the leg/thigh sections will be roasted to perfection. Remember that I told you we could cut your cooking time in half for many dishes? Remember when I told you the shape of the roast is what matters for roasting times?

Here is the one place in the book where I present an entire meal focused on one technique: dry-heat cookery. The following is for a large tom turkey.

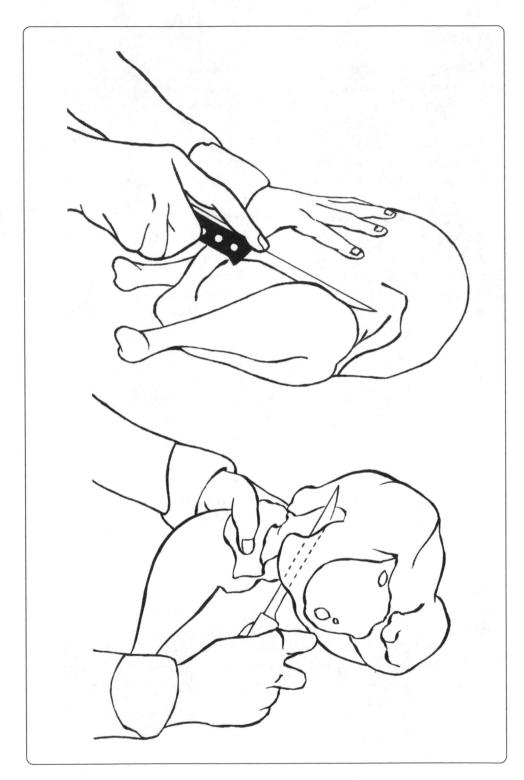

INGREDIENTS

1 turkey, 20–25 lb.
salt, to taste
pepper, to taste
4 tbsp. butter, softened

Method

1. Preheat oven to 450°.
2. Remove giblets and neck from turkey and set aside for stock.
3. Cut thighs and legs away from breast of turkey, leaving the legs and thighs attached to each other.
4. Stand turkey on its crop and cut along the last rib on either side of the turkey, all the way to the backbone. Snap the backbone down at this point and cut away from the turkey. Set aside for stock.
5. Salt and pepper turkey, front and back.
6. Loosen skin of breast and thighs and push small bits of the softened butter under the skin.
7. Tuck the wing tips up under the breast to enable it to stand evenly.
8. Place the "three roasts" on a rack in a roasting pan and place in the oven. After 30 minutes, reduce temperature to 350°.
9. Roast for 2 more hours.
10. Check breast temperature with a meat thermometer, near the center of the breasts but not touching the bone. When the temperature reads 170°, the breast is done.
11. Allow 20 to 25 minutes recirculation time before carving.

Note: You may reassemble the bird to a more traditional look by attaching the thigh/leg to the breast with bamboo skewers cut to a length of about 6 inches. First, place the bird on a bed of the dressing; next, place the rest of the dressing in the cavity, then attach the legs and thigh with the skewers.

Here are a few side dishes I usually associate with holiday cooking in the United States. Of course, there are regional differences as well. I am jumping ahead just a little here so that you may have the entire meal in one location, but both the cornbread and the dressing are cooked with the dry-heat technique.

Cornbread

You will find this a little lighter than most cornbreads because of the egg whites folded in. So, if density of cornbread was off-putting to you, try this one.

Yield: This will feed 8 to 10 hungry folks and provide with enough cornbread for your dressing.

INGREDIENTS

3 c. cornmeal
1 tbsp. sugar
1 tsp. salt
½ c. butter, melted
1 c. boiling water
1 egg, separated
1 c. milk
1 c. flour
1½ tbsp. baking powder

Method

1. Thoroughly combine cornmeal, sugar, salt, and butter in a bowl.
2. Cover with the boiling water and allow the mixture to rest for half an hour or so.
3. Stir in egg yolks, milk, flour, and baking powder.
4. Beat egg whites until stiff and fold into mixture.
5. Bake in a 375° oven in a buttered pan approximately 8 by 12 inches for about 35 to 45 minutes.

Cornbread Dressing
(for Turkey or Chicken)

This very basic dressing is made in the South with cornbread. Stale white bread is the more common ingredient in the North. The bread in the dressing need not be "stale" at all. Remember, these dressings were originally devised as a palatable way to use stale breads.

Yield: 6 to 8 portions

> ### What You Need to Know
>
> When you look at a "batch" recipe, like the following dressings, and you wish to know the yield, look at the number of *cups* listed in the ingredients. This figure will give you the approximate number of 8-ounce portions. That's a large portion for most batch items. But hungry folks can eat that much. This is the reason that with many recipes you will see a range of portions, such as "6 to 8."

INGREDIENTS

½ c. butter
1 c. diced celery
1 c. diced onion
1 turkey giblet, chopped
1 tsp. minced garlic
1 tbsp. whole thyme
1 tsp. powdered bay leaves
½ c. minced parsley
4 c. cornbread (page 16)
salt, to taste
black pepper, to taste
½ c. turkey or chicken stock
2 eggs, lightly beaten

Method

1. Melt butter in a pan large enough to hold all ingredients and sweat celery and onion until just tender.
2. Add giblets and cook through.
3. Add garlic, thyme, bay leaves, and parsley to pan and cook until garlic softens.
4. Add cornbread to pan and thoroughly mix all ingredients.
5. Add salt, pepper, and stock. Combine completely.
6. Remove from heat and add eggs. Combine thoroughly.
7. Cool before stuffing bird—unless you plan to put the bird in the oven immediately.

What You Need to Know

You may add cooked sausage, any kind of nuts, mushrooms, shrimp, or oysters to this dressing if you like. Approximately 1 cup of any of them would be about right. I always bake the dressing separate from the bird. Bake in a 375° oven for about 30 to 45 minutes or until the dressing reaches an internal temperature of about 170°.

Oyster Dressing

Here is another option for your dressing. This is my all-purpose oyster dressing. You may serve it as a side dish with sautéed or fried seafood, or you may stuff game or fowl with it.

Yield: 6 to 8 portions

INGREDIENTS

½ c. butter
2 finely chopped yellow onions
1 c. finely chopped celery
1 c. thinly sliced green onions
1½ tbsp. minced garlic
4 dozen oysters, roughly chopped (reserve oyster liquor to be
    added later)
½ c. finely chopped parsley
black pepper, to taste
¾ c. grated peccorino, romano, or parmesan
3 c. garlic croutons
1½ c. oyster liquor
¾ c. chopped pecans

Method

1. Melt the butter over medium heat.
2. Sauté the onions, celery, green onions, and garlic until translucent, stirring frequently.
3. Gradually add the chopped oysters. Cook about 4 minutes, constantly stirring. Add the parsley; stir.

4. Lower the heat and simmer for 5 minutes. Add the cheese and pepper; stir.
5. Remove from the heat and begin stirring in the croutons a little at a time.
6. Add the pecans and oyster liquor and stir.
7. To serve as a stand-alone casserole, bake in a buttered casserole dish in a 350° oven for about 20 minutes.

What You Need to Know

Garlic croutons: Take a loaf of aging French bread and trim off the crust. Cut the bread into ¾-inch cubes. Heat ¼ cup of extra virgin olive oil in a sauté pan. Add 2 tablespoons of minced garlic. When the first bits of garlic begin to turn brown, pour the oil through a sieve and remove the solid pieces of garlic. Cool the oil slightly. Toss the croutons in a bowl with the oil and salt and pepper to taste. Spread the croutons on a sheet pan and bake in a 450° oven for 10 minutes. Use these in salads, soups, and dressings. Hide them. They will magically evaporate otherwise.

Haricot Verts

Here I have illustrated the essentials of the "harder vegetable technique." Complete details will be found on page 184. The "true" French *haricot verts* are small green beans related to the Blue Lake bean. They are greener and rounder than the Kentucky Wonder type. If you are able to find these beans, great; if not, the two I mention here will be just dandy.

Yield: 8 to 10 portions

INGREDIENTS

3 lb. green beans, Blue Lake or Kentucky Wonder
2 gal. boiling water
2 tbsp. salt
4 tbsp. butter
salt, to taste
black pepper, to taste

Method

1. Tip and, if necessary, string the beans. Cut into diagonal pieces about 1 inch long.
2. Place beans in boiling, salted water, and simmer until just tender—not soft—about 5 to 6 minutes.
3. Drain beans and shock under cold running water.
4. Dry beans.
5. Melt butter in a pan large enough to hold all the beans.
6. Place beans in pan with butter; toss and heat through.
7. Add salt and pepper.
8. Serve immediately or hold in a warm place until service.

You may add a little minced garlic or any fresh herb you like to the pan near the end of the cooking. Toasted almonds or diced fresh tomatoes are an excellent addition as well.

Turkey Giblet Gravy

Take a minute and go look at the velouté on page 291. You will discover that the "gravy" you are making here is actually a turkey velouté, one of the five mother sauces. Also, although I call this "giblet" gravy, you might actually use the giblets in the dressing and omit them entirely from the gravy.

What You Need to Know

What is the difference between a *sauce* and a *gravy*? A gravy is a sauce, but a sauce isn't necessarily a gravy. To be called a gravy, a sauce must be made with pan juices as an ingredient.

Yield: A little over 1 quart

INGREDIENTS
1 oz. turkey "drippings"
2 tbsp. butter
¼ c. minced onion
3 oz. flour
salt, to taste
black pepper, to taste
5 c. hot turkey stock
cooked turkey giblets, chopped

Method

1. Remove turkey from roasting pan and keep warm while you make the gravy.
2. Place drippings and butter in a sauce pan over medium heat.
3. Add minced onion and sweat until soft.
4. Add flour, incorporate thoroughly with the fats, and cook until the flour has a "cooked" aroma. Do not color.
5. Add hot stock and incorporate completely with a wire whip. Should the sauce be too thick, add a little more stock until the desired consistency is obtained.
6. Add giblets, warm through, and check the seasoning.

Turkey Stock

This is the basic white (chicken) stock (page 286) but with turkey as the key ingredient.

Yield: 1 gallon

INGREDIENTS

back and giblets from a turkey
4 carrots, washed and roughly chopped
4 ribs celery, washed and roughly chopped
1 onion, roughly chopped
2 garlic cloves, smashed
3 bay leaves
1 tsp. whole thyme
1 parsley sprig
6–8 whole peppercorns
1 gal. cold water

Method

1. Place all ingredients in a stockpot and bring to a boil.
2. Reduce to a simmer and cook, covered, for 2 hours. Skim occasionally.
3. Strain through a fine sieve and skim all visible fat from surface.
4. Use immediately or freeze or refrigerate.

Whole-Berry Cranberry Sauce

This sauce bears no resemblance to the jelly-like aspic that is rigid and has ridges in it. This is truly a "sauce."

Yield: About 4 cups

INGREDIENTS

1¼ c. water
1½ c. sugar
12 oz. fresh cranberries
1 orange orange zest
1 oz. orange liqueur

Method

1. Place water and sugar in a saucepan and boil for about 5 minutes.
2. Add cranberries and simmer for 5 minutes.
3. Skim top of sauce and add orange zest and liqueur. Chill for at least 2 hours.

Pie Crust

Here is a good pie crust that may be quickly prepared in a food processor.

INGREDIENTS

2½ c. flour
1 tbsp. sugar
2 c. butter, *very* cold, cut into pea-sized pieces
¼ c . shortening, cold, cut into pea-sized pieces
1 tsp. lemon juice or cider vinegar
about 3 oz. ice water

Method

1. Place the flour, sugar, and salt in the processor and pulse just enough to mix.
2. Add butter and shortening and pulse until you have a coarse texture, which should take only a few seconds.

3. Add lemon juice or vinegar. Pulse again briefly.
4. Remove from processor and divide into two balls. Roll one out for your pie and freeze the other.

Pumpkin Chiffon Pie

This "chiffon" pie is considerably lighter than the traditional pumpkin pie.

INGREDIENTS

1 pie shell, baked
1 tbsp. unflavored gelatin
½ c. fresh orange juice and water, equal parts
1 c. brown sugar
2 c. pumpkin purée, fresh or canned
1 tsp. cinnamon
½ tsp. each ginger and cloves
3 egg yolks
½ tsp. salt
3 egg whites
2–3 tbsp. sugar
1 tbsp. orange zest
1 c. heavy cream

Method

1. Combine orange juice and water. Add gelatin and dissolve.
2. Place brown sugar, pumpkin, spices, egg yolks, and salt in a saucepan. Simmer until thickened, stirring all the while. Add orange zest.
3. Remove from heat and stir in gelatin mixture. Refrigerate.
4. Whip egg whites and gradually add sugar.
5. Whip cream.
6. Fold eggs whites into pumpkin mixture. Fold in half of the cream.
7. Place filling in crust and pipe remaining whipped cream on top. Chill.

For more on using uncooked egg whites, see the box on page 171.

Pecan Pie

For many American families, this is an essential Thanksgiving dessert.

INGREDIENTS
4 tbsp. butter
1 tbsp. flour
1 tbsp. cornstarch
¼ tsp. salt
1½ c. Karo syrup
¼ c. molasses
⅓ c. sugar
2 eggs, lightly beaten
1¼ c. pecans
½ tsp. vanilla extract
1 pie shell, unbaked

Method

1. Melt the butter without boiling it.
2. Remove from heat, then add and thoroughly incorporate flour and cornstarch.
3. Return the mixture to the heat and add salt, Karo syrup, and molasses.
4. Bring the mixture to a boil and cook for about 3 minutes. Cool.
5. Blend in beaten eggs, pecans, and vanilla extract.
6. Pour mixture into an unbaked pie shell. (You may garnish the top with pecan halves if you choose.)
7. Bake in a 450° oven for about 10 minutes. Reduce heat to 350° and bake for an additional 30 minutes. The pie will still be just a little jiggly when it is done.

Poulet Roti (Roast Chicken)

Unfortunately, this is a dish I don't see often in the United States these days. With the tender, young chickens available in every supermarket and the ever-increasing availability of free-range chickens, it's a shame. Actually, the rotisserie ovens in those very supermarkets are just about the only place left to see this dish. What you are doing in the following recipe is creating a very slow rotisserie effect. The rotation of the chicken allows the juices to flow around the chicken instead of draining out. The 15 minutes the breast spends embedded in the mirepoix and the liberal application of the butter will prevent it from drying out.

Yield: 4 ½-chicken portions; 8 ¼ chicken portions

INGREDIENTS

2 chickens, fryer or broiler, 2¼–3¼ lb.
4 tbsp. butter, softened
1 tsp. salt
black pepper, to taste
4 c. mirepoix

Method

1. Thoroughly dry the chickens.
2. Loosen the breast skin and push the butter up under the skin with your fingers.
3. Salt and pepper the chickens inside and out.
4. Truss.
5. Add the mirepoix to the roasting pan and place the chickens on top, breast side up, in a pan just large enough to hold them and place the pan in a 450° oven.
6. Roast the chickens for 15 minutes on their backs, then turn them on one side.
7. Roast for 15 minutes on this side, then rotate them to the other side. Roast for 15 minutes.
8. Turn chicken breast side down and roast for 15 minutes.
9. Finish with 15 minutes on the back. Check the temperature with a pocket thermometer. You're looking for 180°. Total roasting time will be 75 to 90 minutes.
10. You may serve the chickens with the pan juices or pan gravy.

What You Need to Know

Mirepoix is a mixture of root vegetables, cut approximately ¾" square—most often consisting of carrots, onions and celery. The usual ratio is two parts of onion to one part each of carrots and celery, but this may be varied according to taste.

Roast Duckling Breast with Blackberry/Cabernet Sauce

Yield: 6 to 8 portions

INGREDIENTS

4 lb., approx. total 6–8 duckling breast
salt, to taste
black pepper, to taste
6 c. duck stock
½ c. clarified butter
2 c. dry red wine (inexpensive cabernet)
¼ c. balsamic vinegar
2–3 c. blackberry/cabernet sauce (below)

Method

1. Clean breasts and lightly prick with a fork.
2. Thoroughly dry and salt and pepper the duck breast.
3. Make duck stock using same procedure as for turkey stock. Make sauce.
4. When you have completed the sauce, heat butter in as many skillets as are needed to hold the duck pieces comfortably. Do not crowd the pieces. When the butter is quite hot, place the duck pieces, skin side down, in the skillets. Cook until golden brown on both sides.
5. Place skillets in a 450° to 500° oven. The duck pieces are skin side up now. Roast for approximately 15 minutes. Deglaze with red wine and vinegar.
6. Serve duckling with blackberry/cabernet sauce, a starch, and a vegetable or two.

Blackberry/Cabernet Sauce

I developed this sauce (and variations of it) using other wines and berries in 1981 while I was chef at Mudd's restaurant in San Ramon, California. The idea of the sauce is rooted in the traditional game sauces. I have substituted honey for sugar. The sauce should be balanced between sweet and sour, with a little zing provided by the ginger.

Yield: About 1 quart

What You Need to Know

In this instance, you will make duck stock with bones and trimmings. Follow the basic stock-making rules on pages 284–287. You may make either the brown or the white (chicken) stock. You will probably want to go with the white since the cooking time is much less.

INGREDIENTS

2 c. stock made from duck bones and trimmings (see the turkey stock on
    page 21 or the section on stocks begining on page 284)
2 c. cabernet sauvignon (not too expensive but something you
    would drink)
¼ c. tomato purée
1 tbsp. minced fresh ginger
1 tbsp. minced garlic
11 oz. blackberry preserves
¼ c. honey
¼ c. balsamic vinegar
3 tbsp. arrowroot
¼ c. orange liqueur
salt, to taste
black pepper, to taste
¼ pt. fresh blackberries, if available

Method

1. Place stock, 1½ cups of the cabernet, tomato purée, ginger, garlic, the honey, and balsamic vinegar in a saucepan. Simmer for 10 minutes.
2. Add preserves to sauce pan and simmer an additional 10 minutes.
3. Push the sauce through a sieve to remove the bits of ginger and garlic and any berry seeds. Return to sauce pan.
4. Combine arrowroot with remaining ¼ cup of wine and thoroughly combine. Add to sauce. Add liqueur.
5. Simmer over low heat, whisking periodically until sauce is translucent and has a sheen.
6. Add salt and pepper.
7. Add fresh blackberries at the last minute to warm through. Do not permit them to break down in the sauce.

Roast Goose

Several years ago, I was invited to the Mississippi University for Women in Columbus to do a series of holiday cooking demonstrations. Not knowing whether I would be able to obtain a goose in Columbus, I stowed a frozen goose in my bag along with my set of knives. This was prior to September 11, 2001. When I attempted to board the airplane in Memphis, the x-rays were inconclusive. The security guard saw something that looked like a small dead animal, plus a collection of lethal weapons. Moe called Larry and Curly, and we sorted it out.

Yield: There is not much meat on a goose. I would not count on it feeding more than 4 comfortably.

INGREDIENTS

1 goose, 5–6 lb.
2 c. mirepoix (page 25)
1½ c. brown stock (page 285)
salt, to taste
black pepper, to taste
1 c. dry red wine
2 tbsp. butter

Method

1. Thoroughly dry goose.
2. Place mirepoix in a roasting pan.
3. Pour in ½ cup of the brown stock.
4. Salt and pepper goose, inside and out.
5. Stuff goose lightly with Christmas goose stuffing (page 29).
6. Truss.
7. Place goose on its breast on the mirepoix.
8. Roast at 425° for 20 minutes. Turn goose on its side and roast for an additional 20 minutes.
9. Turn goose on other side and roast for about 20 minutes.
10. Turn goose on its back and finish roasting for an additional 20 to 30 minutes.
11. Remove goose from roasting pan and disjoint.
12. Remove all but 2 tablespoons of fat from roasting pan.
13. Place roasting pan on high heat on a burner and deglaze with red wine and remaining stock.
14. Reduce by half, add butter, swirl in, thoroughly incorporate, and serve with goose.

What You Need to Know

"Disjoint" is a term we throw around pretty casually in my business. What does it mean? When you literally remove one body segment from the one next to it, at the place where they join, you are disjointing. In the case of fowl, it means removing the leg and the thigh from the carcass and then, sometimes, further removing the leg from the thigh, always by cutting through the joint. You will not need a cleaver or jackhammer to do this. Your knife will slide smoothly through the joint if you have found it.

Christmas Goose Stuffing

Yield: About 8 cups

INGREDIENTS

about 60 chestnuts, warmed and peeled
2 c. chicken or brown stock
6 stalks celery
½ lb. ham, slightly smoky, minced
¾ c. butter
6 spicy sausages, casing removed
½ lb. bacon, blanched and sliced into lardons
2 c. diced onions
½ lb. mushrooms, sliced
1 tsp. whole thyme
3 bay leaves
½ tsp. whole sage
½ tsp. coriander
½ tsp. mace
½ tsp. salt
black pepper, to taste
2 eggs, lightly beaten
4 tbsp. minced parsley

Method

1. Poach chestnuts in the stock with one or two ribs of the celery. Bring to boil and reduce to simmer. They should be soft in approximately 30 minutes. Dice the remaining celery.
2. Sauté the sausage, bacon, onions, and mushrooms with the thyme, bay leaves, sage, coriander, mace, salt, and pepper in the butter.
3. Remove chestnuts from the stock and drain. Crush one-half of the chestnuts lightly.
4. Cool sausage mixture and chestnuts to room temperature and combine thoroughly with the egg and the lightly crushed chestnuts.

5. Stuff the bird loosely with this mixture.
6. Reduce the liquid in which the chestnuts were poached to just a few table-spoons. Serve the remaining chestnuts in this sauce.

ROASTING VEGETABLES

I often accompany roast meats and fowl with a side dish of simple roasted veg-etables. I place them right in the pan with the roast so they absorb its flavor.

INGREDIENTS

3 parsnips, peeled and quartered
3 medium carrots, peeled and quartered
8 potatoes, red or white, B-size
2–3 white turnips, peeled and quartered
¼ c. olive oil
8 boiling onions, peeled
8–10 garlic cloves, peeled
1 sprig fresh thyme
½ c. butter, cut small
1 tbsp. minced Italian parsley
salt and black pepper, to taste

What You Need to Know

In this instance, the word "boiling" designates a size. A *boiling onion* is smaller than an *onion* but larger than a *pearl onion*. It averages about 1½ inches in diameter.

Method

1. Preheat the oven to 375°.
2. In a large bowl, toss the parsnips, carrots, potatoes, and turnips in 1 table-spoon of the olive oil, plus a little salt and pepper, until coated.
3. Sauté all vegetables briefly in a pan large enough to hold them. This sears the outside so that they retain flavor and nutrition.
4. Arrange the vegetables cut side down in a large pan or alongside your roast. Turn the vegetables two or three times during cooking to prevent burning.
5. Roast until a fork easily penetrates the vegetables. Strew the butter over the vegetables, toss, and roast for another 10 minutes.
6. Garnish with the parsley.

2

Grilling

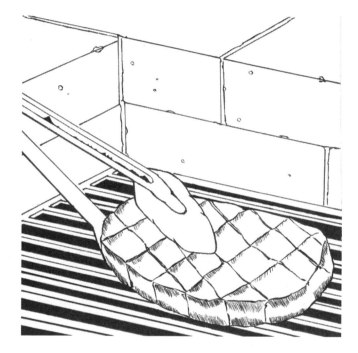

The noun "grill" almost certainly comes down to us from Old French and means now, as it did in the 17th century, "gridiron." The word "broil" is, in some areas, used to describe the same cooking technique. It, too, most likely comes from Old French for "to char" or "to burn" and has existed in English since the 14th century. Forget that I mentioned that part about "burn." Let's begin with a definition of grilling.

In order to be called "grilled," food must be cooked on a "grid" of some sort. The words "grill" and "broil" are interchangeable. The principle is this: A heat source, such as electricity, gas, charcoal, or mesquite wood, heats the grid; the grid "marks," sears, and cooks the food. Then the dry, hot air from the heat source takes over and finishes the cooking by convection. Any food to be grilled must already be tender, as this technique will not tenderize the food to any appreciable extent. Nearly any naturally tender food may be grilled.

THE CANON OF THE GRILL

1. With both of the "tender food" cooking methods, dry heat and fat, any food you wish to brown (caramelize) must be completely dry on its surface. Even if you've had the food basking in a marinade, you must dry it. As long as there is moisture present, you are not cooking above 212° until you boil the water away. If you are applying heat to the water on the surface of the food instead of the surface of the food, the food will begin to "steam" on the surface, not brown (caramelize). This tends to create a "grayish" appearance that's not terribly appealing to the eye. As you will see, the same rule applies to roasting and sautéing as well.

2. Season the food before you cook it. The food will be much more receptive to the seasonings in its raw state, as the outside has not been sealed off by the heat source.

3. To achieve the classically accepted diamond-shaped grill marks, the food is placed on the grill at a 45° angle to the grids. Once on the grill, the food is moved only three times. After about one-quarter of the cooking time, the food is carefully lifted with a set of tongs or a spatula, *not* a fork, and turned 90° to the opposite 45° angle to the grids. When approximately half the cooking time has elapsed, the food is turned over, and the same procedure is repeated on the other side. Once you can see the grill marks, you can make a determination as to which side of the food will be the "presentation" side. As a general rule, chefs cook the presentation side first. But we leave ourselves the option of changing our mind.

4. Keep the grill clean. Have a wire brush on hand to clean the grids frequently. Keep an oil of some kind near the grill. Apply this oil periodically to "season" the grill, much as one seasons cast-iron cookware. After cleaning the grill, apply the oil with a towel.

5. With four of the cooking methods you must make allowances for carryover, or retained, heat. This is particularly important with grilled foods since they are small, and the carryover heat can change the food from one degree of doneness to the next. The juices inside the food require varying time periods to recirculate. If you cut into a New York steak immediately after you remove it from the grill, it will have the appearance of being more cooked toward the outside of the meat and less cooked toward the center. It will also literally spurt its juices out onto the plate or cutting board. If, on the other hand, you allow the food, the New York steak in this instance, to rest for 4 to 5 minutes in a warm place, the juices will redistribute themselves evenly

throughout the steak, the entire inside of the meat will have the same degree of doneness, and the juices will have retreated into the tissues and not nearly so readily disgorge themselves. This is the most commonly ignored procedure and, at least as far as your guests' perception in terms of taste and quality is concerned, perhaps the most important. Depending on the size of the food cooked, different recirculation periods are required.

6. Brown is beautiful. Black is ugly. Or, to caramelize is not to carbonize. Caramelization occurs when you cook the surface carbohydrates present in food. Some browning also occurs as fats present in the food break down. Keep open flames away from the food. If your grill flares up, you may have to move the food. Keep a mister handy. The flames will carbonize, or burn, the food. Carbon is undesirable for several reasons, the most important of which is the substantial evidence for its being carcinogenic. Additionally, it doesn't taste good and isn't attractive. Hopefully, you care about health or aesthetics, preferably both.

7. Do not use a fork to stab and turn the food on the grill. This procedure will permit the juices to flow from the food. Grilling or broiling, and I use those two terms interchangeably, and roasting use "dry heat" to accomplish the same end: cooking the food.

8. In roasting, the food is cooked first and then portioned. In grilling, the food is portioned first and then cooked. Rarely do we grill any food that contains more than two or three portions per piece.

What You Need to Know

"Broiling" has two meanings. The first is synonymous with "grilling." The second is a mid-20th-century development. When stoves were manufactured with broilers beneath the oven, this configuration, which dispensed dry heat from above, was termed a "broiler." Thus, this cooking technique became "broiling." The commercial kitchen now has a device called variously either a top-fired or an over-fired broiler. While food may be effectively "broiled" in this environment, there is no possibility of grill marks.

The professional kitchen has another device in which direct gas heat is dispensed from above—the salamander. Usually used for browning, gratinéeing, or just heating, this tool will also "puff" omelets. Both pieces of equipment feature a sliding tray on which a cook places the food.

Here you will begin to learn the very basic "grills." You will grill steaks, the firmer-fleshed fish: halibut, salmon, sea bass, and swordfish. I do not recommend you grill the softer-fleshed fish, such as flounder or sole, until you are quite accomplished at this technique. Brochettes and kebabs are included here. Everyone seems to want to grill vegetables and pizzas now. I will oblige. Shellfish and poultry will not be left out. I will give you some guidance about which sauces to use with which grilled foods.

American Mixed Grill

Typically, none of these meats will be more than 1 inch thick and will take no more than 10 minutes to grill. You may have the lamb chops cut thicker if you choose. If you are using charcoal, you will, of course, have to allow time for the coals to mature. Basically, on any of the grills, plan on 30 minutes of heating.

Yield: 6 to 8 portions

INGREDIENTS

12–16 lamb chops cut from the rack
6–8 boneless, skinless chicken breast
6–8 spicy sausages (chaurice, andouille, Italian, or whatever you like; do use a sausage that weighs about 4 oz., in a casing), split
1 bunch watercress

What You Need to Know

The lamb chops and the sausage will probably tend to be somewhat fatty, so you will have to watch for flare-ups. Keep a spray bottle such as you might use to mist plants handy and spray the source of the flames when they appear. Should a conflagration develop, move the food until you have extinguished it.

The problem with the boneless breast of chicken is just the opposite. Having virtually no fat, it will tend to dry out on the grill. Mark it quickly and move it to a cooler part of the grill. I really prefer to grill chicken with the skin still on it.

Method

1. What I like about this particular mixed grill is the fact that the lamb, chicken, and sausage should grill in approximately the same amount of time.
2. Follow all the rules for grilling and ensure that your grill is quite hot. Place the lamb chops, boneless chicken breast (flattened slightly with the side of

a knife), and the sausage, cut side down, on the grill at the same time and at the prescribed 45° angle.

3. Grill for about 2 minutes and turn to the other 45° angle.
4. Grill for about 2 minutes and turn all the meats over.
5. Turn the meats 90° to finish the grilling. Hopefully, you have attractive diamond-shaped grill marks on the chicken, lamb, and sausage.
6. Remove the meats from the grill.

If you wish to turn this into a true mixed grill, add a few lamb kidneys and sweetbreads on skewers to the dish.

THE STEAK

This may well be the simplest grill of them all. Just follow the general guidelines for grilling at the beginning of this chapter. Turn the steak when you observe small droplets of blood on the surface of the steak. The temperature of the grill is driving the moisture to the top of the steak. Now is the time to seal the second side. Remember the diamond-shaped grill marks? The best way to tell if a steak is grilled to your satisfaction is to feel it. The manner in which chefs determine the degree of doneness of a piece of meat is by touch. Use the tips of your fingers to press down on the top of a steak. The softer the feel, the rarer the steak; the harder the feel, the more well done. After you have done this a few times, you'll become quite accurate. This method will also provide you with a much better steak since you are able to avoid cutting into it, thereby preventing the juices from escaping.

The amount of time required to grill a steak is dependent on three factors: the thickness of the meat, the texture of the meat, and the temperature of the fire.

Those of you who enjoy your steak *exsanguine* will need to place it on a cooler spot on the grill so as not to char it on the outside.

One of the easiest, fastest, and tastiest finishes for a steak is a mixture of fresh chopped herbs, a little minced garlic, and a squeeze of lemon. Toss all this into a sauté pan with some butter and brush it on or pour it over the steak while it is resting.

Sauces that go well with a grilled steak include béarnaise (page 297) and marchand de vin (page 299).

Some Other Meats You Will Want to Grill

Most of the cuts we call "chops" are perfect for grilling. Pork chops and lamb chops are both wonderful when properly grilled. Follow the basic guidelines for grilling and do not overcook! Veal chops do well but tend to dry out and have little marbling. I love grilled sausages.

Pork and lamb tenderloins also show well on the grill. A coating of oil helps keep them moist.

Bone a leg of lamb and try this dish.

Boneless/Grilled Leg of Lamb with Pesto and Raspberry/Zinfandel Sauce

When I was executive chef at Mudd's restaurant in San Ramon, California, in the early 1980s, I often put game dishes on the specials menu. While not precisely game, this one proved to be so popular that I added it to the regular menu. The food we were doing there has since come to be known as "California Nouvelle." We had a 10-acre organic garden and shared produce with Chez Panisse and Green's. The wines we offered and cooked with were all produced in California. The basil for the pesto was grown in our garden, as were all the fresh herbs we used.

Yield: 8 to 10 portions

What You Need to Know

How to Butterfly a Leg of Lamb

The butcher can do this for you, but it is simple to do yourself if you have a sharp boning knife. There are only three major bones to be removed: the *aitch* bone, femur, and shank. Chefs and butchers use the expression "slash-boned" for this method of boning. The biggest advantage is the fact that you will have meat done to three different degrees of doneness after cooking because the three muscles are of different thicknesses.

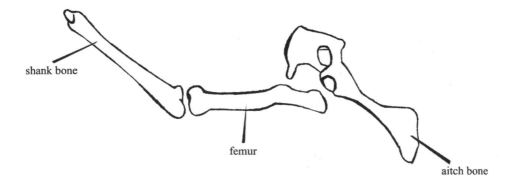

shank bone

femur

aitch bone

Also, I am not entirely sure I believe those who say that the popliteal gland imparts no flavor or taste when cooked. You must bone the leg to remove it.

Imported lamb is less expensive than American lamb, and the range-fed varieties will be much smaller and have a gamier taste. Just a matter of personal preference.

Step 1. Remove the aitch bone. Your aim is to free the meat around the irregular part of the aitch bone, then around the hip joint. Use the tip of your knife to sever the ball-and-socket joint so you can free and move the aitch bone slightly away from the femur. Work closely around the aitch bone, back to the tail bone end, being careful not to slash into the meat. Remove aitch bone.

Step 2. Remove the femur. With the tip of your knife, mark a straight line from kneecap to the ball end of the femur. Now cut down into the meat along this line until you touch the femur bone. Open the meat up along the length of the bone to expose the femur, stroking your knife closely along the bone at all times. Free the meat from the kneecap and knuckle joint.

Step 3. Remove the shank bone. Continue cutting close to the shank bone down its length. Remove the femur and shank bone together. You now have a "slash-boned" leg.

Step 4. Lay the slash-boned leg of lamb out flat, skin-side down. You will see three separate and distinct muscles. Using a boning knife, start from the inner side of the thickest part of the leg (the topside) and make a horizontal cut through the middle of it, taking your knife almost to the outer edge. Fold the top flap out flat, like opening a book. Do the same with the other thick part of the leg (the thick flank). Between two of the muscles, you will see a pocket of fat. Within this pocket will be the popliteal gland. Cut this entire fat pocket out of the leg, and the gland will come away with it. Remove the "fell," the whitish skin covering on the outside of the leg, but leave a thin fat cover on the skin side.

INGREDIENTS

1 boneless leg of lamb
½ c. extra virgin olive oil
2 tbsp. lemon juice
salt, to taste
black pepper, to taste
1 c. dry zinfandel
½ c. pesto

Method

1. Open the leg of lamb and flatten it. Place it in a glass or stainless container.
2. Make the pesto (page 39).
3. You are now ready to marinate the leg of lamb. Pour the olive oil over the leg. Squeeze the lemon juice over the leg. Salt and pepper the leg and rub them in. Pour the red wine over the leg and finally, using a rubber scraper, spread the pesto over the lamb.
4. Dry the lamb with a towel and place in a roasting pan in a preheated 500° oven.
5. Roast for 20 to 25 minutes. The lamb should be very rare—about 130° on a meat thermometer.
6. Now you are ready to grill the lamb. There are two options here: You may grill the flattened leg whole, or you may slice it into serving portions, on which you may create the diamond-shaped grill marks.

What You Need to Know

You will notice that I recommend this technique with the grilled chicken, too. This preliminary "roasting" is designed to ensure that you do not serve raw lamb or chicken. Larger pieces of food are very difficult to grill properly. They tend to want to burn on the outside and remain raw inside.

Raspberry/Zinfandel Sauce

I developed this sauce in 1981, specifically for the previously mentioned lamb dish, while I was executive chef at Mudd's restaurant in San Ramon, California. The idea of the sauce is rooted in the traditional game sauces. I have substituted lemon for vinegar and honey for sugar. The sauce should be balanced between sweet and sour, with a little zing provided by the ginger.

Yield: A little over 1 quart

INGREDIENTS
2 c. stock (made from the bones and trimmings of the varmint for which the sauce is intended)
2 c. zinfandel (not too expensive but something you would drink)
¼ c. tomato purée
1 tbsp. minced fresh ginger
1 tbsp. minced garlic

¼ pt. fresh raspberries
11 oz. raspberry preserves
¼ c. honey
¼ c. lemon juice
3 tbsp. arrowroot
salt, to taste
black pepper, to taste

Method

1. Place stock, 1½ cups of the zinfandel, tomato purée, ginger, garlic, half the raspberries, the honey, and the lemon juice in a sauce pan. Simmer for 20 minutes.
2. Add preserves to sauce pan and simmer for an additional 10 minutes.
3. Push the sauce through a sieve to remove the bits of ginger and garlic and the raspberry seeds. Return to saucepan.
4. Combine arrowroot with remaining ¼ cup of wine and thoroughly combine. Add to sauce.
5. Simmer over low heat, whisking periodically until sauce is translucent and has a sheen.
6. Add remaining raspberries at the last minute to warm through. Do not permit them to break down in the sauce.
7. Add salt and pepper to taste.

Pesto

This aromatic purée from Genoa is spectacular with lamb. We'll use it later with fettuccine. A mixture of cheeses is most often used in Italy. I love it with just the parmesan. Please buy good well-aged "fresh" parmesan, one that isn't sold in a green cardboard cylinder.

Yield: About 1½ cups

Ingredients

4 oz. fresh basil leaves, stems removed
¼ c. pine nuts
6 garlic cloves
black pepper, to taste
¼ c. extra virgin olive oil
⅔ c. parmesan
salt, to taste

Method

1. Place basil, pine nuts, garlic, and pepper in food processor.
2. Turn on processor and add oil in a thin stream. Process until a purée has been obtained.
3. Remove mixture from food processor and combine with cheese in a mixing bowl. Taste before adding salt, as some parmesans are quite salty.
4. This stores quite well in the refrigerator. Make at least the quantity listed here. You'll regret not having it if you don't.

Note: The boned leg of lamb is also quite good with the dry rub (page 9) and the barbecue sauce (page 10).

Lamb Shish Kebab

Many cultures have meat-on-a-stick dishes and a few shellfish dishes, too. All have their own names for them. *Shish kebab* comes from Turkish words literally meaning "skewer" and "roast" meat. Probably invented by nomadic tribes, small pieces of questionable game were easy to marinate and transport and quick to cook, requiring very little fuel for the fire. Shish kebabs are now seemingly omnipresent. Asian cultures have *satay*, or roasted skewered meats served with a dipping sauce often made with peanuts. Japan has *yakitori*, which is grilled, skewered fowl. In France, they are called *brochettes*, meaning "skewer." Bamboo skewers are best and safest. Soak them in cold water for an hour or so before you impale anything with them.

INGREDIENTS

2 green bell peppers
2 yellow onions
2–3 lb. leg of lamb, cut into 1½-in. cubes
½ c. olive oil
2 tbsp. minced fresh oregano
1 tbsp. minced fresh mint
6 garlic cloves, crushed
1 c. dry red wine

Method

1. Light the grill and preheat for 30 minutes before you are ready to cook.
2. Cut the peppers first in halves and then in thirds lengthwise.

3. Remove the seeds and cut each piece across. You will now have 12 pieces of pepper.

4. Peel the yellow onions and cut in half across the middle. Cut each piece in quarters. Peel the layers so that you have 6 pieces about the same size as the green pepper pieces.

5. Place the peppers and onions in a large mixing bowl along with the lamb. Make a marinade of the olive oil, oregano, mint, garlic, and red wine. Pour over the meat and vegetables. Toss and marinate 2 to 3 hours or overnight in the refrigerator.

6. Arrange on skewers in this order: onion, meat, green pepper, meat, onion, meat, green pepper, meat. End with an onion. Use two skewers to prevent the meat and vegetables from spinning. Grill until lightly browned on all sides, approximately 15 minutes.

Serve on a bed of Rice Pilaf (page 156).

GRILLING POULTRY

Cooking poultry on a grill is fraught with entirely different problems than a cook encounters when grilling meats. Of the poultry available during the majority of the year, there are two basic categories: (1) those birds consisting of two different kinds of meat and (2) those consisting of a uniformly colored flesh throughout. The former category encompasses the regular old chicken, turkey, and "Cornish hens," plus some of the more exotic chickens available, such as the *poussin*. These birds have dark meat and white meat. The dark meat tends to be more moist when we cook these birds in any fashion since the tissue has a better blood supply to the muscles used more often, such as legs and thighs. Most of these domestic birds don't have the occasion to use the muscles of the breast or wings very often, so the flesh is not engorged with blood and appears much lighter.

The other category of handy fowl, represented most reliably by the duck, consists of an almost uniform coloration throughout the bird. The pheasant, quail, and partridge fall into this category as well. This latter category is actually easier to grill since you don't have to make allowances for the different cooking times.

Thai Chicken Satay

Thai cooking has taken this country by monsoon. Here is a Thai version of the original Indonesian *Satay*.

INGREDIENTS

2 lb. chicken breasts, skinned, boned and cut crosswise into ½-inch strips
8–10 shallots, peeled and rough-chopped
3–4 garlic cloves, rough-chopped
1–2 stalks lemon grass, chopped
3–4 pieces fresh ginger, cut across the grain about ¼-inch thick and smashed
1 tsp. turmeric
½ tsp. kosher salt
2 tbsp. light brown sugar
1 tbsp. tamarind juice
1 tbsp. coriander
1 tbsp. butter, melted
1 tbsp. sweet soy sauce
1½ c. coconut milk
bamboo skewers, as needed

(Method)

1. Using a mortar and pestle, grind together shallots, garlic, lemon grass, and turmeric powder into a fine paste. Add sugar, salt, and tamarind juice. Mix well.
2. In a bowl, mix the paste with chicken and add butter. Mix well again. Marinate for 2 to 3 hours.
3. Thread four to five pieces of chicken onto each skewer.
4. Cook over a charcoal fire or under a broiler until browned. Baste often with coconut milk during the cooking process. Serve with Satay Sauce (below) and boiled rice.

Satay Sauce

INGREDIENTS

2 tbsp. red curry paste
½ c. shallots, fried
1 tsp. chili powder
½ cup roasted peanuts, ground

3 c. coconut milk
2 tbsp. light brown sugar
1 tbsp. tamarind juice
kosher salt, to taste
2 tbsp. peanut oil

(**Method**)

1. Heat a sauté pan or wok on medium high, then add oil. Stir-fry the paste, fried shallots, and chile powder until aromatic.
2. Add peanuts, sugar, tamarind juice, salt, and coconut milk. Reduce heat and simmer gently until oil rises to the surface. Spoon into small serving bowl.

Fried Shallots

INGREDIENTS

12 shallots, peeled and sliced
1 tsp. kosher salt
1½ c. peanut oil

(**Method**)

1. Heat wok or saucepan on medium high and add oil.
2. Add salt.
3. Stir in sliced shallots and fry until golden brown and crisp.
4. Drain on paper towels and cool.

Grilled Chicken

I am not a big fan of the boneless, skinless chicken breasts that now appear in every supermarket meat case on the planet. They will dry out if you are not careful when you grill them. I do use them in sautés, always marinating them first. Two principal flavor enhancers are fat and salt. Fat also keeps meat and poultry from becoming dry.

Young chickens, weighing between 2 and 2½ pounds each, often called "broilers," are available in every supermarket in the United States and are the right choice for grilling. You will need to allow half a chicken per person. Grilling the chicken on a fire that is too hot is the most common error here. If you are using charcoal, do not cook directly over the coals. The fat rendered from the skin—and the butter—will make your broiler flare. Make a hollow down the middle of the coals and grill your chicken over this trough. This will provide a temperature that should be just right to brown and crisp the skin and at the same time cook the inside of the chicken completely. Remember, you are attempting to have both the dark meat completely cooked and the light meat moist. If you are using gas or electricity, adjust the height of the grid from the heat source.

Yield: 6 to 8 ½-chicken portions

INGREDIENTS

3–4 chickens
½ c. clarified butter or cooking oil
salt, to taste
black pepper, to taste

Method

1. Split the chickens. The neatest manner in which to do this is with a large chef's knife or kitchen shears. Cut down either side of the backbone and remove it. Use it for stock. Remove the last two joints from the wing. They tend to burn. Use them for stock as well. Thoroughly dry the chickens and salt and pepper them.

2. Be sure your grill is hot but not too hot. Baste the skin side of the chicken with the butter. Place the chicken, skin side down, on the grill; grill for half the cooking time, or one-quarter, if you desire the diamond-shaped grill marks. The skin should be golden brown and marked when you turn the chicken.

3. Baste the second side with the butter. Turn the chicken to the second side and grill until the meat next to the bone is no longer pink. Do not thrust a fork into the chicken, as this will permit the juices to escape.

What You Need to Know

If you are cooking a large number of chickens, pre-roast them on a sheet pan in the oven first. After seasoning and basting them, place them skin side up on a sheet pan and place this pan in a very hot oven. Roast the chicken for about 15 minutes and remove. This procedure may be done hours ahead and will reduce the grilling period by about two-thirds. Then grill as just explained.

Pollo Fra Diavolo

This is a spicy Italian variation on the basic grilled chicken.
Yield: 8 ¼-chicken portions

INGREDIENTS

2 chickens, quartered
½ c. butter, melted
2 tbsp. extra virgin olive oil
1 tbsp. crushed red pepper
½ tsp. minced fresh ginger
3 tbsp. finely minced yellow onions
3 tbsp. minced parsley
1 tbsp. minced garlic
salt, to taste
2 c. tomato sauce (page 294) with a little crushed red pepper

Method

1. Dry chicken thoroughly.
2. Combine butter, oil, pepper, and ginger in a mixing bowl.
3. Marinate chicken in the butter mixture for 15 to 20 minutes.
4. Purée onion, parsley, and garlic with a few teaspoons of the butter mixture.
5. Grill chicken on a hot grill, about 6 minutes per side. Baste with the butter mixture periodically.
6. Remove the breasts from the grill to a serving platter or a casserole, place them on a bed of the tomato sauce, and spread each of the breasts with the onion purée mixture.
7. Bake for 5 to 6 minutes in a 400° oven.

Serve this with one of the risottos (pages 157 and 158) and a simple sautéed vegetable such as broccoli. Or you might serve the Italian potato salad (page 176).

GRILLED FISH AND SHELLFISH

All seafoods are naturally tender foods—abalone is the exception, but you aren't likely to find it, anyway. (Call me if you do!) Grilling is a perfect cooking method for most of them.

Grilled Swordfish or Tuna (or Shark)

These seafoods are usually purchased pre-portioned, but I will also tell you how to portion them in case you buy a "chunk."

Swordfish is the one fish with which we have had good success feeding those who don't normally eat a lot of fish. Sadly, there is much concern about mercury levels in swordfish these days. I do hope this concern abates, as this was probably the most popular grilled fish I sold in restaurants over the years. Swordfish does not have the texture most people usually associate with fish. It has a firmness more often thought of in association with meat. If tuna is the chicken of the sea, then swordfish, certainly, is the steak. The contrast between the dark brown grill marks and the light-colored flesh of this fish makes an especially striking presentation.

Swordfish, the most popular of the billed fishes, is one of the easiest of fish to grill. The flesh of the shark is comparable, if usually darker, and it is becoming more available. This fish is also particularly easy to deal with since it has very few bones, and the ones present are large and easily seen. Swordfish is sold in chunks by weight. The best is center cut with no belly flap (the belly flap hangs down from the fish and is where the fish stores extra fat). The center cut is the most expensive cut. This piece is from near the center or the widest part of the fish. You may be able to purchase meat from the tail for a little less. There is nothing wrong with this meat; it may take two pieces to make a portion, though.

The chunk of swordfish will need to be cut into portions. If you bought a quarter-round or half-round piece, this is quite easy to do. Simply turn the swordfish with the rough, skin side down and slice the fish from the inside out to the skin. If you have the entire round of the swordfish, cut it into quarters; if you have half, cut it in half. This will make your portions the size of one-quarter of the round. Make the slices between ¾ and 1 inch thick. If you have been dealing with an average size fish, your portions should weigh between 6 and 8 ounces.

Should you purchase a chunk of tuna, it is even easier to portion since there will be no bones or cartilage to navigate. It will probably have a wedge shape similar to the swordfish. Proceed as with the swordfish.

Several years ago I was fishing in Puerto Escondido, Mexico. Our party caught two sailfish, each weighing about 120 pounds. The anatomy, I was pleased to discover, was quite like that of the swordfish. Of course, I had to deal with the innards of these fish. My point is that if a fisherman you know presents you with whole fish "in the round," clean them as soon as possible after they are out of the water. I hung these varmints up and gutted them right after the picture taking.

It doesn't particularly matter in which direction you initially place the swordfish on the grill since the swordfish is not oriented in any particular direction. Just be sure to turn it 90°—to the other 45° angle—a quarter of the way through the cooking time.

Grilled Salmon

There is now some variety in the types of salmon available in most parts of the country. My personal favorite is the king salmon, whose range includes Washington State, Oregon, and northern California and Alaska. Charters are available in northern California, and you may, if in the area, enjoy going after them yourself. Then again, you may not! Not very long after your boat passes at dawn under the Golden Gate Bridge, you will encounter an interesting stretch of water known locally as the "Potato Patch." If you are at all suscepti- ble to motion sickness, I would strongly suggest you gobble your favorite motion sickness pill before this fateful encounter. I always ate a handful myself and then watched the he-men chumming off the back of the boat as we passed through the Potato Patch.

The charters are not inexpensive, and there exists the distinct possibility you may not catch a salmon. I once asked a good friend if he wanted to go salmon fishing, and he replied that he had discovered—and preferred—an experience analogous to salmon fishing. He set his alarm for 3:30 A.M., arose, went into the bathroom, threw up, took out a hundred-dollar bill, set it on fire, and went back to bed: a fairly close approximation of some of the salmon fishing expe- ditions in which I have participated, except for the going-back-to-bed part. If you can find wild salmon, buy it.

Although salmon is certainly not the most difficult fish to grill, it requires some care. If you have fileted the fish yourself, you will now have two nice long pieces of salmon. If you haven't, I hope you have been able to find a butcher who performed this procedure for you. You now need to portion the filets. Begin at the larger end and make slices through the filet, on the bias, at a 45° angle at 4-inch intervals. Continue until you have reached the tailpiece. What this method of portioning will do is provide you with servings of salmon that have the same shape on both sides (front and back) and will grill uniformly. A 6- to 10-pound fish will provide you with 8 to 12 servings, weighing between 6 and 8 ounces each.

The total grilling time for a portion of salmon prepared in this manner should be no more than 7 or 8 minutes. For fish, the grill should be quite hot and well seasoned. Place the salmon, rounded side down, on the grill at the pre- scribed 45° angle; turn it to the other 45° angle after 1½ to 2 minutes. Check the down side of the salmon for the grill marks, and if they are sufficiently dark, turn it to the second side and continue the standard grilling procedure until the fish just begins to flake.

The beurre blanc (page 298), hollandaise (page 295), or the béarnaise (page 297) sauces all go well with this grilled salmon. Of course, if you are trying to avoid fats, the salmon is wonderful with just a little lemon squeezed over it.

I had an experience once where I was flown to Dallas to cook for a Braniff Airlines board of directors meeting. The menu given to me included prime rib as the feature entrée, and the rest was a fairly typical buffet format. No one let me know that the person chairing the meeting, Jay Pritzker of Hyatt Hotels, was on the Pritikin Diet at the time. I scrambled around and found some salmon and poached it for him. I made him a sauce with a dilled sour yogurt. He said he loved it.

Grilled Halibut

The halibut is the largest member of a family of fish known as the *pleuronectoids* and is fairly widely available these days. Other members of this family are sole, flounder, brill, plaice, and, the smallest I am familiar with, sand dabs. This group is composed of the flatfish characterized by its coloration: dark on the topside, light on the bottom. If a predator observes them from the top, they blend in with the depths of the ocean, but if the predator sees them from the bottom, they blend in with the sky. Both of their eyes are on the dark topside of their bodies. This, I believe, is handy when they burrow in the ocean bottom. They will still be able to see everything transpiring above them. Anatomically, they differ quite a bit from the round fish in that each side of the fish yields two filets.

The larger halibut are found in the colder waters off Alaska and have weighed in at 350 pounds. The smaller, warm-water halibut found off the coast of California weigh between 5 and 25 pounds for the most part. Halibut are the easiest member of the flatfish family to grill, particularly if you follow the method of portioning on the bias as detailed previously. Their flesh is very white and flakes nicely when properly grilled.

The Beurre Blanc would augment the halibut nicely. One of the fried potato dishes would go well with it, as would some of the grilled vegetables.

Split Grilled Lobster

The United States and France are the only two countries I know of that have both of the two main varieties of lobster in the world available in their coastal waters. Off the Northeast coast, we Americans harvest the Atlantic lobster or Maine lobster, or, in French, *homard*. This is the cold-water lobster with the large claws and the small tail. From the waters off the coast of southern California comes the warm-water lobster, the spiny lobster, which is also called the rock lobster, Mexican lobster, or, again, in French, *langouste*. This lobster is characterized by having a larger tail and no front claws. When you have the frozen lobster tail in a restaurant, you are having the rear end of this crustacean, probably from Australia or South Africa. The French catch the homard, slightly smaller than our Atlantic lobster, in the cold waters of the English Channel off the coasts of Brittany and Normandy. They harvest the spiny lobster off the Mediterranean coasts of France. Many of these come from South Africa and Australia as well.

In most parts of the country, you will be more apt to locate the Maine lobster than the spiny. Buy them live if at all possible. If all you have available in your part of the country is lobster tails, you will likely have two options. Most chefs buy cold-water tails from the Atlantic lobster. They will be somewhat smaller than the tails from the spiny lobster, but we tend to like both the flavor and the texture a little better.

Yield: 6 to 8 portions

Ingredients

6–8 live Maine lobsters, approx. 1½ lb. each
¾–1 c. clarified butter
2 tbsp. lemon juice
salt, to taste
white pepper, to taste
½ tsp. cayenne pepper

Method

1. There is a small indentation just at the rear of the lobster's head. Insert a paring or boning knife here to sever the spinal cord. I believe this to be the most humane (lobsterian?) manner in which to dispatch the lobster, but who among us really knows?
2. Using a 10-inch chef's knife, split the lobster down the middle from the bottom side. Do not cut all the way through the shell on the topside. Open the lobster. You will find yourself confronted by an intestinal tract, a stomach sac, a tomalley (or green liver), and perhaps some coral-colored roe. Aficionados consume the tomalley and the roe. Toss the stomach and the intestinal tract.
3. Combine the clarified butter, lemon juice, salt, white pepper, and cayenne pepper.
4. Brush the flesh side of the lobster with the butter mixture and place the lobster on the grill, flesh side down. Grill 3 or 4 minutes, turn 90°, and grill another 3 or 4 minutes. Turn the lobster over with the shell side down, brush the flesh again with the butter, and grill approximately another 2 minutes.
5. Serve with ramekins of the butter mixture for dipping. Serve with a lobster cracker, which looks a lot like a nutcracker.

What You Need to Know

If you really want to go all out, have a modified clambake. Place oysters, mussels, and clams on the grill to "bake." Grill some of the vegetables and corn (page 51) and serve one of the side-dish salads. Make one of the breads. Have some good wine.

Italian Grilled Shrimp

I once did this dish for a party during the winter. I was outside cooking. They were inside drinking. Take my advice and do it during the summer months.

INGREDIENTS

1½ lb. large shrimp/prawns
½ c. olive oil
2 cloves garlic, crushed
black pepper, to taste
kosher salt, to taste
lime juice of 1 or 2 limes
¾ c. garlic butter (below)

Method

1. Split each shrimp on underside down to tail, trying to avoid cutting too deeply into the meat. Devein leaving shell intact.
2. Put shrimp in bowl with remaining ingredients except garlic butter.
3. Cover and refrigerate at least 2 hours.
4. Push two bamboo skewers through each shrimp and grill shrimp about 6 inches from coals over a low charcoal fire. The use of two skewers will prevent the shrimp from spinning around when you turn them.
5. Turn frequently. This procedure will take about 7 to 8 minutes. Serve on skewers with garlic butter.

Garlic Butter

INGREDIENTS

¾ c. butter, melted
1 tsp. Worcestershire sauce
1 tbsp. lemon juice
¼ tsp. Tabasco
2 cloves garlic, mashed
kosher salt, to taste

Mix all ingredients well and serve.

Grilled Curried Sea Scallops

Be sure to buy the large sea scallops.
   Yield: 6 portions

INGREDIENTS

1½ lb. sea scallops
2 tbsp. sesame oil
3 tbsp. curry powder
kosher salt, to taste
fresh cracked black pepper, to taste
2 tbsp. oil for grill

Method

1. In a large bowl, combine the scallops with the sesame oil and toss to coat. Add the curry powder and salt and pepper and toss again.
2. Preheat the grill. Oil the grill. Place the scallops on the grill; grill until the scallops are just cooked through, 3 to 4 minutes.

Scallops will have lost their translucency and will be opaque all the way through when they are done.
   Serve on a bed of the rice pilaf (page 156), accompanied by the raita (page 138).

GRILLING VEGETABLES

Choose firmer vegetables that take well to grilling, such as peppers, eggplant, tomatoes, corn on the cob, button mushrooms, and the summer squashes. Follow these steps:

1. Clean and trim the vegetables. Cut large ones into halves or slice them into large sections.
2. Parboil the harder vegetables, such as small White Rose or Red Rose potatoes, before grilling.
3. Remove silks from corn but leave husks on and soak in ice water for about 1 hour before grilling.
4. Marinate vegetables for 15 minutes before grilling or, alternatively, just brush them lightly with clarified butter or oil so they don't stick to the grill. Prepare a medium-hot fire in the charcoal.
5. Put the vegetables directly on the grill grid or on skewers.

6. Begin with the vegetables that take the longest to cook—denser vegetables such as potatoes or peppers will take longer than moisture-filled ones such as tomatoes.

7. Turn the vegetables often, brushing on more marinade or butter as needed. The vegetables are done when they can be easily pierced with a fork.

Marinade: Combine 2 parts olive oil and 1 part lemon juice with 1 peeled and crushed garlic clove. You may add any fresh herbs you like, such as rosemary, thyme, basil, and marjoram. You may also try different oils—walnut or sesame—and different vinegars—balsamic, red wine, or rice vinegar. Flavored butters, such as chile butter, garlic butter, and herb butter, are quite good with grilled vegetables.

GRILLING BREAD

Bruschetta

Here's one of the grilled "starches" I mentioned. This is the original Roman "garlic bread." Its quality depends entirely on the quality of the olive oil and the bread. The name "bruschetta" means to cook over coals. You will need to first make the Italian bread (page 113).

Yield: 12 slices

INGREDIENTS

12 slices Italian bread, sliced 1½ in. thick
6–12 garlic cloves, crushed
¾ c. extra virgin olive oil
salt, to taste
black pepper, to taste

Method

1. Toast the bread on both sides on a hot grill.
2. Rub the toast well with the garlic, again, on both sides.
3. Soak the slices with the olive oil and add the salt and pepper.
4. Serve immediately.

You may melt some cheese on the bread or place sun-dried tomatoes or pesto on top of it.

Grilled Pizza

As with the grilled lamb (page 36) and grilled chicken (page 43), you are actually grilling and "baking" (we were roasting there) here. You will need a few tools for this treat—a grill with a cover, a hot fire, and a pizza peel.

Method

1. Fire up the grill. The fire should be very hot. The ashes should be white/gray. Allow the grill enough time to heat up. While the grill is heating, make the pizza dough (page 88).
2. Roll or press out the dough.
3. Place the dough on a peel you have either floured or covered with cornmeal. I like the cornmeal crust.
4. Carefully slide the dough off the peel onto the grill.
5. This first side of the dough will probably cook quickly, so keep an eye on it.
6. Slide the peel under the dough to loosen it. Look at the bottom. If the dough is getting crispy, you are ready to move on.
7. You may see some air pockets forming in the dough. Pop them. You should also see grill marks.
8. Using your peel, remove the dough from the grill and turn it over onto a floured work surface so that the grill-marked side is up.
9. Carefully coat the top of the dough with olive oil. Place your favorite toppings on the pizza.
10. Slide a floured or cornmealed peel under your pizza and slide it onto the grill. Cover the grill immediately. Check every few minutes. Usually when the cheese (if you put cheese on the pizza) is melted, the pizza is ready.

Baking

Remember the distinction between roasting and baking? Chefs call it *roasting* when we cook meat or poultry completely surrounded by dry heat. Do not "roast" seafood, as the flesh is too delicate and would disintegrate or dry out. There are, however, many baked seafood dishes. We call a dish "baked" if it is a meat, poultry, or seafood item to which we have added a liquid, a sauce, or a crust or if the dish is a grain, starch, or vegetable dish. Consequently, there are even baked meat dishes, such as Beef Wellington, in which we add a crust between the heat source and the meat. All casseroles are baked dishes.

SEAFOOD

Oysters Rockefeller

Antoine's restaurant in New Orleans, where Jules Alciatore conceived this dish in 1899, will not divulge its recipe for this dish of baked oysters. The dish originated, so the story goes, as an attempt to replace snails, which were in short supply, with oysters. Jules gave the name "Rockefeller" to the dish, after John D., because it was so rich. Every proprietor of Antoine's since Jules has made the same claim that there is no spinach in the dish. They do use a purée of some type of "greens."

INGREDIENTS

3 dozen oysters
1 lb. bacon, finely minced
½ c. butter
2 bunches green onions, minced
3 c. spinach, cooked, drained, and minced
1 c. minced parsley
2 c. finely minced celery
3 tbsp. minced garlic
2 tbsp. minced cilantro

3 tbsp. minced fresh anise
½ c. minced fresh basil
½ c. Pernod or Herbsaint
Tabasco, to taste
1 tbsp. Worcestershire sauce
salt, to taste
black pepper, to taste
1 c. bread crumbs

Method

1. Shuck oysters.
2. Sauté bacon until browned and crisp. Drain.
3. Melt half a stick of butter and sauté all vegetables for 4 or 5 minutes.
4. Deglaze with the Pernod.
5. Add Tabasco, Worcestershire, salt, and pepper.
6. Either cool before finishing dish or immediately top the oysters and bake.
7. Place approximately one tablespoon of the purée on top of each oyster and dot with remaining butter. Place oysters on a bed of rock salt in a shallow baking pan.
8. Bake in a 500° oven for about 10 minutes or until top is lightly browned.

Oysters Bienville

Jean Baptiste Le Moyne, Sieur de Bienville, is considered to be the founder of the city of New Orleans in the year 1718. He was on Iberville's original expedition to the mouth of the Mississippi in 1698. He was governor on and off until 1743, when he left Louisiana. His name is all over New Orleans, and this baked oyster dish is without doubt the most succulent monument to his name. The Bienville Sauce here also goes quite well with grilled fish and may be used with fish baked en papillote. The dish was conceived at Arnaud's restaurant.

INGREDIENTS

3 dozen oysters, shucked
1 c. butter
1 bunch green onions, minced
½ lb. mushrooms, thinly sliced
1 tbsp. minced garlic
½ lb. shrimp, minced
½ c. dry white wine
2 tbsp. lemon juice

½ c. flour
2 c. chicken stock
½ c. heavy cream
salt, to taste
white pepper, to taste
Tabasco, to taste

Method

1. Place the shucked oysters on a bed of rock salt in a shallow baking dish.
2. Sweat (cook until the vegetables exude their juices) the green onions, mushrooms, and garlic in one-half of the butter.
3. In a separate pan, make a roux with the remaining butter and the flour. Do not allow the roux to color.
4. Add the shrimp to the vegetables and cook until they color.
5. Deglaze the shrimp mixture with the white wine.
6. In a separate pan, make a light roux with the remaining butter and the flour. Do not allow the roux to color.
7. Add chicken stock to shrimp and vegetable mixture. Heat through.
8. Thoroughly incorporate the roux in the shrimp mixture.
9. Season with salt, pepper, and Tabasco.
10. Either cover the oysters with the Bienville Sauce and bake immediately or chill the sauce for later baking.
11. Sprinkle the bread crumbs on top of the oysters. You may dot with butter if you choose.
12. Bake in a 500° oven for about 10 minutes or until lightly browned on top.

Barbecue Oysters

In certain areas, you may not always be able to purchase fresh oysters in the shell. You should be able to find the fresh-shucked oysters in a jar, though. Hopefully, you will be able to procure some oyster shells in which to make the dish. If not, small casserole dishes will do. Check the dates on the jar.

If you were able to get—and shuck—the shell oysters, sprinkle a little of the dry rub on each before you put them in the refrigerator. Let them "marinate" at least a couple of hours. Overnight is fine, too. If you have the jar oysters, drain them, dry them, and place them in a bowl with a tablespoon or so of the rub.

INGREDIENTS

3–4 dozen Eastern oysters
dry rub (page 9) as needed
approx. 2 c. barbecue sauce (page 10)
1 c. flour (for the jar oysters)
½ c. extra virgin olive oil (for the jar oysters)
6 c. rock salt (for the shell oysters)

Yield: 6 to 8 appetizer portions

Method

1. Preheat your oven to 500°.
2. Place about a tablespoon of the barbecue sauce on each oyster and place in the oven. The oysters will stand up better and hold heat better if you place them on a bed of rock salt.
3. Bake for 10 to 12 minutes. Serve immediately with French bread (page 106).

Coulibiac of Salmon

(Coulibiac de Saumon à la Russe)

Coulibiac is an enclosed Russian savory "pie." A wide variety of fillings may be employed, ranging from ground meats to salmon or sturgeon. Whatever fillings are chosen, they are always arranged in strata. Various doughs are also used, with the two most common being puff paste and brioche. Coulibiac is most often made as a large party dish, but here, as with the Wellington, you have a recipe for individual Coulibiacs.

INGREDIENTS

1 lb. salmon filet, cut into 2-in. squares
salt, to taste
white pepper, to taste
¾ c. clarified butter
½ lb. mushrooms, finely minced
1 c. finely minced yellow onion
1 recipe brioche dough (page 58), firm
1 recipe rice pilaf (page 156), cooled to room temperature
3 hard-cooked eggs, grated
1 egg, lightly beaten

Method

1. Dry the salmon pieces and sauté them in 2 ounces of the hot clarified butter until they appear "cooked" on the outside. Remove from pan.
2. Combine the onions and mushrooms and sweat in 2 ounces of the clarified butter until the onions are soft. Place in a sieve and drain.
3. Divide the brioche dough into six to eight pieces. Roll each out into a square (or as close as you can get to a square) about 6 inches in each direction.
4. Place a bed of the rice pilaf in the center of each brioche square.
5. Place two or three pieces of the salmon on each bed of rice.
6. Place 2 or 3 tablespoons of the mushroom/onion mixture on top of the salmon.
7. Place a tablespoon of the grated egg on top of the mushroom mixture.
8. Finish with another layer of the rice pilaf.
9. Fold the dough up around the filling and pinch closed. Brush with beaten egg.
10. Invert the Coulibiac onto a baking sheet on which you have placed a piece of parchment paper that you have buttered.
11. You may, if you wish, decorate the top with a lattice of brioche scraps.
12. Bake in a 400° oven for about 40 minutes or until golden brown.

Coulibiac is one of those dishes with which you don't really need a side dish since it covers most of the food groups. I would not serve a starch, just a simple sautéed vegetable or possibly a salad.

Alternatives: You may, if you choose, follow some or all of these options. Make a mousse of whitefish or salmon to place in the center. You may surround this with the fileted salmon, crêpes, or blanched spinach leaves.

Firm Citron-Fennel Brioche

Brioche is an ancient French "cake-bread" that was probably conceived in Brie several hundred years ago and may, at one time, have contained that city's noted cheese. Brioches are baked in all shapes and sizes and are not, typically, eaten with a substantial meal but are consumed as daytime "snacks." The version I give you here has rather more flour than the classic brioche recipe since we are using it to encase food. That's why I call it "firm." Make this the day before you wish to use it.

INGREDIENTS

¾ c. warm water
½ oz. dry yeast
¾ c. warm milk

32 oz. flour
¾ oz. salt
6 eggs
1 zest of lemon
1 zest of orange
½ tbsp. ground fennel
3 c. butter, softened

Method

1. Dissolve the yeast in the warm (115°) water with a pinch of sugar to "jump-start" the yeast.
2. Place yeast and water in mixer bowl with the warm milk. Allow this mixture to "work" for a few minutes.
3. Start mixer on low speed and gradually add flour over a 2- or 3-minute period. Add eggs, one at a time.
4. Add salt, lemon zest, orange zest, and fennel, mixing all the while.
5. Add butter gradually in small pieces. Continue mixing for 5 to 10 minutes after all the butter has been added.
6. Place brioche in a buttered bowl and allow to rise until doubled in volume.

Homard Thermidor

I am not sure who invented this dish. There are several theories ranging from one of Napoleon's cooks to Delmonico's restaurant in New York. I do know, though, that it was among the last meals served on the *Titanic*, the day before it went down, on April 14, 1912.

Yield: 6 to 8 portions

INGREDIENTS
6–8 live Maine lobsters, 1¼–1½ lb. each
3 c. shellfish stock
1 c. dry white wine
1 tsp. chervil
1 tsp. tarragon
1 tbsp. minced shallots
1 recipe béchamel (page 292)
1 tbsp. dry mustard
salt, to taste
white pepper, to taste
2 tbsp. parmesan

Method

1. Split lobsters down the center and clean.
2. Grill lobster halves.
3. Reduce the stock, wine, chervil, tarragon, and shallots until you are left with approximately 1 cup of liquid.
4. Beat mustard into béchamel.
5. Combine reduction and béchamel.
6. Remove lobster meat from shells.
7. Place some of the sauce in the shells—do not quite fill.
8. Place the lobster meat back in the shell and coat with sauce.
9. Sprinkle parmesan over sauce and brown under a salamander or bake in a very hot oven until browned on top.

And here is a dish with a combination of seafood, poultry, meat, vegetables, and starch all baked together.

MEATS AND POULTRY

Paella Americana

This baked Spanish classic was probably developed in or around Valencia. The original was very different from the modern paella. There may have been no seafood at all in the original, but it did contain snails. I call my version here "Americana," as opposed to the original *Valenciana*, because we pull ingredients from all over the country to put it together.

INGREDIENTS

2 whole chickens, disjointed
¾ c. extra virgin olive oil
2 andouille sausages, sliced into 1-in. disks
1 lb. pork loin, cut into ¾-in. dice
2–3 Atlantic lobster, cleaned and cut into 6 pieces
12–16 shrimp, 16–20s, peeled and deveined
12–16 clams and/or mussels, scrubbed
1½ c. diced yellow onion
2 tbsp. minced garlic
1 c. diced red bell pepper,
1 c. diced green bell pepper
2 c. tomatoes, peeled, seeded, and chopped

4 c. converted rice
3 qt. boiling stock
salt, to taste
black pepper, to taste
1 c. fresh peas, hulled

Method

1. Dry and salt and pepper the chicken pieces. Sauté them in ¼ cup of the olive oil until golden brown. Remove from skillet.
2. Sauté the sausage pieces and pork in the oil until well browned. Remove.
3. Sauté the lobster pieces until the shell is red. Remove.
4. Add remaining oil to pan and sauté the onions and garlic.
5. Add peppers and sauté for about 1 minute.
6. Add tomatoes.
7. Add rice and coat with the oil.
8. Add boiling stock, salt, and pepper.
9. Place all in paella and add peas.
10. Arrange seafood neatly on top of rice mixture and cover.
11. Bake about 25 minutes in a 400° oven. Remove from oven and allow to rest for 10 minutes, still covered. Serve with lemon wedges and chopped parsley.

Pot Pie of Smoked Chicken and Wild Mushrooms

I conceived this dish when I first arrived in Memphis and opened a restaurant. I obtained the chickens from a smokehouse in the Ozarks and the mushrooms from a grower in Meridian, Mississippi. Since you may not always be able to obtain fresh shiitake mushrooms, I've included the method for reconstituting the dried ones here.

Yield: 6 to 8 portions

INGREDIENTS

2 oz. dried mushrooms (shiitake, *shimeji*, etc.)
4 tbsp. clarified butter
3 medium carrots, diced
2 c. small fresh peas
1 c. diced green onions
2 tsp. leaf thyme
1 or 2 bay leaves
1 tsp. salt

black pepper, to taste
3 c. smoked chicken
2 pt. cold chicken stock
3 tbsp. cornstarch or arrowroot
1 c. heavy cream
short paste or puff paste, as needed

Method

1. Bring about 2 quarts of water to a boil and pour it over the dried wild mushrooms. Allow them to steep for 30 to 40 minutes. If you are using shiitakes, you will need to remove the tough stems. Dry the mushrooms.
2. Sweat the carrots in the butter until just soft. Add the peas. If they are small, they will take only a minute or two.
3. Add mushrooms and sweat briefly.
4. Add green onions and sweat briefly.
5. Add thyme, bay leaves, salt, and pepper.
6. Add smoked chicken and incorporate thoroughly.
7. Add 3 cups of the stock and bring to simmer.
8. Thoroughly mix the cornstarch or arrowroot in the remaining cup of stock.
9. Simmer until starch clears and mixture thickens.

This is the point to stop if you are making this dish ahead.

You may now place the mixture in a shallow casserole (or several of them if you wish to serve individual portions) and top with the pastry dough. If I am using puff paste, I bake it ahead until it puffs and then place it on the mixture and reheat in the oven. If one selects the short paste (recipe follows), bake it right on top of the pie for 20 to 25 minutes in the oven. Using a paring knife, make a few vent holes in the top.

Short Paste

INGREDIENTS

16 oz. flour
1 tsp. salt
1 c. butter, softened
cold water, to moisten

Method

1. Sift flour and salt together.
2. You may make this dough by hand in a bowl or with a mixer or food processor. We prefer the processor.
3. Work the softened butter into the flour.
4. Add just enough water so the dough will form a ball.
5. Wrap the dough in plastic wrap and allow it to rest in the refrigerator for 30 minutes.
6. This recipe will give you enough dough for a full-size baking pan. Roll the dough out quickly to a rectangle of about 16 by 20 inches. Drape the dough over the baking pan containing the filling. Press gently down with the palm of your hand on the edges of the pan to cut off the extra dough.

Arroz con Pollo (Chicken and Rice)

A simpler Spanish classic than the Paella.
    Yield: 6 to 8 portions

INGREDIENTS

4 lb. chicken, cut into small pieces
½ c. olive oil
2 onion, diced
¼ c. minced garlic
salt, to taste
black pepper, to taste
½ c. minced parsley
1 c. diced pimento
1 c. salsa
1 tsp. paprika
saffron, pinch
1½ qt. chicken stock
½ c. dry white wine
3 c. long grain rice
¼ c. minced parsley

Method

1. Salt and pepper the chicken.
2. In a large, deep pan, sauté the chicken until golden on all sides.

3. Remove to a warm platter.
4. Add the onion and sweat until the onion is soft. Add garlic and parsley.
5. Add the pimentos, paprika, salsa saffron, salt and pepper, stock, and wine and bring to a boil.
6. Add the rice and simmer, uncovered for about 20 minutes, stirring until the rice is semidry but some liquid remains.
7. Bury the chicken in the rice. Cover and bake about 20 minutes.

Cassoulet

Anatole France is among the writers who have extolled the virtues of this most expensive baked or, more properly, stewed bean dish. Nearly everyone who cares is in agreement that this dish originated in the province of Languedoc. Beyond that, there is considerable discussion, with three cities all claiming bragging rights: Toulouse, Castelnaudary, and Carcassone. If you drew a line due southeast from Toulouse to the Mediterranean, it would go through all three cities.

Incidentally, just east of this line is the city of Narbonne. My mother was from southern Indiana, and there is a small town there that was founded by French settlers and named after a town in the south of France, Narbonne. The locals, as time went by, had more and more difficulty pronouncing the name of this town as the area became less and less French. If you look on the map, you will see a town in southern Indiana called "Gnaw Bone."

All three versions of the dish contain beans, pork, ham, and bacon. The cassoulet of Castelnaudary might have mutton and/or partridge included as well. Baked beans à la Toulouse is probably the most distinguished of the three, for it contains *confit d'oie* (preserved goose) and sausages.

In Toulouse, they rear a large (*grosse*) goose, primarily to obtain its fatted liver (*foie gras*). The flesh of this big bird is quite unsuitable for roasting, and rather than leave the countryside littered with the carcasses of rotting fowl, the inhabitants turn the goose cadavers into confit d'oie. I use the more readily obtainable duck for our cassoulet.

INGREDIENTS

2–3 lb. pork shoulder, roasted and visible fat removed
2 lb. small white beans, boiled and soaked
1 duck, disjointed and sautéed
1 lb. bacon, cut into lardons and sautéed
1½ lb. spicy sausage, whatever you like
½ lb. lightly smoked ham, medium dice
2 c. thinly sliced onion, sautéed in butter
¼ c. minced garlic

3 c. peeled, seeded, and diced tomatoes
4 bay leaves
1 tbsp. whole thyme
3 c. dry white wine
1 qt. brown stock
¼ c. brandy
1 tbsp. salt
black pepper, to taste

Method

1. Cut the pork shoulder into 2-inch squares.
2. Discard the water in which the beans were boiled and soaked.
3. Place the beans in a stock pot with the duck back, half the bacon, two or three pieces of the pork, three or four slices of the sausage, half the ham, the onions, the garlic, tomatoes, bay leaves, thyme, wine, brown stock, brandy, salt, and pepper. Bring to a boil and simmer for 1½ hours.
4. Beginning with the beans, make alternating layers of the beans and various meats in a casserole. Pour in just enough of the liquid to come to the top.
5. Cover the top with the mixture of bread crumbs and parsley and dot with butter.
6. Bake in a 425° oven for about 30 minutes, crack the crust that has formed, and push it gently into the casserole. Cover the top again with the bread crumb and parsley mixture and dot with butter.
7. Bake for an additional 20 to 30 minutes or until the crust forms again. Serve in the casserole.

Individual Beef Wellington
(Filet de Boeuf Wellington)

Arthur, the first Duke of Wellington, who died in 1832, has had trees, boots, and apples named for him as well as this dramatic—and hearty—"baked" beef dish. *Foie gras* (goose or duck) is very expensive. You may wish to substitute a pâté. As to the puff pastry, I am including the recipe for the ambitious among you, but, again, there are one or two premade frozen brands that will suffice quite admirably. Should you want to prepare this dish for two, four, or even six people, you need not purchase the whole beef tenderloin. Buy filet mignon steaks 2 inches thick and trim them of all visible fat and sinew. This is one of the advantages of preparing the individual Wellingtons as opposed to the traditional entire tenderloin. The tenderloin is the most tender muscle in the steer. It does not "do the locomotion."

Yield: 8 to 10 portions

INGREDIENTS

1 tenderloin of beef, "peeled," 4–5 lb.
salt, to taste
black pepper, to taste
4 tbsp. clarified butter
6–8 puff pastry, 4- by 8- by ¼-in. squares
6–8 oz. paté de foie gras (or foie gras)
6–8 oz. duxelles

Method

1. Remove the "head," "tail," and any remaining silver skin from the tenderloin. Cut the remaining center portion of the tenderloin into pieces approximately 2 to 2½ inches thick. Dry the pieces thoroughly and salt and pepper them.
2. Heat the clarified butter until quite hot, in a fry pan, in a sauté pan, or, as I prefer, on a griddle.
3. When browned on all sides, drain pieces of beef on a cake rack over a drip pan.
4. Cut the foie gras into cubes of approximately 1 inch and place squarely in the center of each of the pieces of puff pastry.
5. Place a spoon of the duxelles on top of the foie gras.
6. Press the piece of tenderloin down on top of the duxelles and foie gras, flattening them slightly.
7. Using a sharp knife, remove a 1-inch square from each of the corners of the puff pastry. (This will prevent the Wellington from being too "doughy" on the bottom.)
8. Fold the two side flaps, as you face it, up over the bottom. Then fold up the two end flaps and pinch to seal.
9. Invert the Wellington and place it on a baking sheet.
10. Bake in a 450° oven for approximately 12 to 15 minutes or until golden brown.

The Wellington may be served with a brown sauce derivative or, if you are feeling particularly decadent, the béarnaise sauce (page 297). I like the Pommes de Terre Duchesse (page 79) as a side here, too. You could actually bake everything for this meal if you choose to include one of the timbales (pages 70–71) also.

CHEESES, EGGS, VEGETABLES, AND STARCHES

Baked Goat Cheese with Pesto

I began cooking with goat cheese from Sonoma County in California in about 1980 and have come up with several dishes that show off this fairly mild cheese to its best advantage. The Montrachet style of French goat cheese is similar and widely available in supermarkets today. Either will suffice for the following dish. There is also an excellent goat cheese that is made in Tennessee. This recipe may seem somewhat involved. Trust me here. Try it.

Yield: 6 to 8 portions

INGREDIENTS

6–8 pieces of goat cheese, cut or formed into wheels about ¾ in. thick
   and 2½ in. across
¼ c. extra virgin olive oil
½ c. pesto
½ c. vinaigrette dressing (page 170)
6 c. mixed salad greens (romaine, butter, Bibb, etc.)
1 c. bread crumbs
12–16 Calamata olives, pitted
12–16 sun-dried tomatoes
½ c. finely minced yellow onion
12–16 croutons

Method

1. After you have cut or formed the goat cheese (if you cut the cheese, use a stainless knife which you dip in hot water after each cut), spread some of the olive oil on a baking sheet before you set the cheese wheels on it.
2. Drizzle the remaining olive oil over the top of the cheese.
3. Spread a thin layer of the pesto over the top of each wheel, covering them completely.
4. You may marinate the cheese overnight in the refrigerator if you choose or 2 or 3 hours at room temperature.
5. Make the vinaigrette dressing.
6. Wash and dry the salad greens.
7. Make the croutons (page 68).
8. Dip the goat cheese in the bread crumbs and place the goat cheese in a very hot oven on a sheet pan (or, if you are just doing a few, use a pie pan) and

bake for 4 or 5 minutes or until the goat cheese begins to slide when you shake the pan.

9. Toss the salad greens with the vinaigrette and place them on salad plates.
10. Garnish with the Calamata olives, sun-dried tomatoes, minced onion, and, finally, around the edges of the plate, the croutons.

What You Need to Know

To make the croutons, take one baguette and slice it thinly. Place ¼ cup of butter and ¼ cup of extra virgin olive oil in a skillet with 1 tablespoon of minced garlic. Heat. Using a basting or pastry brush, paint the croutons with this mixture. Bake until the croutons are golden brown. You might want to make more of these than the recipe indicates. They have a way of disappearing.

There may be something that doesn't like a wall, but I know no one who doesn't like a properly baked potato. Even a lot of the fast-food joints have figured this one out. There really is a right way to do this. Here it is.

How to Bake a Potato

The first thing you must do is select the right kind of potato for baking. The Russet potato is the one you want. The Idaho potato is the same thing with a good marketing board. The Russet potato has a high starch and solids content and will "fluff" much better than the White or Red Rose varieties.

1. Preheat your oven to about 450°.
2. Wash the potato. Dry and rub some kosher salt into the skin. You may also rub the potato with butter or oil if you choose, but it is not necessary.
3. Impale the potato with a fork three or four times.
4. Place the potato in the middle of the oven on the oven rack.
5. Bake for approximately 1 hour.

If you need to hold the potatoes for a while, you may now wrap them in foil. Never bake a potato in foil! This will not allow the starches to fluff. Once the potato is baked, you may hold it for a while in foil to retain heat.

Foil will not allow steam to escape and the potato will steam, not bake. The attraction of the baked potato is the fluffiness of the starch. Most baked potato aficionados do not cut the cooked potato with a knife in order to maintain the lightness of the fluffed starches. "Serrate" the potato down the middle with a

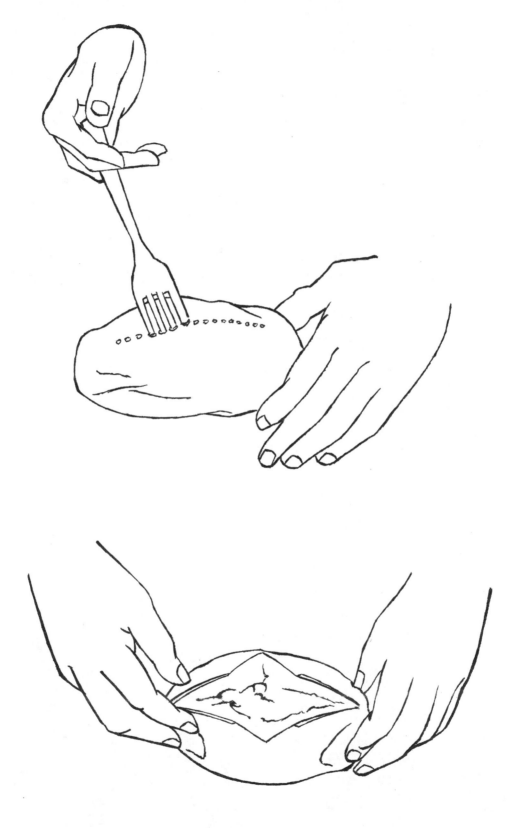

fork, press on both ends with your thumb and forefinger, and the potato will "pop" open for you. Load it up!

Timbales

Timbale is the name of a tapered cooking vessel as well as a number of dishes made in those vessels. Most often, the dish will be in a custard base. The timbale technique is a great way to make a vegetable dish ahead and hold it for a period of time. This is like a mini-quiche, only the quantity of custard is proportionately much less than in a true quiche. Delicate vegetables, like the spinach, will not break down once they are in the custard. If you are just making a few timbales, use custard cups. If you are cooking for many, use muffin pans. When using the latter, I spray the muffin tins with a pan spray *before* buttering. This will ensure that the timbales will release cleanly. Here are a couple of spinach-based timbales.

Spinach and Goat Cheese Timbales

I've prepared this dish for very large parties—up to 250. It will hold for several hours without breaking down.

Yield: About 12 timbales

INGREDIENTS
¾ c. minced onion
½ c. butter
3 c. cooked, well drained, and chopped spinach (about 8–9 bunches fresh spinach)
8 eggs
1 c. goat cheese
½ c. sour cream
2 c. half-and-half
black pepper, to taste
kosher salt, to taste
½ tsp. freshly grated nutmeg
cayenne pepper, to taste

Method

1. In a frying pan or sauté pan, sweat onion in butter until soft.
2. Add spinach and thoroughly incorporate. Drain mixture in a sieve and allow to cool.

3. In a bowl, crumble goat cheese into eggs. Beat eggs, goat cheese, and sour cream together.
4. Blend in half-and-half and add to spinach mixture.
5. Add all seasonings and mix well.
6. Using a pastry bag without a tip, pipe into well-buttered timbale molds. If the mixture seems a little thin, use a ladle.
7. Bake at 475° in a boiling water bath for about 30 minutes. Carefully turn out of molds and serve.

Italian Spinach, Feta, and Potato Timbale

This timbale incorporates both a starch and vegetable.
　　Yield: About 12 timbales

INGREDIENTS

　　2 c. Italian spinach (page 216)
　　2 c. mashed potatoes (page 162)
　　½ c. feta cheese
　　2 eggs, lightly beaten
　　1 c. half-and-half

Method

1. Combine cooked, drained spinach, and mashed potatoes.
2. Add feta cheese.
3. Combine beaten egg with half-and-half.
4. Combine egg mixture with spinach mixture.
5. Butter inside of six timbales or custard cups.
6. Using a pastry bag, pipe the mixture into the timbales.
7. Bake at 475° in a water bath for about 30 minutes. Carefully turn out of molds and serve.

Quiche

This is the classic custard dish that is the ancestor of the timbales.

Quiche Conundrums

Many of the same verities apply here as for the soufflé (page 73).
　　Always use *cooked* food in quiche. Whatever filling you choose for the quiche will not cook in the custard mixture.

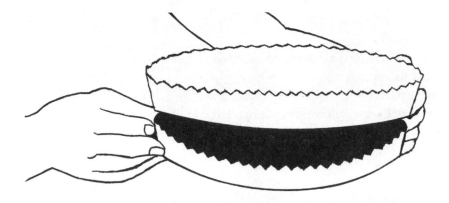

As with the soufflé, again, just about anything you like or have left over from a previous meal may be put into a quiche. Unlike the soufflé, though, the food need not be puréed. A certain "chunkiness" in the ingredients provides interest and texture to the quiche.

Drain any excess moisture from the ingredients before adding to the quiche.

I like a spinach and feta cheese quiche. Mushrooms are great as well. Onions are good. Use your imagination.

Quiche Lorraine

You may be surprised that the quiche is probably a German, not a French, dish. The word *quiche* was at one time spelled *kiche* from the German word *kuchen*. The present French province of Alsace-Lorraine is conceded to be the birthplace of the quiche. Under Bismarck, Alsace-Lorraine was part of the German Empire. The original quiche was probably just a savory custard of eggs and cream in a pastry crust. My version is what most people think of when they hear the name *Quiche Lorraine*, a savory custard tart with cheese and bacon.

Yield: 1 10-inch quiche; serves 6 to 8

INGREDIENTS

1 recipe short paste (page 62)
12 oz. bacon, sliced in pieces 1 in. long
8 oz. Emmenthaler (Swiss) cheese, grated
1 pt. half-and-half
4 eggs
salt, to taste
black pepper, to taste
nutmeg, to taste

> ### What You Need to Know
>
> Notice the ratio of half-and-half to the large eggs. A large egg weighs 2 ounces. The ratio is two large eggs for every cup of dairy product. Eight large eggs beaten into a quart of a dairy product and then cooked will give you custard—every time. Try to store that in your memory bank.

Method

1. Line a pan with the short paste. The pan I think makes the most dramatic presentation is the fluted quiche pan with the removable bottom. You may, of course, make quiche in any tart, *tartelette*, or even a pie pan. "Blind-bake" this crust for 10 minutes in a 375° oven. You do this by lining the dough with aluminum foil and filling the foil with dried beans so that it conforms to the shape of the pan.
2. Blanch the bacon in boiling water for about 5 minutes.
3. Dry the bacon and sauté it until browned. Drain and pat it on paper towels.
4. Spread the bacon and the cheese over the bottom of the dough.
5. Beat the cream, eggs, salt, pepper, and nutmeg together in a bowl. Pour the cream mixture in on top of the bacon and cheese.
6. Bake in a 375° oven for 45 to 60 minutes. Test the center with a piece of dried pasta. If the pasta comes out clean, the quiche is done.

> ### What You Need to Know
>
> Although I am providing you with the recipe for a short-paste crust for the quiche, it is not the crust I prefer. I like the texture and ease of handling of frozen puff pastry much better. Buy the 10- by 15-inch sheets if they are available in your area. You will not have to take the additional step of "blind baking" if you use the puff pastry.

The Savory Soufflé

The soufflé is a mixture of béchamel (page 292), savory or sweet; eggs; and puréed, cooked, drained food and/or cheese. That's it.

I know of no better example of the value of technique than the making of a soufflé. To make a savory soufflé, you need one recipe, not a separate recipe for each new dish issued by the Soufflé-of-the-Month Club. Once you understand these few simple rules, soufflé making becomes child's play (a gifted child, you

understand). The French noun *souffle* (without the accent mark) means "breath" or "breathing." The soufflé is a light dish, puffed up, as if it had inhaled air, which is precisely what the egg whites do when beaten.

The recipe given here is for a soufflé dish, which holds approximately 8 cups.

INGREDIENTS

½ recipe béchamel (page 292)
6 egg yolks
1½ c. grated cheese or purée (or both)
8 egg whites
1 tbsp. butter, softened
¼ c. parmesan

What You Need to Know

When you separate eggs and wish to whip the whites, you must take care to allow *no* yolk in with the whites. Any fat present will prevent the whites from incorporating the air with which you are attempting to infuse them. On the other hand, you can be a little sloppy in recipes that call for egg yolks because a little white will have virtually no effect on the dish.

Method

1. Make the béchamel.
2. Separate eight large eggs.
3. Grate cheese or make vegetable, meat, or shellfish purée.
4. Beat egg yolks into tepid béchamel, one at a time. This will give you a fairly thick batter.
5. Incorporate cheese and/or purée into béchamel.
6. Whip egg whites until quite stiff. Fold into béchamel.
7. Butter bottom and sides of soufflé dish.
8. Put parmesan in soufflé dish and roll it around until it completely coats the dish. Shake out any extra.
9. Bake soufflé in a 375° oven for about 35 minutes. The top should have browned nicely at this point, and the inside of the soufflé will be "set."

If you remove the soufflé too soon, it will implode almost immediately. A sure method with which to tell if the soufflé is cooked in the center is to insert a strand of dried pasta into the soufflé. If it comes out dry, the soufflé is ready. Even if the soufflé is properly cooked, it has a shorter life span than the mayfly. It may hold for 5 to 10 minutes at the most. Eat it now!

What You Need to Know

If you are making a cheese soufflé, nothing more than the grating is required. If, however, you wish to make a soufflé containing a purée of vegetables, fish, shellfish, or even meat, there are a couple of additional steps involved. First, the food must be previously cooked. Second, the 1½ cups is the *net* amount. If you are using spinach, for instance, you will probably need to begin with 4 to 5 cups of raw spinach to achieve the net amount of 1½ cups. Third, you will need to make sure the purée has no extra water in it. Place the purée in a sieve and press firmly on it with a rubber scraper, squeezing the water out. Alternatively, you may place the purée in a kitchen towel and wring it dry.

Cheeses

Swiss cheeses—Emmenthaler or Gruyère—are excellent choices for a soufflé. Basically, any hard or medium-hard cheese you fancy will do well. Both cheddar, in moderation, and goat cheese make wonderful soufflés. Go light on the cheddar, though, because of the fat content.

Purées

Spinach is a quite popular soufflé. Really, any vegetable you enjoy will make a tasty soufflé as long as you cook, purée, and drain it. Salmon, lobster, shrimp, and even clams will be quite successful. I have even made a soufflé with grits.

Pimiento, Jalapeño, and Bean Frittata

The frittata is a baked, open-face Italian omelet. Again, once you master the basic technique, let your imagination be your guide as to ingredients.

Note: This is one of those sauté dishes that is finished in the oven.

Yield: 4 to 6 portions

INGREDIENTS

2 red peppers, roasted and peeled
2 jalapeños, roasted and peeled
7–8 green beans, washed and trimmed
½ c. thinly julienned yellow onions
½ c. parmesan
2 tbsp. extra virgin olive oil
6–8 eggs, lightly beaten
salt, to taste
black pepper, to taste

Method

1. Cut pimiento into a medium julienne.
2. Slice jalapeños into disks about ¼ inch thick.
3. Blanch beans in boiling water until tender, about 10 minutes.
4. Sweat onions in olive oil until soft and translucent. Remove from heat.
5. Arrange beans over onions.
6. Arrange peppers over beans.
7. Sprinkle with about one-quarter of the cheese.
8. Carefully pour eggs over all.
9. Add salt and pepper.
10. Sprinkle with the rest of the cheese.
11. Bake in a 425° oven for about 10 minutes or until puffed and browned.
12. Cut into desired number of portions and serve.

Tortilla de Patata

And our last omelet is the Spanish take on the versatile egg. Read this recipe carefully!

There is not a bar or a party in the Basque country that doesn't offer *tortilla de patata*. You will see it in every tapas bar in the larger cities in Spain, too. This very popular dish is excellent accompanied by a glass of wine, but it can also be cut into larger pieces and served as a light entrée with green salad, making a fine light meal for vegetarians, especially. Tortilla de patata is also common picnic fare, perfect for sandwich filling.

Note: This sauté, too, is finished in the oven.

Yield: 8 portions

INGREDIENTS

1½ c. olive oil
1½ c. chopped onion
4 potatoes, thinly sliced
salt, to taste
black pepper, to taste
6–8 eggs

Method

1. In a large skillet, about 10 inches in diameter, heat the olive oil over medium-high heat. Add the onion and sauté it for about 5 minutes until it is light golden. Add the potatoes and season them to taste with salt and pepper. Reduce the heat to medium and cook the potatoes for about 15 minutes longer, stirring, until they are tender.
2. Raise the heat to medium-high, cook the potatoes for 1 or 2 minutes longer until they are lightly browned, crisp on the outside, and soft on the inside. Using a large slotted spoon, remove the potatoes and onion from the pan and drain them in a colander onto paper towels. Let the oil in the pan cool slightly, then pour off all but about 3 tablespoons.
3. In a large bowl, beat the eggs lightly. Add the potatoes and onion and mix well. Set the mixture aside for a few minutes.
4. Heat the skillet over high heat, tipping the pan to ensure that the oil is evenly distributed. When it is very hot, pour the egg mixture into the pan. Use a spatula to spread the mixture evenly in the skillet. Shake the pan gently to prevent sticking and burning and cook the omelet for 2 or 3 minutes longer until the eggs begin to set around the edges.

5. Lay over the skillet a plate that is slightly larger in diameter than the skillet. Using one hand to hold the plate in place, invert the omelet onto it. Do this over a clean work surface for insurance.

6. Return the empty skillet to the stove, add another 2 tablespoons of the reserved oil, and heat it over high heat. When the oil is hot, slide the omelet off the plate and into the pan, the uncooked side facing down. Shake the pan gently to prevent sticking, and cook the omelet for 1 minute. Reduce the heat to medium and cook for about 3 minutes longer until the omelet is set.

7. Place the omelet in a 375° oven for about 10 minutes.

8. Slide the omelet onto a serving plate and let the omelet cool. Cut into eight pieces and serve.

Yorkshire Pudding

In 1747, in *Mrs. Glasse Cookery*, appears the first recipe I know of for this standard side dish for the English roast beef: "Take a Quart of Milk, four Eggs . . . make it up into a thick Batter with Flour, like a Pancake Batter." I can't improve on that, other than to be a bit more precise.

Yorkshire, the largest county in the north of England, is historically known for its pigs, stone, and the following delectable starch. Traditionally, the pudding was made in a large pan placed under a "joint" rotating on a spit. The drippings from the roast fell into the pudding and flavored it. I think you will find it much easier to handle if you try it our way, in the muffin pan.

Yield: 6 to 8 portions

INGREDIENTS
4 eggs
2 c. milk
2 c. flour
1 tsp. salt
black pepper, to taste
beef drippings, as needed

Method

1. Beat eggs and milk together in a bowl.

2. Incorporate the flour, salt, and pepper into the eggs and milk. Permit the batter to rest, covered, in the refrigerator while you are preparing your roast.

3. Heat two muffin pans in a 375° oven for about 5 minutes.
4. Pour about 1 teaspoon of the drippings from a roast into each of the cups in the muffin tins.
5. Using a ladle, fill the muffin cups approximately three-quarters full with the batter.
6. Bake in a 375° oven for 15 to 20 minutes or until puffed, browned, and set. Do this while you are allowing your roast to rest so the juices in it may recirculate in the meantime. Serve with the roast.

Pommes de Terre Duchesse

While this dish actually combines two of the techniques, boiling and baking, when more than one cooking technique is involved in preparing a dish, I will usually list the dish within that technique we see when the dish is set before us. Here, we see a "baked" potato dish. A French version of "mashed" potatoes, these are also "milled." The addition of the eggs provides both color and body. When you pipe these from a pastry bag, they will hold their shape when baked. This is an excellent "do-ahead" dish, as the piping and initial baking may be done hours ahead, and the last baking, which colors and finishes the potatoes, takes just a few minutes.

Yield: 8 portions

INGREDIENTS
3 lb. Russet potatoes, peeled and quartered
water, to cover
1 tsp. salt
white pepper, to taste
½ c. half-and-half
1 egg
2 egg yolks
nutmeg, pinch
4 tbsp. butter

Method

1. Boil potatoes until just soft, usually, about 20 to 25 minutes, in the water, to which you have added the teaspoon of salt.
2. Put the potatoes through a food mill and place them in a stainless bowl. Stir constantly over low heat for 2 to 3 minutes to drive off any excess moisture.

3. Add salt and pepper.
4. Beat in half-and-half to form a creamy texture—not too thin. Do not be too dogmatic about adding all the liquid. The potatoes must be stiff enough to stand on their own.
5. Thoroughly incorporate eggs and yolks.
6. Add nutmeg and butter.
7. Place potato mixture in a pastry bag with a star tube. Pipe onto a sheet pan.
8. Bake the potatoes in a hot oven for about 10 minutes. They will not be brown yet.
9. Hold them in a warm place until just 5 or 10 minutes before you are ready to serve them. Brown them in a very hot oven.

What You Need to Know

About this "piping" thing—it takes a little practice. Twist the top of the pastry bag shut and get a grip on the bag. Use your other hand to guide the bag. Try to stay perpendicular to the surface on which you are piping.

Gratin Jurassien

No, this is not a dish of raptors with cheese. It is another make-ahead, nifty French potato dish. I've used this as a starch in several restaurants.

Yield: 6 to 8 portions

INGREDIENTS

6–8 Russet potatoes, peeled and sliced ⅛ in. thick
6 tbsp. clarified butter
1 c. parmesan
1½ c. heavy cream
salt, to taste
white pepper, to taste

Method

1. Spread a thin layer of butter in a baking dish.
2. Lay one shingled layer of the potatoes in the dish.
3. Season the layer with the butter, cheese, salt, and pepper.
4. Repeat twice more.

5. Finish the top off with a layer with the cheese.
6. Carefully pour in the cream around the edges to avoid dislodging the layers. Dot the top with butter.
7. Bake in a 350° to 375° oven for about 60 minutes. The top should be golden brown and the potatoes in the middle creamy.

Note: Do not attempt to make more than three layers, or the potatoes will not bake in the 60 minutes.

Oven-Baked Potatoes

Some would call these "roasted" potatoes. I like to reserve the term "roast" for meats and poultry.
　　Yield: 6 to 8 portions

INGREDIENTS

6–8 80-count baker potatoes, peeled and quartered
½ c. clarified butter or olive oil
salt, to taste
black pepper, to taste
1 tbsp. minced garlic
2–3 tbsp. minced parsley

What You Need to Know

The Russet or Burbank potato is sold in a carton. The size is indicated by how many potatoes are contained in a standard-sized carton holding approximately 50 pounds of potatoes. The sizes run from about a 40-count (the largest) to a 120-count (the smallest.) The 80-count is a good-size all-round cooking potato; it weighs about 10 ounces.

Method

1. Heat the butter or oil in a sauté pan until quite hot.
2. Sear the potatoes in the hot fat until just browned on the outside, 4 or 5 minutes, tossing or stirring all the while.
3. Place in a 425° oven for about 35 minutes. Every few minutes, agitate the pan to ensure the potatoes are browning (caramelizing) uniformly. When the potatoes are nearly done, sprinkle the garlic over the potatoes.

4. When the potatoes are brown and crisp on the outside and soft on the inside, remove them from the oven, sprinkle the parsley over them, and serve.

Italian Baked Potatoes

I learned this dish from a German chef.
   Yield: About 10 portions

INGREDIENTS

8–10 Russet potatoes
2 tbsp. butter, softened
approx. 1½ qt. chicken stock
salt, to taste
black pepper, to taste
1 tbsp. minced garlic
1½ c. parmesan

Method

1. Peel potatoes and slice thinly, about ¼-inch thick. Hold in a bowl of cold water until ready to assemble dish.
2. Butter a rectangular baking dish large enough to hold potatoes.
3. Place potatoes—standing on edge—in rows in baking dish; leave no spaces between the potatoes or the rows. You may have to slice an additional potato to fill out your pan.
4. Bring stock to boil and add garlic, salt, and pepper.
5. Carefully pour stock over potatoes. Use enough stock to come to within ½ inch of tops of potatoes.
6. Bake in a 400° oven for approximately 30 minutes or until potatoes are soft and a golden brown crust has formed on the top.
7. Uniformly strew the parmesan over the top of the potatoes and bake for an additional 30 minutes.

How to serve: Lift a 1½- to 2-inch section of the potatoes out of the pan with a set of tongs. Place on plate and press down as you tip the tongs to the side, "fanning" the potatoes slightly.

Herb-Roasted Potatoes, Dijon

Yeah, yeah, I know. I slipped into the "roasted" potato thing here. Shut up. Here is a more adventuresome version of the oven-baked potatoes.

Yield: 6 to 8 portions

INGREDIENTS

1 c. Dijon mustard
¾ c. extra virgin olive oil
2 tsp. oregano
2 tsp. basil
1 tsp. crushed red pepper
12–14 small Red or White Rose potatoes
salt and black pepper, to taste

Method

1. Combine all ingredients—except potatoes and ¼ cup of the olive oil—in a bowl.
2. Wash and dry potatoes and remove a small band of the skin around the center of the potato.
3. Heat remaining olive oil in a sauté pan.
4. Cook potatoes until they are just beginning to caramelize. Add Dijon mixture to pan and toss, thoroughly coating potatoes.
5. Roast at 450° for about 40 minutes. Serve with any hearty roasted meat or poultry dish.

Lasagne al Forno

A party dish, this lasagne is a hybrid born of the very rich lasagne of southern Italy and the more reserved version served in Emilia-Romagna. This recipe will fill what chefs call a full-size "hotel" pan (about 20 by 12 inches and 2½ inches deep) and will feed about 20 people. If you are going to go through this much trouble, make a lot! Make the Ragu alla Bolognese well in advance of preparing the dish.

Yield: About 16 to 20 portions

INGREDIENTS

8 c. Ragu alla Bolognese (page 269)
3 c. béchamel sauce (page 292)
1 recipe fresh pasta, cut in 4-in. strips

1 lb. grated mozzarella
1 c. parmesan
2 lb. ricotta

Method

1. Make Ragu alla Bolognese. (I hope you have this already!)
2. Make béchamel.
3. Using a full-size hotel pan, place a thin layer of the Ragu on the bottom of the pan.
4. Place a layer of the noodles over the sauce.
5. Place a thin layer of the sauce over the noodles.
6. Spread béchamel over the sauce.
7. Mix the three cheeses together and spread a layer of them over the béchamel.
8. Place a layer of noodles over the cheeses and repeat steps 6, 7, and 8. Coat the last layer with béchamel.
9. Sprinkle parmesan on top and bake in a 450° to 475° oven for 30 minutes. Rest lasagne 10 minutes before cutting.

How to Bake a Winter Squash

The best method for making the winter squashes is to bake them. The winter squashes are far too firm to sauté. Winter squash, including butternut, acorn, delicata, and pumpkins, are very tasty and quite nutritious. Here is what I have found to be the best way to prepare winter squash, either to eat plain as it comes from the oven or for use in other recipes.

1. Cut squash in half, scoop out the seeds, and put in a baking pan, face down with about ¼ inch of water in the pan.

2. Bake at 375° for 20 to 45 minutes (depending on squash size). Test by poking with a fork to tell when it's done—it should be soft.

3. Serve just as it is or scooped from its skin and mashed up with butter and some brown sugar. Raisins, maple syrup, or nuts are also fine additions.

Aubergines à la Provençale

This dish from the south of France is one of the few baked vegetable dishes (other than timbales) I have used in restaurants over the years. If you get small eggplants, you will be able to "hold" them without them breaking down for a couple of hours after cooking.

Yield: 6 to 8 portions

Ingredients

3–4 small eggplants
2 tbsp. lemon juice
1 tbsp. salt
1–2 c. peeled, seeded, and diced tomatoes
¼ c. extra virgin olive oil
1 tbsp. minced garlic
1 tbsp. pesto
2 tbsp. minced parsley
black pepper, to taste

Method

1. Cut eggplant in half lengthwise.
2. Sprinkle a little salt and spread a little of the lemon juice over the cut halves.
3. Bake in a 450° oven for 10 minutes.
4. Remove from oven and cool slightly. Carefully scoop out the flesh, leaving ¾ inch on all sides. Dice flesh.
5. Sweat eggplant and tomatoes in olive oil.
6. Add garlic and pesto (page 39) and continue to sweat.
7. Add parsley and remainder of lemon juice.
8. Add salt and pepper to taste.
9. Fill hollowed eggplant halves with mixture and bake in a 450° oven for 10 minutes.

Melanzane alla Parmigiana

You will be hard-pressed to find a "red sauce" Italian restaurant that does not include this dish in the bill of fare. Sadly, the eggplant is usually swathed in a dense egg batter before frying. This procedure creates a *very* heavy dish. You merely dry and lightly flour the eggplant. If you have read your chapter on frying, you know what oils to use, what temperature to use, and how to fry anything without it becoming fat laden. That knowledge will come in quite handy here.

Yield: 8 to 10 portions

INGREDIENTS

4 fried eggplants (below)
1 qt. Roma tomatoes, diced
1 tbsp. minced garlic
½ c. minced parsley
salt, to taste
black pepper, to taste
2 c. grated mozzarella
1 c. parmesan
1 tbsp. whole oregano
2 tbsp. butter

Method

1. Butter half a full-size hotel pan and put down a layer of eggplant.
2. Mix the tomatoes, garlic, and parsley.
3. Place a thin layer of the tomato mixture over the eggplant.
4. Salt and pepper the eggplant. Sprinkle a little oregano over.
5. Place a layer of the cheeses over the tomatoes.
6. Continue with layers until you have exhausted the eggplant.
7. Finish with eggplant with a little parmesan sprinkled over the top. Dot with butter and bake at 425° for about 30 minutes. You may need to skim some fat and/or water from the dish while it is baking. Allow the dish to "set up" for 5 or 10 minutes before serving.

How to Fry Eggplant

Here's an easy way to prepare eggplant. Peel the eggplant and slice it across into 1-inch-thick slices. Salt. Place the slices on a cooling rack over a pan. Place another pan on top of the eggplant and add some weight to it. This will squeeze out much of the water in the eggplant. Thoroughly dry the eggplant and dredge it lightly in all-purpose flour. Shake off excess. Preheat peanut oil to 350°. Fry slices until they are just beginning to brown, 4 to 5 minutes. Drain.

Cannelloni

This stuffed pasta dish probably originated in northern Italy, in Piedmont. You will notice the ingredients are remarkably similar to those in lasagne.

Yield: 8 to 10 portions

INGREDIENTS

1 recipe egg pasta (page 165)
1 recipe stuffing (below)
1 recipe Ragu alla Bolognese (page 269)
1 recipe béchamel (page 292)
½ c. parmesan
4 tbsp. butter, softened

(**Method**)

1. Preheat oven to about 400°.
2. Make the pasta and roll as thinly as possible. Cut into rectangles about 3 by 4 inches.
3. Make the stuffing.
4. Make the meat sauce.
5. Make the béchamel.
6. Blanch the pasta for about 30 seconds in boiling water. Cool, flatten, and dry.
7. Place approximately 1 tablespoon of stuffing on each pasta rectangle and spread evenly.
8. Roll the strip into a cylinder on the shorter side.
9. Place in an oiled baking dish and cover with a layer of the Ragu.
10. Cover with the béchamel.
11. Strew the cheese over the top and dot with butter. Bake for about 15 minutes.

Cannelloni Stuffing

INGREDIENTS

½ yellow onion, diced
3 tbsp. extra virgin olive oil
½ lb. lean ground beef (or veal)
¼ c. minced ham
1 egg yolk
1 c. parmesan
1¼ c. ricotta
¼ c. béchamel (page 292)

nutmeg, pinch
salt, to taste
black pepper, to taste

Method

1. Sauté onion in the olive oil until translucent.
2. Add ground meat and sauté until cooked.
3. Strain to remove fat.
4. In a mixing bowl, combine meat mixture with ham, egg yolk, parmesan, ricotta, béchamel, nutmeg, salt, and pepper.

Pizza

In Italy there are very stringent rules that must be followed if one is to be a traditional licensed pizza maker, one who makes the "Traditionale Garantita Pizza Napoletana." The Ministry of Agriculture specifies temperatures, types of flour, and ingredients and that the pizza be baked in a wood-fired oven. I'm not going to be quite so Draconian. The Italians use a "00" flour for their pizza crust. While you may purchase this in specialty stores or buy it on the Internet, it really isn't necessary in order to make a great pizza. I use a combination of all-purpose and bread flour, though you will get a perfectly acceptable pizza with either. Do get a pizza stone, and do get your oven as hot as it gets!

Pizza Dough

Yield: 2 10-inch pizzas

INGREDIENTS

1 oz. dry yeast
2¾ c. warm water
5 c. all-purpose or bread flour
1 tsp. salt
½ tsp. white pepper
¼ c. extra virgin olive oil

Method

1. Dissolve yeast in warm water (about 110°). Allow this mixture to "work" for about 10 to 15 minutes. Place mixture in mixer.
2. Thoroughly blend flour, salt, and white pepper together.

3. Turn mixer onto low speed. Gradually add flour, salt, and pepper mixture to yeast mixture in mixer. Stop adding flour when the dough pulls away from the sides of the mixer and forms a ball on the dough hook.
4. Add olive oil in a stream. Add remaining flour, if any, just until the dough does not feel tacky to the touch.
5. Place the dough in an oiled bowl, cover, set in a warm place, and allow it to rise for about an hour or until doubled in volume.

Sauce for Pizza

Yield: 1 quart

INGREDIENTS

2 c. tomato sauce (page 294)
1 c. Roma tomatoes, seeded and chopped
1 c. juice from tomatoes
1 tsp. whole oregano
1 tbsp. chopped fresh basil
1 tsp. minced garlic
½ tsp. salt
black pepper, to taste

Method

1. Place all ingredients in a saucepan.
2. Simmer for 5 minutes.

Pizza (Individual)

INGREDIENTS

5 oz. pizza dough (page 88)
½ oz. parmesan
4 oz. pizza sauce (above)
3 oz. grated mozzarella
extra virgin olive oil, drizzle
1 tsp. minced fresh basil

Method

1. Using your fingers, spread the dough out to an approximate 10-inch circle. Place it either on a pizza peel, on a tile, or in a pan before adding any toppings.
2. Drizzle olive oil over the dough and spread it with your fingers. Spread parmesan evenly over the dough.

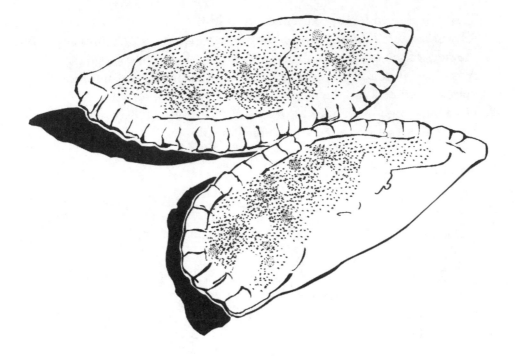

3. Put pizza sauce on dough with a ladle, beginning in the middle of the dough and spreading the sauce outward toward the edges. Leave a 1-inch border with no sauce all around the pizza.
4. Spread mozzarella evenly over the sauce.
5. Drizzle a little olive oil over all.
6. Sprinkle basil over all. (I like to let the pizza sit for a few minutes at this juncture so the border of dough around the edge will rise slightly.)
7. Bake in a very hot oven, 450° to 500°, for approximately 10 to 12 minutes.

Note: You may add any toppings you like to this basic pizza. Always add cooked meats. The harder vegetables should be lightly blanched before adding to the pizza.

Calzone (Individual)

INGREDIENTS

4 oz. pizza dough (page 88)
½ oz. parmesan
2 oz. pizza sauce (page 89)

6 oz. filling

   (Possible fillings: mozzarella, goat cheese, sausage, garlic, pesto,
   prosciutto, salami, Swiss cheese, provolone, sun-dried tomatoes,
   olives, onions, cheddar cheese, fresh tomatoes, and just about
   anything else you like to eat!)

1 egg, lightly beaten

½ tsp. garlic oil

Method

1. Roll dough out into an oval about ¼ inch thick.
2. Spread parmesan over center of dough. Place sauce on parmesan.
3. Place filling on top of sauce.
4. Fold calzone over so the filling is enclosed and the edges meet.
5. Decoratively crimp edges.
6. Wash with beaten egg.
7. Bake in a very hot oven for about 15 minutes or until golden brown.
8. With a spoon, spread the garlic oil over the top of the calzone.

BAKING BREADS

Risen Breads and Doughs

Long called "the staff of life," bread has been a nutritious element in Western cookery for thousands of years. Until the wild yeasts were harvested, bread was a pretty unpalatable, heavy food. Once these yeasts came into the picture, the outlook for bread became much rosier. Bakers leaven doughs in three basic manners: the straight dough method, the sponge method (both of which rely on yeast), and the base/acid method, which involves a chemical reaction with baking powder (soda) and acid.

You will notice that many of the measurements for the doughs, both here and in the dessert chapter, are given by weight. If you will invest in a small, inexpensive kitchen scale, your abilities as a baker will improve overnight. In professional bakeries, usually dealing in somewhat larger quantities than the average home cook, quantities are all determined on a scale. If you want the results achieved by these professional bakeries, weigh your ingredients.

Yeast and baking powder (or soda) are the two principal ingredients needed to *lighten* doughs. Without one of them, you would get flat, heavy, unpalatable bread. Both perform precisely the same function: when mixed with a liquid, carbon dioxide is given off as a by-product. The carbon dioxide attempts to escape from the dough, pulling the dough up. This is why doughs rise.

Flours tend to be irregular. They cannot be counted on to have the same moisture content from one batch to the next. Also, if you live in an area with high humidity, the flour will have a higher moisture content. Because of these varying factors, virtually no yeast dough recipe is intended to be executed literally in all locations. After doing a little baking, you will learn the adjustments that need to be made in your area. We are always looking for a texture. All the following doughs are intended to be made in an electric mixer equipped with a dough hook.

There are two basic methods for making yeast dough: the straight method and the sponge method. For now, we will concern ourselves only with the straight method.

The Yeast Dough Straight Mixing Method

Place these ingredients in the mixer in the following order:

1. *Liquid*. The liquid should always be warm, but not above 138°—the temperature at which the yeast will be destroyed.
2. *Yeast*. All the quantities in the recipes are for active dry yeast. If you are using fresh yeast, use about twice as much.

3. *Sugar.* A little sugar added to the water and yeast mixture in any dough will activate the yeast more quickly and initiate the feeding frenzy that produces as a by-product the desirable carbon dioxide.

4. *Flour* (and salt). If you sift the salt with the flour, it will be more evenly distributed throughout the dough. For most recipes, do not add the salt before this stage, as it will retard the growth of the yeast. The critical point here is to add the flour after the liquid and to adjust the quantity accordingly to ensure you have a nice smooth dough ball.

5. *Proteins.* The proteins will almost invariably be whole eggs, egg whites, or egg yolks. Add them one at a time and be sure each is thoroughly incorporated before adding the next.

6. *Fats.* The fats give a smoother texture to the dough and should always be added last. They include shortening, butter, and cooking oils.

You may well need to incorporate more flour to pull your dough together. Add it very slowly, and as the dough pulls away from the side of the mixer, look for smooth, clean sides on the mixing bowl.

Texture

This is one of the keys to making good breads. When the dough has begun to pull away from the sides of the mixing bowl and cling to the dough hook, the bread dough is nearly ready.

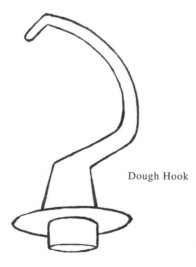

Dough Hook

What You Need to Know

Most quality mixers will arrive equipped with three basic attachments: a paddle, a dough hook, and a whip. I use the dough hook for all *stiff* doughs. By that I mean doughs in which I wish to develop the maximum gluten. This will be principally breads and rolls. The paddle is useful for making anything of a batter consistency and the whip for incorporating air into egg whites or cream.

The dough will still be somewhat tacky at this point. Continue adding flour, just a little at a time, until the dough is smooth to the touch. At this time, the sides of the bowl should be quite clean. This is the texture for which we aim on nearly all breads. For making the french bread, the onion rolls, the white rolls, and the challah, you should not have to put any flour out on the counter or bench.

Mixing and Kneading

The two components of flour about which we need concern ourselves when we make yeast doughs are starch and gluten. Pastry flours have less gluten and are

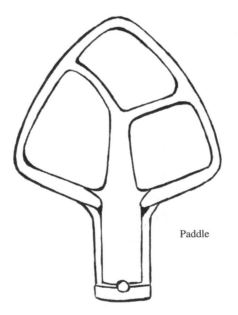

Paddle

Whip

"softer." Bread flours have more and are "harder." All-purpose flour, which we specify for many of the recipes in this book, is a balance between the two. "Softer" flours would be better for pastries and "harder" for breads. The gluten in bread flour helps hold the escaping carbon dioxide in the bread, and this is what causes the dough to rise.

You have no doubt noticed when reading a recipe for pie dough or biscuits that you were enjoined to mix the dough just enough to combine the ingredients. The more you handle the dough, the more you will develop the gluten in the dough. The more you develop the gluten, the more elastic the dough will be. This elasticity is a desirable trait in bread and not nearly so in pastries or biscuits.

Bread doughs may be removed from the mixer and kneaded by hand, or they may be left in the mixer and kneaded with the dough hook in many instances. When engaging in the latter practice, you must be careful not to permit the temperature in the mixer to reach a point where it kills the yeast. Bread doughs require kneading to develop the gluten.

Rising and Proofing

All yeast doughs will need to rise at least once, preferably twice. You will get a certain amount of "oven-spring" in the oven, but it will be minimal. Most yeast doughs will rise in about an hour in a warm room or in 12 to 24 hours in a refrigerator for the first rising.

Place most doughs in a stainless mixing bowl to let them rise. Lightly coat the inside of the bowl with oil or butter before placing the dough in it. Form the dough into a uniform ball and place it in the mixing bowl. Turn the dough over; you have now coated the top of the dough with a little of the fat. This will keep the dough from "crusting" or drying out. Cover the bowl with a piece of plastic wrap. This will create the moist environment the yeast prefers. Also, as the carbon dioxide escapes from the dough, you will be able to see it "blowing up" the plastic wrap. This will tell you how active your yeast is.

Between risings, when you punch the dough down, you will need to knead it for a minute or two to redevelop the gluten. Shape the dough either into rolls or a loaf before the second rising. The second rising will not take quite as long as the first rising.

I've included quite a few rolls and breads in this book. I think that once you grasp the essentials of baking breads, you will see the need for a fairly large repertoire of these. You will notice there is a panoply of soups as well. I periodically teach a class on breads and soup as a complete meal. The students are *always* asking me for a greater variety of both. I think I've included enough to keep you busy for a while. Very few foods are more satisfying than fresh bread warm from the oven.

Rolls are a little easier to make than loaves, so we will begin with a few of them here.

What You Need to Know

You will notice in the following recipes that we have several *washes*. The wash, a coating for yeast breads and rolls, will determine the texture of the surface of the roll or bread as well as its color. The most common washes are egg yolk, egg white, whole egg, butter or oil, and water. All the egg washes should be diluted by whipping in 1 teaspoon of cold water per egg. This will ensure even spreading. A small pastry brush is best for this task. No one wash is always right for any given yeast roll or bread. Experiment and see what you like.

One last note here before I get into the recipes. In several of the recipes, I ask you to butter or oil the pan on which you are baking. That's fine; there's absolutely nothing wrong with that. But most often, I use parchment paper myself. Just a matter of personal preference—also, you add no fat to the bread with the parchment paper, and it keeps the pan clean.

Yeast Rolls

This is a very simple roll which makes a good accompaniment to almost any meal. This is also the only roll recipe I am giving you here where the rolls will actually be touching each other after they rise. I use what we call a *half sheet* pan for this roll.

Yield: About 24 2-ounce rolls

What You Need to Know

The half-sheet pan, approximately 12 by 17 inches, will fit in most home ovens. The full-sheet pan, approximately 17 by 24 inches, will not. If you plan to do a lot of baking, I recommend you go to your local restaurant supply store and get several half-sheet pans. This same store will likely have a supply of parchment paper. Get some. I prefer this to the sprays and baking mats.

INGREDIENTS

1 oz. dry yeast
2½ c. warm water
6 tbsp. sugar
7½ c. sifted bread flour
1½ tsp. salt
¼ c. shortening
1 tbsp. butter, melted

Method

1. Thoroughly blend yeast and warm water (about 115°–120°) and add 1 tablespoon of the sugar. Put this mixture in the mixing bowl and allow it to "work" for 5 to 10 minutes.
2. Sift together the flour, sugar, and salt.
3. While the mixer is running on slow speed, gradually add the flour mixture, a little at a time, to the bowl.
4. Combine the vegetable oil and the melted butter and add them to the mixing bowl gradually.
5. Place the dough in a large buttered bowl, cover the bowl with plastic wrap, and permit it to rise until doubled in volume.
6. Divide the dough into 2-ounce rolls and place them close together, five across, nearly touching, until you run out of space, on a half-sheet pan lined with parchment paper.

7. Allow the rolls to rise again until doubled in volume.

8. Bake in a 350° oven for about 25 minutes. Brush the tops of the rolls with unsalted, melted butter and bake approximately 10 minutes more.

> ### What You Need to Know
>
> To make a roll with a smooth surface, using your fingers, gather the ball so you have one small "seam" at the center of the roll. Invert the roll; press the roll against the work surface with the bottom of your palm, holding the seam to the surface; and gently push away from you, and you will discover the upper surface to be smooth.

Onion Rolls

This is as close as I have seen to a "foolproof" bread recipe. The professional students who have studied with me over the years love this bread for its flavor, texture, and the consistent results. Try it as a sandwich or dinner roll. You will need to weigh these ingredients.

Yield: About 24 2-ounce rolls

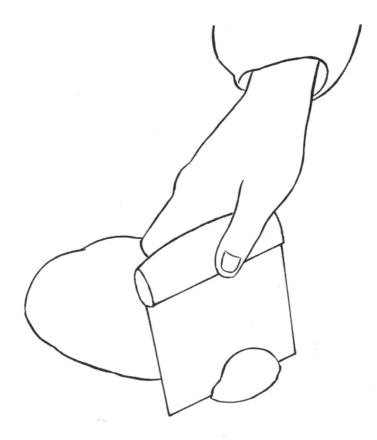

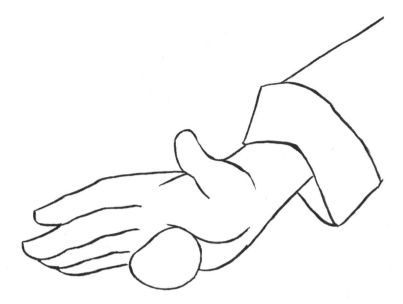

Ingredients

12 oz. warm water
1 oz. dry yeast
2½ oz. sugar
1 lb., 6 oz. bread flour
¼ oz. salt
1 egg
2½ oz. vegetable shortening
¼ c. finely minced yellow onion

Method

1. Combine water, yeast, and sugar in mixer bowl. Permit mixture to work for 5 minutes or so.
2. Sift flour and salt together. With mixer running on low speed, gradually add flour to water and yeast mixture.
3. When flour is thoroughly incorporated, add egg.
4. Add shortening.
5. Add onions and permit dough hook to knead the dough for a minute or two. Remember you are looking for a texture. If you need a little more or less flour, make the adjustment.
6. Place the dough in a warm place, covered with plastic wrap, and allow it to rise until it has doubled in volume.
7. Punch the dough down and weigh it into 2- or 3-ounce portions. Form these into rolls—round or oval. Round is best for sandwiches.

8. Place the rolls on a sheet pan on which you have placed parchment paper, wash them with a whole egg wash, and permit to rise again until doubled in volume.
9. Bake in a 375° oven for 15 to 20 minutes or until golden brown.

White Rolls

This is a good, basic roll appropriate for most dinners. At Mudd's we made this and the whole-wheat roll our staples.

Yield: About 24 2-ounce rolls

INGREDIENTS

24 oz. warm water
2 oz. dry yeast
1 tbsp. sugar
2¾ lb. bread flour
1 oz. salt
2 egg whites
1 oz. shortening

Method

1. Combine warm water, yeast, and sugar in mixer. Allow mixture to "work" for 5 to 10 minutes.
2. Sift flour and salt together.
3. Run mixer on slow speed with dough hook.
4. Gradually add flour to mixer bowl.
5. Add egg whites.
6. Add shortening and thoroughly incorporate.
7. Place dough in an oiled bowl, cover, and allow to rise in a warm place until doubled in volume.
8. Punch dough down and form into 2- to 3-ounce rolls. Place on a sheet pan with parchment paper.
9. Slit tops of rolls diagonally and paint with water. Allow rolls to double in volume and bake in a 375° oven for about 20 minutes.

Guastelle
(Italian Rolls)

I learned this from an Italian baker in the San Francisco area in the late 1960s. I have been making it ever since.

Yield: About 24 2-ounce rolls

INGREDIENTS

2 c. water
½ c. peanut oil
¼ c. sugar
1½ tbsp. salt
1½ c. warm water
1½ oz. dry yeast
2 eggs
8 c. bread flour

Method

1. Bring 2 cups of water to a boil. Pour over oil, sugar, and salt in a bowl. Cool until tepid.
2. Dissolve yeast in warm water.
3. Combine the two mixtures in the mixer.
4. Start mixer and gradually add flour.
5. Run mixer on low speed and add eggs, one at a time. Let rise until doubled in volume.
6. Knead lightly, make into rolls, and crease center with the back of a paring knife. Press all the way down to the pan.
7. Paint with an egg-white wash and sprinkle with sesame seeds.
8. Let rise until doubled in volume and bake in a 400° oven for about 15 minutes.

Heavy Cream Rolls

This roll is actually quite light.
Yield: About 24 2-ounce rolls

INGREDIENTS

1½ oz. dry yeast
1 c. warm water
2 eggs
2 c. heavy cream, room temperature
6–7 c. bread flour
1 tsp. salt

Method

1. Place yeast and warm water in mixer.
2. Combine eggs and heavy cream in a bowl and whip until just mixed.
3. Add egg mixture to mixer.

4. Add flour gradually with mixer running on slow. Add salt about halfway through mixing procedure.
5. Make the dough into rolls and place on sheet pan with parchment paper. Allow the rolls to double in volume.
6. Paint rolls with heavy cream.
7. Bake in a 425° oven for about 15 minutes.

Leavening with Baking Powder or Baking Soda

Single-acting baking powder produces all its bubbles when it gets wet. Double-acting baking powder produces bubbles again when it gets hot.

Some recipes call for baking soda rather than baking powder. These recipes will almost invariably include a liquid acid like buttermilk or yogurt to react with the baking soda to produce the bubbles. We use baking powder rather than yeast in some recipes principally because it is much faster.

What You Need to Know

Baking powder normally has three constituents: an *acid*, a *base*, and filler of some sort. All three need to be dry powders that can be mixed together. The three most common ingredients are baking soda (the base), cream of tartar (the acid), and cornstarch (the filler). The basic idea here is the same as with yeast: you want to produce bubbles of carbon dioxide to lighten the dough. When you add a liquid to baking powder, a reaction begins between the acid and the base, and the resulting solution produces carbon dioxide.

Blueberry Muffins

When I lived in New York, I had blueberry muffins for breakfast three or four days per week. When I was in Paris, I had croissants and bread with strawberry preserves several days per week. Strong French roast coffee, a fresh bread of some kind, and a piece of fruit will get my engine going in the morning.

Yield: About 18 muffins

INGREDIENTS
1½ c. blueberries
3 c. flour
1 tbsp. baking powder
1 tsp. salt
½ c. sugar
½ c. dark brown sugar

½ c. butter, melted
3 eggs
1 c. milk

Method

1. Wash, dry, and pick over blueberries. If using frozen blueberries, drain well in a colander.
2. Sift together flour, baking powder, salt, and granulated sugar in a mixing bowl.
3. Stir in brown sugar.
4. In another bowl, combine eggs and milk. Beat.
5. Carefully incorporate egg mixture into dry ingredients. Do not overmix. Once you add your liquid, the reaction begins. Carefully incorporate blueberries.
6. Fill two 12-muffin muffin pans approximately two-thirds full with the batter, and bake in a 400° oven for about 20 to 25 minutes.

Buttermilk Biscuits

This makes a very light, tasty biscuit. Remember: knead quickly.
Yield: About 12 biscuits

INGREDIENTS

3 c. flour
1 tbsp. sugar
4 tsp. double-acting baking powder
1 tsp. salt
1 tsp. baking soda
¾ c. butter, chilled and cut into ¾-in. pieces
1 c. buttermilk

Method

1. Preheat oven to 425°. Whisk flour, sugar, baking powder, salt, and baking soda in large bowl to blend.
2. Using your fingertips, rub the ¾ cup of butter into dry ingredients until mixture resembles coarse meal.
3. Add buttermilk and stir until evenly moistened.
4. Using 2 ounces of dough for each biscuit, drop biscuits onto baking sheet, spacing 2 inches apart. Alternatively, you may shape the dough into a

round or rectangle by hand and carefully cut out the biscuits with a cookie cutter.

5. Bake until biscuits are golden brown on top, about 15 minutes. Cool slightly. Serve warm.

These are great—and fast—for breakfast. Of course, southerners eat them for every meal and with just about anything. I like them with soups.

Before we jump into making loaves, I am going to give you a valuable, if time-consuming, recipe. Puff pasty can be used for every course in a meal. It is one of our most important pastry doughs. This is only for the most ambitious among you, as very good frozen puff pastry may now be purchased in most supermarkets.

Puff Pastry
(Pâte Feuilletée)

No one knows who devised puff pastry. Several nationalities stake a claim; Austria may have the best. The first mention of this light, flaky pastry in English was in a book by Sir Hugh Plat, published in 1609 and titled *Delights for Ladies*. The recipe today remains virtually unchanged. It is the pastry dough used for Napoleons and Beef Wellington. It may also make an appearance as a garnish for a soup or main course.

I must warn you about this recipe. Both patience and space are required. It is very time and space consuming. Most restaurants purchase their puff pastry, either raw or from a bakery, made into individualized portions and shapes. Use this with the Beef Wellington (page 65) and the Smoked Chicken Pot Pie (page 61).

Yield: 4 pounds of puff pastry (this will go a long way)

INGREDIENTS

4 c. butter, softened
1 tsp. salt
2 lb. flour, sifted
2 egg yolks
1 pt. cold water

Method

1. Mix all the butter with about 4 ounces of the flour. Shape into a rectangle approximately 6 by 10 inches and set aside.
2. Mix all remaining ingredients in mixer and allow to rest, covered in the refrigerator for about 30 minutes.

3. Roll this dough into a large rectangle approximately ½-inch thick.
4. Spread the butter and flour mixture over about two-thirds of the dough.
5. Fold the dough so the two ends meet in the center. Fold in half, widthwise.
6. Wrap the dough tightly in plastic wrap and refrigerate. Allow to rest for 30 minutes.
7. Turn the dough 90° from its previous position and roll it out into a rectangle approximately ³⁄₁₆-inch thick. Fold into thirds: this is a *half tour*. Wrap and refrigerate for 20 minutes.
8. Repeat step 7 four more times. This folding will produce over 1,200 layers or so.
9. Wrap and refrigerate. The dough will survive 3 or 4 days in the refrigerator or 3 months of freezing.

Challah

This is the traditional Jewish egg bread, and it is always braided. It is traditionally served after Yom Kippur and at Jewish weddings. If you want to be traditional, sprinkle with poppy seeds instead of sesame.

Yield: 1 large loaf

INGREDIENTS
1½ tbsp. dry yeast
2¼ c. warm water
1 tbsp. sugar
6 c. bread flour
2 tbsp. salt
1½ tbsp. peanut oil
1–2 eggs
1 egg, lightly beaten with a little water
sesame seeds, as desired

Method

1. Combine yeast, warm water, and sugar in bowl of mixer. Allow this mixture to "work" for 5 to 10 minutes.
2. Sift flour and salt together.
3. Make the dough, using the straight dough mixing method.
4. Remove the dough from the mixer and place in a bowl that you have coated with peanut oil. Cover the bowl with plastic wrap and permit it to double in volume in a warm place.
5. Remove one-fourth of the dough and set it aside.

6. Divide the larger piece of dough into three equal pieces.
7. Using your hands, roll the three pieces into "ropes" approximately 1 inch thick and 14 to 16 inches long.
8. Braid these three pieces together and pinch the ends tightly.
9. Place on an oiled baking sheet or on a sheet on which you have placed a piece of parchment paper. Paint with the egg wash and allow this to become a little tacky.
10. Divide the smaller piece of dough into three equal pieces. Roll out and braid as before.
11. Place the smaller braid on top of the larger braid.
12. Paint with the egg wash and sprinkle the sesame seeds over all. Allow to rise until doubled in volume.
13. Bake in a 425° oven for about 35 to 40 minutes.

French Bread

What Americans call French bread the French don't. They don't have "French fries" either. What we Yankees call French bread is usually made in bakeries in France. When I was staying in the Latin Quarter in Paris, just off Place St. Michel, there was a bakery just around the corner. Early every morning, the boy from the *boulangerie* would be off on his bicycle with the long, thin baguettes sticking out of a basket on the back. Breakfast was usually croissants and bread, both still warm from the bakery, with strawberry preserves and good butter. To make what we think of as French bread with a nice light brown, crispy crust and a soft interior, you require an oven with even heat from all sides and some steam in the oven. You will probably have much better success at home by making this dough into a roll. Whatever shape you choose, French bread has only four ingredients. Try to find unbleached, hard-wheat, high-gluten flour for best results.

You may, of course, make this as a loaf. I recommended rolls here because you are more likely to have initial success with them in a home oven.

Yield: About 24 2-ounce rolls

INGREDIENTS

24 oz. warm water
2 oz. dry yeast
1 oz. salt
44 oz. bread flour

Method

1. Make dough, using the straight dough mixing method.
2. Place dough in a buttered bowl, covered with plastic wrap, and set in a warm place until doubled in size.
3. Punch dough down and permit it to double in volume again.
4. Using a scale, weigh the dough into 2- to 3-ounce portions.
5. Shape the dough into ovals and wash with cold water.
6. Using a sharp paring knife, make a shallow diagonal slit in the top of each roll.
7. Permit the dough to rise one more time until doubled.
8. Preheat oven to 425° with a pan containing water sitting on the bottom of the oven.
9. Bake the rolls for 15 to 20 minutes or until light brown in color and crisp.

What You Need to Know

Remember the two basic techniques for making yeast breads: the straight dough and the sponge. There are actually two sponge methods. The "sponge method" is the manner in which all breads were made until Louis Pasteur come up with cultured yeast around the middle of the 19th century. Basically, this manner of bread making entails leaving a "batter" of water and flour out at room temperature to capture the wild yeasts around us everywhere. This method is also called "sourdough." This procedure cannot be rushed; it may take days.

The second procedure involves the same flour and water with an added leavening agent. The agent may be a "starter" or yeast or sometimes both. The rising and fermentation go much faster with this method. Most artisan bakers claim the bread does not develop the character or flavor of the true sourdough method.

Of course, nearly all the breads in this chapter could be made with the sponge or sourdough method. I choose to give you the straight dough method because I would rather you make bread than buy it, and I think most folks are more likely to go with the quicker method. The following two breads profit greatly in terms of both flavor and texture with the sponge method.

Whole-Wheat Bread

Yes, I know, many ingredients, many steps. Try it; you'll like it.
  Yield: 24 2-ounce rolls or 3 large loaves

Ingredients

1½ oz. dry yeast
¾ c. warm water
pinch of sugar
3 c. warm milk
6 tbsp. butter, softened
⅓ c. dark brown sugar
¼ c. molasses
3 tbsp. sesame seeds
3 tbsp. cornmeal
2 eggs, lightly beaten
3 c. whole-wheat flour
1 tbsp. salt
4 c. flour
2 c. flour
butter, melted, to cover

Method

1. Dissolve yeast in water with a pinch of sugar. Allow to "work" for 10 minutes.
2. In a large bowl, combine milk, softened butter, brown sugar, molasses, sesame seeds, and cornmeal.
3. Stir in eggs, the yeast mixture, and 3 cups of whole-wheat flour. Stir this mixture until smooth, cover with plastic wrap and let stand in a warm place for about 30 minutes to 3 hours.
4. Beat in salt and 4 cups of the white flour, one at a time.
5. Turn the dough out onto the bench and knead in the last 2 cups of flour.
6. Place the dough in a butter bowl and brush the top with melted butter. Cover bowl with plastic wrap.
7. Form dough into 2- or 3-ounce rolls and place on parchment paper on a sheet pan, brush with egg wash, and allow to rise until doubled in volume. You may also bake this bread in loaf pans.
8. Bake in a 350° oven for about 30 minutes.

Rustic French Bread

Why "rustic"? Because I needed a name other than "French bread" for this one, and this is close to the way breads were made traditionally.

Yield: 3 large loaves

INGREDIENTS

1 tsp. dry yeast
1 c. warm water
1½ c. bread flour
2 tsp. dry yeast
2 c. warm water
1 c. whole-wheat flour
3 c. bread flour
2 tsp. salt

Method

1. Several hours before baking, prepare the starter. In a medium-sized nonreactive mixing bowl, dissolve 1 teaspoon active dry yeast in 1 cup of warm water. Add 1½ cups of bread flour and mix well. Cover and let sit several hours at room temperature.

2. In the mixer, dissolve the 2 teaspoons of yeast in the 2 cups of warm water. Add the starter mixture, the whole-wheat flour, 3 cups of bread flour, and the salt; stir until well combined. Add the remaining bread flour, ½ cup at a time, mixing well after each addition. When the dough has pulled together, turn it out onto a lightly floured surface and knead until smooth and elastic. Lightly oil a large bowl; place the dough in the bowl and turn to coat with oil. Cover with plastic wrap and let rise in a warm place until doubled in volume, about 1 hour.

3. Grease two 9- by 5-inch loaf pans. Deflate the dough and turn it out onto a lightly floured surface. Divide the dough into two equal pieces and form into loaves. Place the loaves into the prepared pans. Cover the loaves with a damp cloth and let rise until doubled in volume, about 45 minutes. Preheat the oven to 425°. Bake about 30 minutes.

Grissini
(Bread Sticks)

You will find these are quite different from the "bread sticks" in cellophane packages found in many "Italian" restaurants around the country. When fresh from the oven, they are soft and somewhat fragile. As they age a little, they become chewy like soft pretzels. I like them both ways. I suppose these qualify as "loaves," albeit skinny ones.

Yield: 18 to 20 18-inch bread sticks

INGREDIENTS

¾ oz. dry yeast
1 c. warm water
1 c. milk, scalded then cooled
2 tbsp. sugar
2 tbsp. salt
6 c. bread flour
2 tbsp. butter, softened
1 egg white, lightly beaten
coarse salt (optional)
sesame seeds (optional)

[**Method**]

1. Dissolve yeast in water and milk and thoroughly incorporate.
2. Allow yeast to "work" for 5 to 10 minutes.
3. Add salt to flour.
4. Place yeast mixture in mixing bowl and slowly add flour while mixing with the dough hook on slow speed.
5. Shape the dough into a ball and place in a buttered bowl. Cover with plastic wrap and permit the dough to rise until it doubles in volume.
6. Punch the dough down and turn it out onto a floured board. Roll the dough out to a thickness of ½ inch.
7. Cut into narrow strips, place on a buttered sheet pan, brush with egg white, and sprinkle with sesame seeds or coarse salt.
8. Bake in a 425° oven for approximately 15 minutes.

Irish Soda Bread

Here is a loaf leavened with baking soda and buttermilk. Try this with Corned Beef and Cabbage (page 134) or the Irish Stew (page 132).

INGREDIENTS

8 c. flour
1 tbsp. baking soda
1 tbsp. sugar
2 tsp. salt
3 c. buttermilk

Method

1. Sift all the dry ingredients together.
2. Place buttermilk in mixer and gradually add dry ingredients to it—on slow speed.
3. Turn out onto a floured board and knead a few times.
4. Shape into two round, flat loaves.
5. Make several slits across the tops of the loaves.
6. Bake in a 375° oven for 30 to 35 minutes.

Rye Bread

I have adapted this from the rye made in my stepfather's bakery. I began working for him on weekends when I was in high school. I continued during the summers when I was in college. The bakery method was a sourdough sponge, but I think you'll like this one as well.

Yield: About 18 2-ounce rolls or 2 loaves

INGREDIENTS

24 oz. warm water
1½ oz. dry yeast
1 tbsp. sugar
¾ lb. rye flour
2 lb. bread flour
1 oz. salt
1 oz. caraway seeds
1 oz. shortening

Method

1. Combine water, yeast, and sugar in bowl of mixer and allow the mixture to "work" for 5 to 10 minutes.
2. Sift the flours and the salt together.
3. Gradually add the flours to mixer using the dough hook on slow speed.

4. Add the caraway seeds.

5. Gradually add the shortening.

6. Form the dough into a ball and place it in an oiled bowl in a warm place to rise until doubled in volume.

7. Punch the dough down and form either into rolls (2–3 ounces each) or loaves.

8. Allow rolls or bread to double in volume and bake in a 375° oven for 20 to 25 minutes for the rolls and a 350° oven for approximately 35 minutes for the loaves.

Cresca
(Italian Easter Bread)

I learned this from the same baker who taught me the Guastelle. You will cut a cross in the top of the bread.

Yield: 2 round loaves

INGREDIENTS

20 oz. warm water
1½ oz. dry yeast
1 tsp. sugar
7 c. bread flour
1 tsp. salt
½ tsp. black pepper
¾ c. parmesan
3 eggs, lightly beaten
2 tbsp. extra virgin olive oil

Method

1. Dissolve yeast in warm water with sugar.

2. Sift flour, salt, and pepper together. Add cheese.

3. Place yeast mixture in mixing bowl and slowly add flour mixture while running mixer on medium speed.

4. Add eggs.

5. Add olive oil. (More flour may be added at this point if necessary.)

6. Place in an oiled bowl and cover. Allow to rise until doubled in volume.

7. Shape into either two round loaves—and cut a cross in the top of each— or 2-ounce rolls. Brush the top with olive oil and allow to rise until doubled in volume.

8. Bake the loaves approximately 35 minutes in a 400° oven and the rolls about 25 minutes.

Vienna Bread

This was probably the most popular bread in my stepfather's bakery when I worked there as I was growing up. We sold several dozen loaves a day. It has a nice, chewy crust and is a great sandwich bread.

Yield: 2 loaves

INGREDIENTS

1 oz. dry yeast
1¾ c. warm water
1 tbsp. sugar
2 c. milk, scalded then cooled to 125°
1 tbsp. salt
8 c. bread flour
1 egg white, lightly beaten

Method

1. Dissolve yeast in warm water with sugar.
2. Add milk.
3. Sift salt and flour together.
4. Make dough with the straight dough mixing method.
5. Let rise in buttered bowl until doubled in volume. Punch down.
6. Shape into two long loaves. Wash with egg white. Cut shallow slits in the top of the loaves.
7. Let rise again until doubled.
8. Begin baking at 450°. After 15 minutes, lower heat to 400°.
9. Bake for 15 minutes. Remove from oven. Glaze again with egg white. Return to oven until golden brown and done, about 10 minutes.

Multipurpose Italian Bread

Of course, there are many, many Italian breads. This one is versatile. I use it to make bruschetta, the grilled, original Roman garlic bread, all the time. I make it both as a loaf and as rolls, too.

INGREDIENTS

2 lb. warm water
1½ oz. dry yeast
1 oz. sugar
3½ lb. bread flour
1 oz. salt
¼ oz. malt syrup (optional)

Method

1. Use the straight dough mixing method (page 93).
2. Place in an oiled bowl, cover with plastic wrap, and allow dough to rise until doubled.
3. Place a pan of boiling water on lower shelf of oven.
4. Make dough into loaves, slit the tops, wash with water, and allow to rise again.
5. Bake at 425° until browned and done.

Spanish Bread

This is a very light bread—one I usually make with paella.

INGREDIENTS

3 c. water
1 tbsp. salt
2 tbsp. sugar
½ c. butter
10 c. bread flour, sifted
1½ oz. dry yeast
1⅓ c. warm water

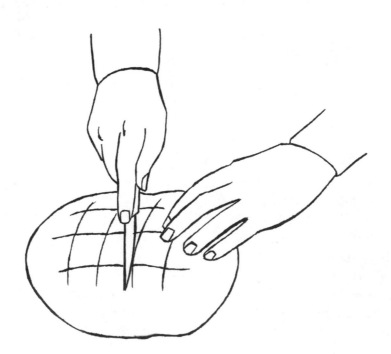

Method

1. Bring first four ingredients to a boil and cool.
2. Place flour in mixer.
3. Dissolve yeast in the 1⅓ cups of warm water—with a pinch of sugar.
4. Add liquids to flour gradually with mixer on medium speed.
5. When dough begins to "ball," it is ready. Place in an oiled bowl and allow to double.
6. Make into three round loaves. Cut a cross in the top of each and brush with melted butter. Let rise until doubled.
7. Bake at 450° for 10 to 15 minutes. Lower heat to 400° and bake until done, about 20 minutes.

What You Need to Know

Although I asked you to simply cut a cross in the tops of the loaves, I usually slice a "crosshatch" pattern in the top of this bread. To do this, make four or five evenly spaced light slices in one direction. Then do the same across the slices you have made, alternating the end from which you begin so you are "pulling" your rectangles in opposite directions.

Gannat
(Cheese/Potato Bread)

At first glance, you might think this a quite heavy bread. It is light! Try it; you'll like it.

Yield: 3 loaves

INGREDIENTS

1½ oz. dry yeast
1 c. warm water
1 tbsp. sugar
8 c. bread flour
2 tsp. salt
¾ c. butter, softened
2 c. Gruyère or other cheese
1½ c. mashed potatoes
4 eggs
1 c. milk, scalded

Method

1. Place yeast, water, and sugar in mixer.
2. Add flour, a little at time, until about 3 cups have been added.
3. Combine salt, butter, cheese, mashed potatoes, eggs, and milk (cooled).
4. Add above mixture to mixer a little at a time.
5. Add remaining flour.
6. Allow mixer to knead dough until a smooth ball is formed.
7. Place in an oiled bowl and allow to rise until doubled. Punch down. Make into three loaves and place in loaf pans. Allow to double again.
8. Bake in a 400° oven until browned, about 30 minutes.

Italian Roll for Muffuletta

This bread is good for just about any sandwich.
Yield: 8 rolls

Ingredients
2½ c. warm skim milk (about 125°)
2½ tbsp. dry yeast
¼ c. sugar
7–8 c. bread flour
2 tsp. salt
½ c. extra virgin olive oil
2 eggs
1 tbsp. extra virgin olive oil

Method

1. Combine milk, yeast, and sugar in mixer and permit to "work" for a few minutes.
2. Begin adding flour, a cup at a time. Add salt a little at a time as you add the flour.
3. Add olive oil, in a stream.
4. Add eggs, one at a time.
5. Add flour as needed until a bread dough consistency is reached.
6. Oil a bowl with the tablespoon of olive oil. Place the dough in the bowl and allow to rise until double in size.
7. Divide dough into eight equal-sized pieces. Shape into balls.
8. Press or roll each ball into an 8-inch round.

9. Paint each with the remaining olive oil.
10. Place dough on sheet pans and allow to double again. Bake for about 15 to 20 minutes in a 425° oven.

You may sprinkle the rolls with sesame seeds if you like them.

Pumpernickel

Difficult as it may be to believe, this bread is, I have read, named after a 15th-century German baker named "Pumpernickel." The story has it that he made a very coarse, dark bread with rye flour during a period when there was no wheat flour available. Bakers make it quite differently now.

INGREDIENTS

2 c. warm water
1 oz. dry yeast
½ c. molasses
2 tbsp. caraway seed
2 tbsp. shortening
2½ c. rye flour
1 tbsp. salt
4 c. bread flour

Method

1. Dissolve yeast with warm water in mixing bowl.
2. Add molasses and caraway. Add shortening.
3. Mix flours and salt thoroughly together before adding to mixing bowl with other ingredients.
4. Run mixer slowly while adding flour mixture to bowl.
5. Place dough in a buttered bowl covered with plastic wrap and allow to rise until doubled.
6. Sprinkle a sheet pan with cornmeal. Make two round loaves. Brush with water and allow to rise until doubled.
7. Bake at 450° for about 15 minutes. Lower heat to 400° and bake about 20 minutes more.

Focaccia

This is the bread I see more and more in Italian restaurants. Serve it with some good olive oil into which you have ground a little black pepper.

Yield: 4 nice loaves

INGREDIENTS

2½ c. warm skim milk, scalded (about 125°)
2½ tbsp. dry yeast
¼ c. sugar
7–8 c. bread or all-purpose flour
2 tsp. salt
½ c. extra virgin olive oil
2 eggs
¼ c. extra virgin olive oil
1 tbsp. kosher or coarse salt

Method

1. Combine milk, yeast, and sugar in mixer and permit to "work" for a few minutes.
2. Begin adding flour, a cup at a time. Add salt a little at a time as you add the flour.
3. Add olive oil, in a stream.
4. Add eggs, one at a time.
5. Add flour as needed until a bread dough consistency is reached.
6. Allow to rise in an oiled bowl until double in size.
7. Divide dough into four equal-sized pieces. Shape into balls.
8. Press or roll each ball into a 10- to 12-inch round or oval.
9. Paint each with the remaining olive oil.
10. Sprinkle with the kosher or coarse salt.
11. Place dough on sheet pans and allow to double again. Bake for about 15 to 20 minutes in a 425° oven.

You may top the focaccia with just about anything you like: thinly sliced onions, parmesan cheese or other cheeses, sun-dried tomatoes, basil, or oregano.

We'll wrap up our baking section with a few tried-and-true desserts. These baked sweets that follow are those that guests have shown a preference for in restaurants I have done over the years. They are all crowd-pleasers.

Carrot Cake

This has been a popular item for me in several restaurants over the years. I am sure the main attraction is the rich cream cheese icing.

Yield: 1 cake

INGREDIENTS

3 c. minced carrots (in food processor)
2 c. brown sugar
4 eggs
1¼ c. peanut oil
1 tsp. vanilla
2 c. flour
2 tsp. baking soda
½ tsp. salt
1 tsp. baking powder

Method

1. Thoroughly combine carrots, sugar, eggs, oil, and vanilla in mixer.
2. Sift together flour, baking soda, salt, and baking powder.
3. Gradually add flour mixture to carrot mixture. Blend thoroughly.
4. Bake at 350° for about 45 minutes in springform pan.

Cream Cheese Icing for Carrot Cake

INGREDIENTS

1 lb. powdered sugar
8 oz. cream cheese
½ c. butter
1 tsp. vanilla

Method

1. Cream all ingredients together.
2. Ice the cake.

Dark Chocolate Cake

I tell my students to learn as many chocolate desserts as possible. Chocolate never goes out of style and is nearly universally loved.

Yield: 1 cake

INGREDIENTS

2 c. flour, sifted
1 c. dark brown sugar
1 c. sugar
¾ c. cocoa powder
1 tsp. baking soda
2 tsp. baking powder
1 tsp. salt
2 eggs, large, beaten
1 c. half-and-half
½ c. peanut oil
1 tsp. vanilla extract
2 tsp. brandy
1 c. boiling water
chocolate buttercream (below)

(Method)

1. Heat oven to 350°. Prepare cake pan.
2. In a large mixing bowl, sift together dry ingredients.
3. Using a wire whisk, mix together all liquid ingredients except boiling water.
4. Add liquid ingredients to dry; when incorporated, add boiling water in a stream.
5. Pour batter into prepared pan and bake for 35 to 45 minutes.
6. Allow the cake to cool and cut in half. Trim if necessary. Spread one-third of buttercream over bottom layer. Ice outside of cake with remaining buttercream.

Chocolate Buttercream

This is a very basic buttercream recipe—you will see others that add vanilla, heavy cream, and even eggs.

INGREDIENTS

2 c. butter, softened (but not melted!)
4½ c. powdered sugar, sifted
3 tbsp. cocoa powder

[**Method**]

1. Using the paddle attachment on the mixer, beat the butter in a mixer until light and fluffy.
2. Add the sugar slowly while beating.
3. Gradually add cocoa powder.

Chocolate Bread Pudding for a Party

This has been a very popular dessert in several of the restaurants where I was chef.

Yield: 20 portions

INGREDIENTS

2 c. heavy cream
16 oz. semisweet chocolate, shaved or chopped
1⅓ c. sugar
10 eggs, separated
1 c. butter, cut into small pieces
2 tbsp. vanilla extract
4 c. white bread crumbs

[**Method**]

1. Bring cream to a simmer.
2. Process chocolate in food processor.
3. When chocolate is grated, add cream, slowly, in a stream to the food processor.
4. Add approximately half the sugar to the processor.
5. Add egg yolks, one at a time.
6. Add butter and vanilla and continue processing.
7. Remove the mixture from the processor and, in a mixing bowl thoroughly blend the chocolate mixture with the bread crumbs.
8. In the mixer, whip the egg whites until soft peaks form.
9. Continue whipping as you add the sugar until the mixture is stiff and glossy.
10. Beat one-third of the egg whites into the chocolate mixture to lighten it.
11. Fold remaining egg whites into the mixture.
12. Turn the mixture out into a full size 2½-inch-deep hotel pan that has been buttered and coated with sugar. Knock out excess.
13. Place the hotel pan inside a deeper hotel pan in which you have placed an inch or two of water. Bake in a 350° oven on the middle shelf for approximately 45 minutes or until the pudding is just set.

Sabayon

This custard/sauce is called *sabayon* in France and *zabaglione* in Italy. It may be served warm in a coupe over fresh fruit but is also used as a sauce and served warm, cold, and even frozen. A "coupe" is the shallow glass that many erroneously call a "champagne" glass—supposedly modeled after Marie Antoinette's breast, so the story goes. Sabayon may be made with wine or various fruit juices as a base.

Yield: 6 to 8 portions

INGREDIENTS

4 eggs
8 egg yolks
1⅓ c. white wine or fruit juice
1¼ c. sugar
1 tsp. lemon juice
1 tsp. vanilla
2 tsp. brandy

Method

1. Combine eggs, yolks, and wine or fruit juice and beat together in a bowl.
2. Add sugar and lemon juice.
3. Place in top of a double boiler and whip vigorously over simmering water until mixture thickens, 5 to 10 minutes.
4. Beat in brandy.
5. Serve immediately or beat until cool with a whisk, then chill.

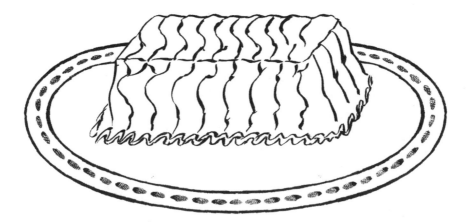

Baked Alaska

The origins of this dessert are in dispute. Speculation ranges from a Swiss pastry chef to a cook in Thomas Jefferson's White House. See the recipes for pound cake (page 124), vanilla ice cream (page 124), strawberry ice cream (page 125), and chocolate ice cream (page 125).

Yield: 8 to 10 portions

INGREDIENTS

1 pound cake (page 124) or Génoise
2 qt. ice cream, chocolate, vanilla, and strawberry
1 oz. Grand Marnier or Cognac
1 recipe meringue (below)

Method

1. Slice the cake into pieces 1 to 1½ inches thick.
2. Arrange the cake on an ovenproof platter—in whatever shape you choose: round, square, rectangular, and so on.
3. Sprinkle about one ounce of the Grand Marnier or brandy over the cake.
4. Shape the ice cream over the cake, completely covering it.
5. Place the meringue in a pastry bag fitted with a large star tube.
6. Decoratively pipe the meringue over the ice cream and cake covering both completely.
7. Bake the Alaska in a 425° oven for approximately 8 minutes or until the "peaks" have browned. When you serve it, flame with a little of the brandy.

The Meringue

INGREDIENTS

12 egg whites
1 tsp. cream of tartar
1–1½ c. powdered sugar, sifted
1 tsp. vanilla extract

Method

1. Whip the egg whites until they froth. Add the cream of tartar and continue whipping.
2. Gradually add the sugar, a little at a time.
3. Add vanilla and continue whipping until mixture is stiff.

Pound Cake

INGREDIENTS

4 c. all-purpose or pastry flour
1 tsp. salt
4 tsp. baking powder
1½ c. butter, softened
3 c. sugar
8 eggs
1 c. milk
2 tsp. vanilla
2 tbsp. Grand Marnier or other flavoring agent

Method

1. Sift flour, salt, and baking powder together.
2. Cream butter and sugar together.
3. Add eggs, one at a time, and incorporate thoroughly.
4. Add flavoring agent and vanilla.
5. Alternately, add flour and milk, blending all the while.
6. Line two loaf pans with parchment paper and add batter.
7. Bake for about an hour at 350°. Test for doneness with a piece of dried pasta.

Vanilla Ice Cream

INGREDIENTS

3 c. heavy cream
1 c. milk
¾ c. sugar
2 tbsp. vanilla extract
4 egg yolks

Method

1. Heat cream, milk, and sugar in a saucepan, stirring until sugar is dissolved.
2. Beat egg yolks together in a bowl.
3. Add about 1 cup of the cream mixture to the eggs, slowly, in a stream, beating all the while. Add mixture back to pan.
4. Whip constantly with a wire whip until mixture thickens. This will take about 6 to 7 minutes on medium heat. Do not boil!

5. Strain the mixture and place it in the ice cream machine.

6. Set machine to maximum time limit and turn on.

Note: The quantities I give in the ice cream recipes fit nicely in my Il Gelatio Italian ice cream machine. All the ice cream recipes will yield about 1 quart.

Strawberry Ice Cream

INGREDIENTS

2 pt. strawberries, washed and hulled
½ c. + 2 tbsp. superfine sugar
3 tbsp. lemon juice
1½ c. heavy cream

Method

1. Purée strawberries in food processor.

2. Combine all ingredients and place in the bowl of the ice cream machine.

3. Turn the machine on and freeze about 25 minutes.

Chocolate Ice Cream

INGREDIENTS

4 oz. semisweet chocolate
1 recipe custard ice cream base (see note below)

Method

1. Shave the chocolate or use the small bits.

2. Slowly melt the chocolate over low heat or in a bain-marie.

3. Slow add the custard base to the chocolate, whisking constantly.

4. Cool.

5. Place mixture in machine and freeze about 25 minutes.

The custard ice cream base is made in the same manner as the vanilla ice cream (page 124). Just omit the vanilla. The base should be warm when you add it to the chocolate.

How Dry I Am

This concludes the section on cooking with dry heat. Remember that *grilling*, *roasting*, and *baking* are the three terms we use in this technique. You grill and roast the same tender foods, meats, poultry, vegetables, and starches. You never roast seafoods; you grill and bake them. You bake grains, vegetables, starches, casseroles, desserts, and fruits.

Carême was probably the first "celebrity chef." Born just before the French Revolution, he wrote several books on cooking techniques and designed some of our modern pots and pans. He may be responsible for the shape of the chef's hat (*toque*). He focused much of his teaching on roasting and baking.

Now that you have this seminal technique under your belt, you are well on your way to being the best cook you can be.

> When we no longer have good cooking in the world,
> we will have no literature, nor high and sharp intelligence,
> nor friendly gatherings, nor social harmony.
> —MARIE-ANTOINE CARÊME

PART II

The Second Technique
Boiling

MEATS, POULTRY, AND SEAFOOD

STARCHES

EGGS AND VEGETABLES

DESSERTS

THIS MAY WELL be the second-oldest cooking technique. But, wait, you say, didn't we need pots and pans first? No. There is archaeological evidence that several thousand years ago our ancestors in the nether regions of what was once the Soviet Union dug pits in the sand at low tide, waited for the seawater to flood the pits at high tide, built fires and heated rocks again at low tide, and pushed the hot rocks into the pits and boiled seafood. Some of the more common terms heard in regard to this technique include poaching, simmering, steaming, blanching, and, of course, boiling. All these terms refer to cooking a food with a liquid without first browning it.

Boiling Basics

1. This is one of the two techniques best for cooking tougher pieces of food, the other being *braising*. This technique is not only for tough pieces of food,

though. Of the five techniques, this is the only one where no caramelization ever occurs. Even with the extraction technique, you have occasion to brown sometimes (for instance, Brown Stock; see page 285).

2. The liquid in which the food will be boiled is brought to a rolling boil. You can see the temperature. The food is added, and the liquid is returned to a boil and then reduced to a simmer. Just about the only time we maintain the rolling boil during the entire cooking period is when cooking dried pasta.

3. The liquid is always salted before the food is immersed in it, not so much to give the food a salty flavor as to aid in retention of the salts naturally occurring in the food. All foods have some salt content. When you place the food in unsalted water, the salts inside the food will attempt to equalize the salinity inside and out. If the salt in the food migrates to the liquid outside, it also pulls flavor and nutrition from the food and deposits them in the liquid. This is exactly what you want in the extraction technique and most definitely what you do not want here.

4. Infuse the liquid while still cold with all the spices, herbs, vegetables (mirepoix), and seasonings in the dish. This will extract flavor from them into the liquid.

5. Simmer. Yes, simmer. If you maintain the liquid at a rolling boil for the entire cooking period, much weight will be lost in, for instance, a large piece of meat or poultry. With smaller pieces of food, there is the danger that the temperature inside the food will also reach the boiling point. In this case, much of the flavor and nutrition would be lost. Thus, you simmer; you do not boil.

What You Need to Know

Beef contains a minimum of 70 percent water. Now what will happen if you boil beef at the rolling boil for the couple of hours it will take to tenderize the tougher cuts of beef? Once the temperature inside the beef reaches the temperature of the boiling liquid, the water inside the beef will begin to boil. Here comes the ultimate irony: by "boiling" beef in a liquid, you can actually dry it out. Bring the liquid to a boil so you can *see* the temperature of the liquid. Then reduce it to the simmer.

What do chefs boil? Large pieces of tough meat lend themselves well to this technique. Pieces from the round and chuck primal cuts are good candidates. The brisket does well. The French do *Pot au Feu*. The Irish and Irish Americans boil Corned Beef and Cabbage. Americans also have a fondness for a boiled dish called Chicken and Dumplings. The French poach *quenelles* as well as a number of classic dishes with chicken breasts. The traditional Irish Stew is an example of a dish of boiled meat. The Italians from the Piedmont region of Italy have given us *Bollito Misto*, a dish usually containing beef tongue, chicken, and sausage with vegetables.

There are many boiled Oriental dishes. In Japanese Sukiyaki, the noodles are boiled with either meat or seafood. The Mongolian Fire Pot is another relatively common boiled Asian dish.

This technique is just as widespread as it has always been but not nearly as popular in Western cuisine as it once was. Modern chefs have access to better-quality meats than our ancestors did. Better quality translates into shorter cooking times. We also have come to prefer our meats and poultry caramelized, and most of the tougher cuts of meat suitable for boiling are braised.

In general, most diners prefer a caramelized beef stew, such as *boeuf bourguinonne,* or a pot roast, like sauerbraten, to a boiled beef. All the same pieces of meat may be boiled or braised. In fact, these comfort foods like stews, Swiss steaks, and pot roasts have become quite popular in many modern upscale dining establishments as well as the more down-home style of restaurant.

On the other hand, Americans prefer many fish and shellfish boiled. Boiled shrimp such as shrimp cocktail or rémoulade; boiled or steamed lobster; steamed clams; poached salmon, sole, or flounder; and boiled crayfish and crabs are among the more popular seafood items.

Chefs boil pastas. We also boil vegetables and other starches. We soft-boil and hard-boil eggs. We also poach them. Eggs are more fragile than most meats and seafoods, and there are some additional precautions you need to observe when cooking them. And they need special handling, which is the reason I've devoted a section to them. Otherwise, the procedures listed here apply to all kinds of foods.

Some chefs prefer steaming vegetables and many starches to boiling. There is some evidence that we lose more vitamins and minerals in boiling than in steaming. This loss, however, can be kept to a minimum by following the proper boiling procedures listed here—and then finding a use for the water in which you have boiled (a soup or sauce, for instance).

Another use of boiling is desalinizing or rehydrating cured meats or seafood. Dry-cured hams require rehydrating, and many salted, cured fish (such as salt cod) need to be preliminarily cooked in a liquid.

A by-product of boiling savory foods is broth. Students often ask me what is the difference between stock and broth. The key is in that word "by-product." Broth is the result of properly cooking solid food in a liquid; consequently, we have retained maximum flavor and nutrition in the food, and very little of those elements has leaked out into the liquid. Still, it is a flavorful liquid with some nutritional value. With stock, on the other hand, we have done everything we know to milk the flavor and nutrition out of the solid food and into the liquid. So stock is an end product we set out to achieve.

MEATS, POULTRY, AND SEAFOOD

Should you notice a distinct paucity of boiled meat and poultry dishes in this chapter, I would like to commend you on your mathematical acuity. While there are many cultures afloat with a raft of boiled dishes, the American culture does not happen to be one of them. We prefer our meat caramelized. Where others might boil, we braise.

Blanquette de Veau

I first had this dish in 1968. A lovely lady prepared it Bellevue, France. If you took the train to Versailles, you quickly passed through here.

Yield: 8 portions

INGREDIENTS

3 lb. veal, rump, rib eye, or shoulder, 1½-in. cubes
1½ qt. veal or chicken stock
1 carrot, quartered
1 onion, peeled and stuck with a few cloves
bouquet garni (below)
6–8 boiling onions
12–16 small mushroom caps
6 tbsp. butter
6 tbsp. flour
salt, to taste
white pepper, to taste
3 tbsp. lemon juice
4 egg yolks
1 c. heavy cream

Note: Bouquet garni may be almost any combination of herbs, spices, and vegetables, but for this recipe we will use the following:

2 sprigs parsley
1 sprig thyme
2 bay leaves
2 stalks celery, cut in 2-in. lengths

Method

1. Place veal in a saucepan or casserole and cover with the stock. Bring to a boil and skim.
2. Add carrot and onion to the pot. Wrap parsley, thyme, bay leaves, and celery in cheesecloth, tie, and add to pot.
3. Cover and simmer for about 1¼ hours. Do not over cook.
4. Add boiling onions to pot and simmer for 15 minutes.
5. Add mushrooms to pot and simmer for 5 minutes.
6. Melt butter in a sauté pan. Add flour and make a blond roux.

7. Remove veal, onion, carrot, bouquet garni, boiling onions, and mushrooms from stock. Discard carrot, large onion, and bouquet garni.
8. Incorporate roux into stock with a wire whip. Add lemon.
9. In a mixing bowl, beat together the egg yolks and cream.
10. Beat about 8 ounces of the sauce into the egg mixture. Add this mixture to the pot and whip thoroughly.
11. Return veal, boiling onions, and mushrooms to the sauce. Check the seasoning and keep warm until service. Do not boil.

Irish Stew

This traditional, simple, and delicious dish is actually not a "stew" at all! It is, rather, a dish of boiled meat, onions, and potatoes, prepared in the *blanquette* manner.

Yield: 8 portions

INGREDIENTS

3–4 medium potatoes, White Rose or Russet type
3 lb. lamb, sirloin or leg, 1½-in. cubes
3 lb. yellow onions, thinly sliced
salt, to taste
black pepper, to taste
1 tbsp. whole thyme
1 or 2 bay leaves
1 qt. beef stock

Method

1. Slice the potatoes into ¼-inch slices (peel the Russet type).
2. Thoroughly dry the lamb pieces so they will hold the spices.
3. Peel and slice the onions cross-sectionally into ¼-inch slices.
4. Place a layer of the potatoes in a casserole dish. Top the potatoes with a layer of the lamb. Place the onions on top of the lamb.
5. Season each layer with the salt and pepper and the thyme as you go.
6. Continue layering until all ingredients are in the casserole. Finish with a layer of the potatoes. Place the bay leaves just under the final layer of potatoes.
7. Add stock.
8. Bring the stock to a boil, reduce to a simmer, cover, and continue to simmer on top of the stove or in the oven for 2 to 2½ hours or until all the liquid has been absorbed and the lamb is tender.

Serve with Irish Soda Bread (page 110) or French Bread (page 106).

Pot Au Feu

Literally translated, *pot au feu* means "fire pot." Practically speaking, it refers to the medieval pot that nearly every family kept in the fireplace for cooking or whatever. Today the "pot au feu" is a one-pot meal, consisting of beef and/or chicken accompanied by vegetables, sausage, and, often, cured or smoked meats. The regional variations are multitudinous. Pickles, mustards, and horseradish are frequent condiments.

Yield: 10 portions

INGREDIENTS

boiling water, to cover
1 rump or round of beef (4–5 lb.)
4 bay leaves
1 tbsp. whole thyme
1 tbsp. peppercorns, crushed
1½ tbsp. salt
6 garlic cloves, peeled and crushed
1 chicken, 2½ lb., trussed
8 carrots, peeled and cut into 2-in. pieces
4 turnips, peeled and quartered
4 leeks, washed and cut into 2-in. pieces
4 onions, quartered
4 stalks celery, cut into 2-in. pieces
1 head cabbage, sliced into thin wedges
2 lb. spicy sausage (such as chaurice), sliced

Method

1. Place the meat in the boiling water in the stockpot.
2. Add the bay leaves, thyme, peppercorns, salt, and garlic to the pot.
3. Return the water to a boil, reduce it to a simmer, and cook, covered, for about 2 hours. Add the chicken to the pot.
4. The trick with the vegetables is to add the hardest and densest first and then add progressively softer vegetables at intervals so that all will be done at the same time. Total simmering time will be less than 60 minutes.
5. Add sausage and simmer for an additional 15 minutes.

Bollito Misto

This dish comes from Piedmont in northern Italy. It is essentially a dish of boiled beef tongue and chicken with some sausages added. Quite often in the American version, you can substitute another cut of beef for the tongue. The American palate is not quite as accepting of the variety meats as is the European.

Yield: 6 to 8 portions

INGREDIENTS

salted, boiling water, several quarts
3–4 lb. beef tongue (or round, brisket, or chuck)
12 whole black peppercorns
3 or 4 bay leaves
4 carrots, peeled and quartered
2 yellow onions, peeled and quartered
4 stalks celery, roughly diced
1–2 chickens, whole or pieces
3 or 4 Italian sausages

Method

1. If you are using the tongue, you will have to blanch it for about an hour and then drain it before proceeding.
2. Add the meat to the boiling water along with all the spices. Reduce to a simmer once it has returned to a boil.
3. Simmer for about an hour. Add vegetables and simmer for about 15 minutes.
4. Add chicken and simmer for another 45 minutes.
5. Slice the meats and chicken and serve on a large platter with some of the broth.

The dish is traditionally served with boiled white beans and potatoes. I like the gnocchi and pesto that comes from a few miles south (Genoa) and a salsa verde.

Corned Beef and Cabbage

There is debate about even this simplest of hearty dishes. Traditionally, the Irish meat of choice (or, actually, of availability) was pork, both fresh and cured, the latter mostly in the form of bacon. Apparently there were some Irish folk who prepared this dish, but it was by no means widespread. It just seems Irish

American to me. The story I like best is as follows: The dish originates on the Lower East Side in New York, the only place I could afford to live when I lived there. In the 19th and early 20th centuries, these neighborhoods were inhabited by Jewish and Irish immigrants. The Jewish population eschewed bacon, of course, and the butchers there had a wealth of cured meats, "corned" beef brisket being one of the less expensive cuts. Irish immigrants began substituting this corned beef for the more traditional bacon with which they had cooked their cabbage.

Should you be concerned about the way your beef is raised, fed, and slaughtered, you might try the "naturally" raised beef from suppliers such as Niman Ranch. Reach deep into your pocket.

Yield: 8 portions

INGREDIENTS

5 lb. corned-beef brisket
½ c. pickling spice
8 medium potatoes, peeled and quartered
1 large white cabbage head, cut into 8 wedges
2–4 garlic cloves, smashed
10–12 whole black peppercorns
3–4 bay leaves
8 carrots, peeled
8 yellow onions, peeled
2 tbsp. butter
1 bunch parsley, chopped

Method

1. Bring several quarts of water to a boil in a large pot. Rinse and wipe corned beef with towels.
2. Place beef in pot and add garlic cloves, black peppercorns, and bay leaves.
3. Bring back to a boil.
4. Reduce heat; simmer 5 minutes. Skim surface. Cover pot and simmer 3 to 4 hours or until corned beef is fork-tender.
5. Add carrots, potatoes, and onions during last 25 minutes. Add cabbage wedges during last 15 minutes.
6. Cook vegetables just until tender. Thinly slice the corned beef across the grain. Arrange slices on platter with cabbage. Brush potatoes with butter and sprinkle with chopped parsley.

> ### What You Need to Know
>
> There are two options if you choose to "corn" your own brisket. There is a dry cure where the spice mixture is rubbed onto the beef. I prefer the wet or "brining" method. Here it is:
>
> Bring 4 cups of water to a boil and add 1 cup of kosher salt. Stir until salt is dissolved. Remove from heat and add ½ cup of pickling spices. Cool. Place brisket in a nonreactive container and cover with the brine solution and refrigerate. Brine for 6 to 7 days, turning the brisket once a day. Your brisket will not have the bright red color of those you buy in the supermarket—unless you have added saltpeter to the brine.

Poaching Poultry

There are very few dishes of poached poultry on our Western culinary palette—seems to do little for our palate. The Chicken and Dumplings (page 138) is by far the most widespread. There is a Gallic penchant for poached chicken that has never translated well into American culture, so I'm including none of the French poached chicken dishes I learned many years ago. In Indian culture, however, just about all the dishes we refer to as "curries" are poached. I'm including here the two poached poultry dishes I prepare most often.

Indian Ginger Chicken

This is a dish I learned to prepare using an Indian maharaja for a friend who acted as guinea pig. He had been Palmer Madden's roommate at Stanford. Palmer was Virginia Mudd's husband. We opened Mudd's restaurant for her. This dish is an authentic "curry." The whole spices in the dish are characteristic of Moghul cooking. All curries are made in the *blanquette* manner. The meat is not caramelized; they are "boiled" dishes.

Yield: 6 to 8 portions

INGREDIENTS

1 c. clarified butter
2 onions
3 tbsp. garlic
3 tbsp. ginger
1 tbsp. turmeric
1 tsp. coriander
1 tsp. cardamom, decorticated

1½ tbsp. whole cloves
8 cinnamon sticks, broken in half
1 tsp. cayenne pepper
1 tsp. cumin
2 tbsp. peppers, minced (serrano, jalapeño, etc.)
6–8 chicken breasts, boned and cut in pieces
3 c. chicken stock
½ c. tomato purée
1 tsp. salt
black pepper, to taste
1 c. yogurt
1 c. flaked, unsweetened coconut
1 c. cashew butter

Method

1. Purée the onion, garlic, and ginger in a processor.
2. Sweat the onion, garlic, and ginger purée in the clarified butter until translucent, about 3 or 4 minutes.
3. Add all dry spices and the peppers and continue to sweat for another 2 or 3 minutes.
4. Add chicken, chicken stock, tomato purée, salt, pepper, yogurt, and coconut.
5. Simmer, covered, 15 minutes. Add cashew butter. Cover.
6. Serve with Apple-Ginger Chutney (below).

Apple-Ginger Chutney

Spicy Indian dishes are usually accompanied by condiments called "chutneys." I came up with this chutney specifically to accompany the Indian Ginger Chicken (page 136).

INGREDIENTS

3 c. peeled and sliced Granny Smith apples
1 c. sliced yellow onion
2 tbsp. minced fresh ginger
1 c. red wine vinegar
1 lemon, peeled, seeded, and minced
2 or 3 hot peppers (serrano, jalapeño, etc.)
1¼ c. brown sugar
1½ tsp. minced garlic
1 tsp. cumin

1 tsp. coriander
salt, to taste
cayenne pepper, to taste
1 c. raisins

Method

1. Place 3 cups of the apples in the food processor with the onion, ginger, vinegar, lemon, peppers, brown sugar, garlic, cumin, and coriander. Process to a coarse purée.
2. Dice remaining apples.
3. Remove purée from processor and add salt, cayenne pepper, diced apples, and raisins. Chill.

These "curried" dishes are also often accompanied by a palate cleanser such as Raita.

Raita

INGREDIENTS

2 large cucumbers, peeled, seeded, and diced
4 Roma tomatoes, seeded and diced
1½ c. plain yogurt
½ c. sour cream
sea salt, to taste
black pepper, to taste
½ c. minced green onion
½ c. fresh mint leaves, chiffonade

Method

1. Combine all.
2. Chill.

Poached Chicken with Dumplings

Yes, this is the famous comfort food Chicken and Dumplings. Made properly, it follows all the technique guidelines. The only portion of this dish that requires a little finesse is the dumplings. The folks I've prepared this for say these are the lightest dumplings they've ever had.

Yield: 8 portions

INGREDIENTS

3 qt. water

2 tbsp. kosher salt

2–3 chickens, whole cut into 2 legs, 2 thighs, and 2 breast pieces, each with skin removed

1 large onion, peeled and cut into large chunks

2 bay leaves

4 stalks celery stalks, trimmed and cut into 1- by ½-inch pieces

4 medium carrots, peeled and cut into 1- by ½-inch pieces

8 boiling onions, peeled and halved

4 tbsp. butter, softened, or chicken fat from the cooked chicken

6 tbsp. flour

1 tsp. thyme leaves

1 c. heavy cream

1 c. fresh peas

½ c. minced parsley

black pepper, to taste

Dumplings

INGREDIENTS

2 c. flour

1 tbsp. baking powder

¾ tsp. salt

3 tbsp. butter

1 c. milk

¼ c. minced fresh herb leaves, such as parsley, chives, and tarragon (optional)

Method

1. Bring the salted water to a rolling boil.
2. Add chickens, bay leaves, carrots, celery, and onions to the pot and return to a rolling boil.
3. As soon as the boil is reached, reduce the liquid to a simmer. Simmer for about 60 minutes or until the chicken is tender. At this point, you may either remove the chicken from the bones and return the meat to the pot or, for a rustic touch, leave the meat on the bones.

Forming the dumplings:

1. While chicken is cooking, mix flour, baking powder, and salt in a medium bowl.
2. Add optional chopped fresh herbs.
3. Heat butter and milk to simmer and add to dry ingredients. Cool to room temperature. Mix with a fork or knead by hand two to three times until mixture just comes together. Note: Do not overknead! Your dumplings will turn out too dense.
4. Form dough into balls or lightly roll out and use the end of a 2-inch cookie cutter to cut the dough into even circles. Set aside.

Adding the dumplings:

1. Lay formed dumplings on the surface of the chicken mixture; cover and simmer until dumplings are cooked through, about 15 minutes. Add heavy cream.
2. Gently stir in peas and parsley.
3. Adjust seasonings, including adding ample amounts of salt and pepper.
4. Ladle portions of chicken, sauce, vegetables, and dumplings into soup plates and serve immediately.

Poaching Fish and Shellfish

We Americans do like boiled seafood as opposed to boiled meat and have a downright love affair with boiled shellfish. Poached salmon fits in very nicely with many of the fad diets rampant in the country today (both the Pritikin and the South Beach diets endorse it). We can't get enough boiled lobster, shrimp, and crabs. And tons of cray (craw) fish are consumed in Louisiana annually.

I subscribe to the Don Ho school of poaching: tiny bubbles. The water temperature should be around 200°. I do not want the rolling boil for the more delicate-fleshed fish, as it tends to toughen them.

Chilled Poached Salmon with Cucumber/Dill Sauce

Most often, you can poach fish in a *court-bouillon*, or "little bouillon." This elixir always contains some acids, usually wine and lemon. I suspect most of the fad diets would eliminate the sour cream here. I won't.

Yield: 6 to 8 portions

INGREDIENTS

2 c. dry white wine
2 c. water
6 whole peppercorns
3–4 sprigs fresh dill
2 bay leaves
1 rib celery, diced
1 lemon, thinly sliced
6–8 salmon filets, ¾ in. thick

Method

1. To make the salmon, combine the wine, water, peppercorns, dill, bay leaves, celery, and lemon in a skillet. Bring to a boil. Cover, reduce heat, and simmer for 10 minutes. Add the salmon to the mixture in the skillet and cook for 10 minutes or until the fish flakes easily.
2. Transfer the salmon to a platter, using a slotted spoon. Cover and chill thoroughly. Discard the liquid mixture remaining in the pan.

Cucumber/Dill Sauce

INGREDIENTS

¼ c. peeled, seeded, and finely chopped cucumber
¼ c. sour cream
⅓ c. plain yogurt
2 tsp. chopped fresh dill
1 tsp. Dijon mustard
6–8 fresh dill sprigs (for garnish)

Method

1. In a medium bowl, mix together the cucumber, sour cream, yogurt, dill, and mustard.
2. Place the filets on individual serving plates. Spoon the sauce evenly over the filets. Garnish with fresh dill sprigs.

I usually serve this with a simple green salad.

Sole a la Nantua

Sole is another fish well suited to poaching. You may substitute flounder. Because the sole has a subtler flavor than the salmon, I use a milder court-bouillon here. This dish can make a spectacular presentation if you take a little care. I once made a presentation with it that was spectacular but not quite what I had in mind. I was substituting for a sick French chef in a cooking school in San Rafael. The students neglected to tell me that the "ears" that held the lid of the food processor were broken. I had the crayfish and mirepoix mixture in the bowl, turned it shut to activate the blade, and then made some grand gesture that required both hands. The lid flew off the processor, and the not-quite-purée flew everywhere. I had a stripe of it right across my chest; it covered all the cooking pots and pans hanging on the wall. Thus is the fate of the substitute teacher. They didn't laugh, though, when I had them wash all the pots and pans and clean the wall and mop the floor. The following procedure is a classic French technique for poaching fish.

Yield: 6 to 8 portions

INGREDIENTS

6–8 filets of sole, 4- to 6-oz. pieces
2 tbsp. minced shallot
1 c. dry white wine
1 c. water
salt, to taste
white pepper, to taste
2 tbsp. butter
12–16 oz. Sauce Nantua (page 143)
6–8 whole crayfish
6–8 sprigs parsley
6–8 lemon wedges

(Method)

1. Dry sole before seasoning.
2. Place shallots, wine, and water in a buttered casserole dish.
3. Fold sole filets in thirds and place in casserole.
4. Cover fish with buttered parchment paper.
5. Bring to a simmer and simmer for about 6 minutes. Do not overcook.
6. Remove and drain fish filets. Coat with sauce and garnish with whole crayfish, parsley, and lemons. You might pipe a border of Pommes de Terre Duchesse (page 79) around this dish for an attractive presentation.

Sauce Nantua

INGREDIENTS

2 c. mirepoix
6–8 crayfish, cleaned
1 c. butter
1½ c. béchamel (page 292)
1 c. heavy cream
salt, to taste
white pepper, to taste
1 tsp. lemon juice

Method

1. Sweat mirepoix and crayfish in the butter until the vegetables are completely cooked.
2. Grind mirepoix and crayfish in food processor until the shells are completely ground.
3. Push the mixture through a sieve or *tamis* until all the bits of shell have been removed.
4. Thoroughly incorporate the crayfish butter and cream in the béchamel.
5. Add lemon.

Cioppino

This dish (pronounced "cha-peeno"), not totally unlike the fish and shellfish "stews" of the southern coast of France or the coasts of Italy, was devised by the fishermen who catch the fish in the dish, in this case, Italian fishermen on the West Coast of the United States. Having prepared this dish in several restaurants in the San Francisco area, I find it travels well with me wherever I go.

Yield: 8 portions

INGREDIENTS

16 clams, littleneck if possible, well washed
2 qt. fish or shellfish stock
1 c. dry white wine
3 tbsp. minced garlic
3 tbsp. minced parsley
3 bay leaves
1 tsp. whole oregano

1 tsp. thyme
salt, to taste
black pepper, to taste
2 lb. tomatoes, peeled, seeded, and diced
1–2 Dungeness crab, cleaned, or 6–8 blue crabs
1 lb. rockfish (rock cod, Pacific snapper, etc.), cut into 1-in. chunks
¼–½ c. parmesan

(**Method**)

1. Place well-washed clams in a large pot.
2. Add stock, garlic, parsley, bay leaves, oregano, thyme, salt, pepper, and tomatoes.
3. Bring to a simmer.
4. Add crab.
5. Cover and simmer until clams open.
6. Add rockfish, cover again, and simmer for about 5 minutes.

Serve in soup bowls with parmesan and additional parsley sprinkled over the top of each bowl. Serve with a salad and sourdough French bread. You may also add some large shrimp if you choose—when you add the rockfish.

Note: Mirepoix is a mixture of approximately equal parts of carrots, celery, and onion, diced to a diameter of approximately ¼ inch.

Coquilles St. Jacques

Coquilles is not the name of a dish, just the French expression for "scallop," be it sautéed, fried, or boiled. There is a legendary tradition associating the scallop and/or its shell with James, one of Christ's first disciples. James and his brother John, whom Jesus called the *Boanerges*, meaning "Sons of Thunder," were fishermen, as were his first two disciples, Peter and Andrew. Pilgrims in the 15th and 16th centuries returning from the shrine of St. James at Compostella were often adorned with scallop shells—as visible proof, I suppose, of the actual visitation. All the Europeans seem to be in agreement here. The Italians call the scallop *Conchiglia di San Iacopo*, and the Germans call it either *Pilgermuschel* or *Jacobmuschel*.

Coquilles St. Jacques à la Parisiennes

Yield: 6 portions

INGREDIENTS

2 c. water
1 c. dry white wine
2 bay leaves
3 tbsp. minced shallots
1 tbsp. lemon juice
salt, to taste
white pepper, to taste
1½ lb. large scallops
2 c. sliced mushrooms
4 tbsp. flour
3 tbsp. butter
1 c. milk
2 egg yolks
¾ c. heavy cream
2 oz. parmesan

Method

1. In a nonreactive pan—not aluminum or copper (stainless lined would be good)—combine water, wine, bay leaves, shallots, lemon juice, salt, and pepper. Bring to a boil.
2. Reduce to a simmer and simmer for 5 minutes.
3. Add scallops and mushrooms. Simmer, covered, for 5 minutes.
4. Using a skimmer, remove scallops and mushrooms from poaching liquid.
5. Raise heat and reduce poaching liquid to approximately 1 cup.
6. Make a light blond roux with the flour and butter.
7. With a wire whip, incorporate roux into poaching liquid.
8. Beat egg yolks and cream together in a bowl. Beat a few spoons of the sauce into the egg mixture, then incorporate the mixture into the sauce in the pan.
9. Check the consistency and the seasoning of the sauce.
10. Return the scallops and mushrooms to the pan.
11. Place the scallops and sauce in an ovenproof dish(es), sprinkle the parmesan over the top, and gratinée.

Steamed Clams

The following is one portion. Get a big pot and practice your multiplication tables to increase it. Here's a little clam lore for those of you who are landlocked. When you hear expressions like "littleneck" and "cherrystone" used in reference to clams, these names are *sizes*, not different kinds of clams. The littlenecks are the smaller, more tender clams.

INGREDIENTS

12–16 littleneck clams, thoroughly scrubbed
½ c. mirepoix
2 c. water
1 tbsp. minced garlic
2 oz. dry white wine
1 tbsp. lemon juice
black pepper, to taste
1 tbsp. minced parsley

Method

1. Place clams in a saucepan with all other ingredients.
2. Bring to a boil, place a lid on the pot, and reduce to a simmer.
3. Cook until all clams have opened. You may give the pot an occasional shake to help them open. Just before serving, add parsley. You may serve the clams

either in the pot in which they were cooked or in a soup bowl with the broth.

Serve with clarified butter to which you have added a little garlic and with a crusty bread.

Boiled Maine Lobster

Every now and then when someone asks me "If you could only eat one food, what would it be?" I reply without hesitation, "Lobster, simply boiled with lots of clarified butter." And that's the truth. It is one of the mysteries of the universe why a bottom-feeding scavenger could taste so good. Turns out, they're not really scavengers, though. They like a lot of the same foods people do: clams, mussels, fish, and crabs. They even have a great fondness for lobster, too.

Yield: 6 portions

INGREDIENTS

2 gal. water
2 bay leaves
1 lemon
1 c. dry white wine
1 tbsp. black peppercorns
¼ cup sea salt
6 live lobsters, 1¼ lb. or bigger
1½ c. clarified butter

(**Method**)

1. To make the court-bouillon, pour 2 gallons of water into a 16-quart stockpot over medium heat. Tie the thyme, parsley, and bay leaves together with kitchen string to make a bouquet garni. Place the herb bundle in the stockpot and secure the end of the string to the pot handle for easy removal.
2. Cut the lemon in half and squeeze the juice into the water, then drop in the halves. Add wine, peppercorns, and sea salt. Bring to a rolling boil.
3. Cut off the rubber bands that secure the lobster claws. Plunge lobsters head first into the stockpot, cover, and boil for 12 minutes for the 1¼-pounders, 15 minutes for the 2-pounders, and so on. Remove lobsters from boiling liquid with tongs.

I serve the lobsters on white linen napkins with 2 ounces of the clarified butter in a ramekin. Pommes Frites (page 248), crusty bread, and a plain green salad are all that's needed to complement the lobster.

Crawfish Boil

The Louisiana crawfish season runs from fall to late spring with Mardi Gras often falling smack at the height of the season. I have done many parties where I cooked 500 pounds of these little critters, and they all disappeared. In answer to your next question, no, you do not have to suck the head to enjoy crawfish.

You are going throw this fête outside. You will need a pot and a propane burner. You will be able to get a 36-quart pot for around 40 bucks. Should you later decide you want to try deep-frying a turkey, you will already have your apparatus for this treat. It will be equipped with a basket in which you will boil the crawfish. The same store will sell you a propane burner. Most of the crawfish pros suggest having an ice chest on hand in which to "finish" the crawfish, that is, allow them to finish their steaming in a closed ice chest.

Yield: 8 to 10 portions

INGREDIENTS

30 lb. live crawfish
20 gal. water
court-bouillon recipe ingredients (page 149), triple recipe
4 onions, peeled and quartered
2 oz. liquid crab boil
4 oz. Tabasco
2 oz. peanut oil
6 lemons, cut in half
5 lb. potatoes, Red or White Rose, B-size
8–10 ears corn, shucked and cut in half
3–4 lb. andouille sausage, cut in 2-in. pieces

(**Method**)

1. Thoroughly rinse the crawfish with cold running water. They aren't called "mudbugs" for nothing.
2. Add court-bouillon ingredients, onions, crab boil, Tabasco, peanut oil, and lemons to the pot. Squeeze them into the water and then throw in the lemon carcasses.
3. Bring to a rolling boil.
4. Add potatoes to the liquid and boil for about 10 minutes.
5. Add corn to pot and boil for an additional 15 minutes.

6. Stab a cook's fork into one of the larger potatoes. If you cannot remove the potato from the pot by lifting straight up, they are done. Lift the basket out and dump its contents into one of your ice chests. Close.

7. You may add one of the proprietary crawfish boils to the pot at this point should you choose.

8. Put the basket back in the pot and add the crawfish to the pot.

9. Boil the crawfish for about 10 minutes, add the sausage, and boil an additional 5 minutes. Remove basket and dump into your other ice chest. Close. Let the crawfish "steam" for about 10 to 15 minutes in the ice chest.

10. While the crawfish are steaming, cover your tables with newspaper or paper grocery bags. This not only lends an authentic rustic element to your party but also aids immeasurably in the cleanup! This would also be the time to cook your crabs and shrimp should you have elected to include them.

11. Here comes the easy part of this meal. Dump your ice chests full of food right onto the paper on the tables.

Serve this meal with a nice crusty bread, chile sauces (pages 276–277), rémoulade sauce (page 151), butter for the bread, potatoes and corn, drawn butter, and lots of bibs and napkins.

As I mentioned earlier, we do have a great fondness for boiled shellfish. The biggest pitfall here is overcooking the shellfish. While they are tender foods by nature, overcooking will change that and toughen them. Don't do it! Most large shrimp will take only between 2 and 3 minutes to cook through. Here is a court-bouillon I use for boiling shrimp.

Court-Bouillon

The "court" in this instance just means a "short," or *quick*, bouillon. The following will be enough to boil 5 pounds of shrimp, crabs, or crayfish. Or it may be used to poach any of the stronger-flavored fish.

Ingredients
4 stalks celery, roughly chopped
12 cloves
1 tbsp. whole thyme
6 bay leaves
1 tsp. whole allspice
1 tsp. mace
1 tsp. crushed red pepper

1 tsp. black peppercorns
2 or 3 sprigs parsley
½ tsp. cumin
6 qt. water
2 tsp. salt

Method

1. Combine all ingredients and simmer for 15 minutes.
2. Add shrimp, crabs, or crayfish and boil until done. The large shrimp will take about 2 to 3 minutes, blue crabs 7 or 8 minutes, and Dungeness crabs 10 to 12 minutes. The crayfish should boil only 5 to 6 minutes.

Shrimp/Crab Louis

This salad/appetizer is quite popular in the better San Francisco, Seattle, and Portland seafood restaurants. I am not sure who invented it or exactly when it was first served. It seems it probably appeared during the first 20 years of the 20th century in San Francisco. The crab Louis was the original; the shrimp came later. You can make your own "chile sauce"; most chefs purchase it, however. The recipe is for one portion. I deviate from my usual multiportion recipes here because I serve this as an "arranged" individual "salad."

INGREDIENTS

6 oz. mixed salad greens
4–6 shrimp, boiled, peeled, and deveined, 16–20s or 21–25s
1 hard-cooked egg, sliced in half lengthwise
2 tomato slices
2 cucumber slices
¼ Hass avocado, sliced
1 lemon wedge
2 Calamata olives
3–4 oz. Louis Dressing (page 151)

Method

1. Toss with a little of the dressing and arrange salad greens on a chilled plate.
2. Arrange shrimp down center of greens.
3. Garnish around edges of greens with remaining solid ingredients.
4. You may either spoon the dressing over the shrimp or present it in a ramekin on the side or both.

You may substitute 4 ounces of Dungeness or lump crabmeat for the shrimp. You may toss the greens first with either Vinaigrette (page 170) or the Louis Dressing before you place them on the plate.

Louis Dressing

Remind you of Thousand Island dressing? It is quite similar but better.
   Yield: About 1 quart

INGREDIENTS

1 qt. mayonnaise
1 c. chili sauce
2 oz. green onion, finely diced
2 oz. bell pepper, finely diced
2 oz. pimiento, finely diced
1 tbsp. lemon juice
1 tbsp. minced parsley
Tabasco, to taste
1 c. heavy cream

Method

1. Combine all ingredients in a bowl.
2. Chill.

Rémoulade Sauce

Originally a French dressing, rémoulade has come to be best known in this country for its New Orleans incarnations. To make his rémoulade, the classic French chef Escoffier merely added chopped gherkins, capers, spices, and anchovies to a previously made mayonnaise. This produces a sauce more like what is now called tartar sauce than the unique emulsion you are going to make here. The following recipe is my version of one of the two types of rémoulade made in New Orleans. The other style is made with hard-cooked eggs, and I am not, I must confess, fond of it. Again you are employing whole eggs. Serve this with boiled shrimp.

INGREDIENTS

3 eggs
2 tbsp. lemon juice
2 tbsp. red wine vinegar
salt, to taste
white pepper, to taste
Tabasco, to taste
5–6 drops Worcestershire sauce
1 tsp. finely minced garlic
1 tsp. grated horseradish
3 tbsp. Creole mustard
1–2 tbsp. paprika
3 c. peanut oil
¼ c. finely minced parsley
¼ c. finely minced green onions

Method

1. Place eggs, lemon juice, vinegar, salt, pepper, Tabasco, and Worcestershire in food processor or blender. Pulse until smooth.
2. Add garlic and horseradish. Pulse again for a few seconds. Add peanut oil slowly in a stream until a mayonnaise-like consistency has been reached.
3. Using a rubber scraper, remove sauce from processor and place in a stainless or glass mixing bowl.
4. Incorporate parsley and green onions.

Shrimp Rémoulade

INGREDIENTS

Court-bouillon (page 149), several quarts
2 lb. gulf shrimp, unpeeled, 21–25s or 16–20s
1 head romaine lettuce, shredded (chiffonade)
2–3 lemons (wedges or crowns)
12–16 cured olives, Calamata or Niçoise
½ bunch parsley, minced
paprika, sprinkle

Method

1. Bring the court-bouillon to a boil, reduce to a simmer, and simmer for about 15 minutes.
2. Bring the heat back up to a rolling boil. Add shrimp.
3. Boil shrimp for 2 to 3 minutes. When they are pink, they are *nearly* done. Feel one. When it is no longer "spongy" and has a firm texture, it is done.
4. Chill shrimp immediately under cold running water in a colander. Add ice to aid in the chilling. If you do not observe this step, the shrimp may still overcook from the residual heat.
5. Peel and devein the shrimp. Do not remove the last tail joint. The tails not only add to presentation but also provide a convenient handle for picking up the shrimp. Even the more dainty among you may find yourself in a situation where your fingers are the best tool.
6. Arrange the shredded romaine on a platter or individual plates. Carefully shingle the shrimp around the romaine, tails all pointing out in the same direction.
7. Finish the garnishing with the lemons, pitted olives, parsley, and paprika.

> ### What You Need to Know
>
> In most places in the country, you will have difficulty finding fresh shrimp. Frozen shrimp come in many different forms. I have tried nearly all of them. If you buy frozen shrimp, buy the "block-frozen" green, headless Gulf shrimp. They are sold in sizes: 21–25 means there will be 21 to 25 shrimp per pound; 16–20 means 16 to 20 shrimp per pound. As a rule, these shrimp are an excellent product, and the shrimp do not suffer badly if frozen in this manner.

STARCHES

There are literally thousands of boiled rice, potato, and pasta dishes. But you just have to learn these few basic techniques to be able to prepare them all. The steamed bread I place at the beginning here is truly worth making. I love it.

Chinese Steamed Lotus Buns

I don't steam many foods. Although I frequently poach, simmer, blanch, and boil, I have developed a certain prejudice against steaming from many years in restaurants watching my cooks overcook just about everything they attempted to steam. These rolls, though, are very good. And if I do steam, I prefer the Chinese bamboo steam baskets. Serve them with the Stir Fry (page 196).

INGREDIENTS

1 oz. dry yeast
6 tbsp. sugar
1 c. warm water (110°)
4 c. flour, more or less for kneading
1½ c. warm milk (110°)
2 tsp. baking powder
¼ c. peanut oil

Method

1. Put yeast and 1 tablespoon of the sugar into a bowl. Pour in warm water, stir, and let mixture stand 5 minutes to dissolve. It should foam and bubble. If it does not, discard and use a fresh package of yeast.

2. Put flour and remaining sugar in a food processor fitted with the metal blade. Turn machine on for 2 seconds to mix ingredients.

3. Combine yeast mixture with warm milk and, while the machine is running, pour milk down the feed tube in a steady stream. Process until dough forms a rough ball. If the ball is sticky, add flour, a tablespoon at a time, and process a few seconds longer until dough pulls cleanly away from sides of bowl. Remove dough to a lightly floured board.

4. Knead, dusting with flour until dough is smooth and elastic, about 2 minutes. Form dough into a ball and put it into a large, lightly oiled mixing bowl. Cover and set in a warm spot. Let rise until it doubles in size, about 1 hour.

5. Punch down dough and turn out on a lightly floured surface. Flatten, then put the baking powder in the center. Fold over edges and knead until baking powder is thoroughly incorporated. Invert mixing bowl over the dough; let rest 10 minutes.

6. Divide dough in half. Cover one-half and roll the other half into a 12-inch-long roll; cut into 12 pieces. Remove 1 piece and cover the rest. Roll the piece into a flat 3½-inch circle. Lightly brush one with oil; fold over to form a half-moon. With the back of a knife, score the half-moons crosswise at ¼-inch intervals.

7. With your finger or a chopstick, make an indentation in the middle of the rounded edge while the thumb and forefinger pinch the middle of the straight edge to form a notch and form a leaf. Place on parchment paper that you have cut to fit your steamer and place in a steaming basket. You will need two baskets, or you'll need to steam two separate batches. Repeat with remaining dough; leave space between buns in the basket.

8. Let rise for 30 minutes or until buns almost double in size, then steam over boiling water for 15 minutes. When done, let cool for a minute before serving.

All pilafs, risottos, pulaus, and so on have one thing in common. Whatever kid of rice you use and whatever ethnicity is involved, they all begin by coating the rice with hot fat.

Rice Pilaf

This is a fairly generic rice pilaf I make. It will go with many sautés.
Yield: 8 portions

INGREDIENTS

4 tbsp. butter
½ c. finely minced yellow onion
½ c. finely minced celery
½ c. finely minced carrot
1 tbsp. minced garlic
1 tsp. minced fresh ginger
1 c. converted rice
2½ c. chicken stock
¼ c. dry white wine
2 tbsp. lemon juice
salt, to taste
black pepper, to taste
1 tbsp. turmeric

Method

1. Melt butter over medium heat in a saucepan.
2. Sweat onion, carrots, and celery until just soft.
3. Add garlic and ginger.
4. Add rice and toss until rice is completely coated with the butter.
5. Add stock, salt, pepper, and turmeric and thoroughly incorporate.
6. Cover pot and simmer over very low heat for about 15 minutes or until liquid is completely absorbed.

Patiala Pilaf

This pilaf comes from the city of Patiala in the state of Punjab. It should be made properly with basmati rice. The dish is characteristic of the Moghul style of cooking that uses whole spices wherever possible.
Yield: 6 to 8 portions

INGREDIENTS

3 onions
2 c. basmati rice
⅓ c. peanut oil
1 tsp. cumin seeds (or ground cumin)

1 tbsp. minced garlic
1 tsp. cardamom pods (or ground cardamom)
1 cinnamon stick, broken
6–8 whole cloves
2–3 bay leaves
4 c. water
2 tsp. sea salt

Method

1. Shred two of the onions paper-thin. Dice the third.
2. Wash the rice.
3. Over medium-high heat in a sauté pan, sauté the shredded onions in the peanut oil until they are caramelized, about 15 minutes.
4. Remove the onions with a slotted spoon and drain them on toweling. They should become crisp when they cool.
5. Add cumin and diced onion to pan. Sauté until brown.
6. Add remaining spices and sauté 1 minute.
7. Add rice and sauté for about 1 more minute.
8. Add water and bring to a boil, stirring often. Add salt.
9. Reduce heat to low simmer and cook rice for about 10 minutes.
10. Cover pan and reduce heat to lowest possible level. Cook an additional 10 to 15 minutes. Fluff rice with a fork and serve with onion shreds strewn over the top of the rice.

Serve with the Indian Ginger Chicken (page 136).

And here are a couple of classic Italian rice dishes.

Risotto Florentina

Yield: 6 to 8 portions

INGREDIENTS
8 oz. lean pork loin, large dice
½ c. clarified butter
2 c. Arborio rice
1 tbsp. minced garlic
¾ c. finely diced onion
2 bay leaves
½ c. dry white wine

5 c. chicken stock
salt, to taste
black pepper, to taste
1 c. white beans, soaked, cooked, and drained
1 c. spinach, chopped, cooked, and drained
¼ c. minced parsley
¾ c. parmesan

Method

1. Caramelize the pork in 3 ounces of the clarified butter. Remove the pork.
2. Add rice to the pan and toss until it is completely coated with the butter.
3. Add garlic and onion and cook until translucent.
4. Add pork, bay leaves, wine, stock, salt, and pepper to the pan. Cover and bake in a 425° oven for 25 minutes.
5. In a sauté pan, sweat the beans and spinach in the remaining butter with a little garlic.
6. Allow the rice mixture to cool for 10 minutes, then toss lightly (using two forks) with the beans, spinach, and parmesan. Serve immediately.

Risotto Milanese

Risotto Milanese dates back to 1574, when a stained-glass artisan named Zafferano added some saffron that he used for coloring his paints to his risotto for his daughter's wedding. In no time, this dish was the talk of the town and still is—or so the story goes. Even if not true, it is a good story. Saffron is the world's most expensive spice. It comes from small purple crocus flowers producing three stigmas per flower that are handpicked and dried. It takes 14,000 of these stigmas to produce 1 ounce of saffron.

Yield: 6 to 8 portions

INGREDIENTS

7 c. chicken stock
4–6 saffron threads (or ⅛ tsp. powdered saffron)
¼ c. extra virgin olive oil
¾ c. minced yellow onions
2 c. Arborio rice
2 tbsp. butter
salt and pepper, to taste
½ c. dry white wine
1 c. parmesan

(**Method**)

1. In a large pot, heat the stock but don't let it come to a boil. Just let it simmer.
2. Heat the oil in a separate heavy-bottomed pot over medium heat.
3. Add the onion and cook slowly until translucent.
4. Stir in the rice until the grains of rice are coated with the oil. This will keep them from sticking together.
5. Cook for a couple of minutes until the rice gives off a nutty smell.
6. Start by adding 1 cup of hot stock, stirring continuously.
7. As the rice absorbs the stock, begin adding ½ cup of stock at a time, stirring continuously until all the stock is used (15–20 minutes).
8. Remove from heat and stir in the wine and saffron threads.

Haricot Rouge et Riz

My mother, God rest her soul, was not the world's greatest cook. This came about more from disinclination than from any lack of ability. Also, she was a working woman. She did, however, prepare one truly wonderful dish: Red Beans and Rice. In New Orleans, it is traditional to eat this dish on Monday. We had it just about every Monday when I was a child. My version is "after" hers.

Yield: 10 to 12 portions

INGREDIENTS

1 lb. red beans, boiled and soaked for 1 hour
3 qt. water
1 lb. ham hocks
2 c. thinly sliced yellow onions
2 c. thinly julienned bell pepper
1 tbsp. minced garlic
2 c. thinly sliced (on the bias) celery
1 c. julienned ham
2 or 3 hot sausage (andouille or chaurice)
1 tsp. cumin
1 tsp. black pepper
1 tsp. cayenne pepper
4 bay leaves
1 tbsp. whole thyme
2 c. peeled, seeded, and chopped tomatoes
½ c. tomato purée
3 c. diced potatoes
salt, to taste
¼ c. minced parsley

Method

1. Drain beans and place in a pot with the water, ham hocks, onions, bell pepper, garlic, celery, ham, sausage (sliced), cumin, peppers, bay leaves, thyme, tomatoes, purée, potatoes, salt, and parsley.
2. Bring the pot to a boil, reduce to a simmer, cover, and simmer for approximately 1 hour. Check the beans, and if they are not yet soft, cook until they are.
3. Remove ham hock from pot and cut meat off the bone and dice. Return to pot.

We like to make our boiled rice separate and serve the red beans in a soup bowl over the rice. I almost invariably serve the Red Beans and Rice with the Muffuletta (see the next recipe).

Muffuletta

The origin of this king of sandwiches is attributed to the Central Grocery in New Orleans. There are multitudinous versions of it now in New Orleans. Here is our favorite.

Yield: 4 *healthy* portions

INGREDIENTS
1 round Italian loaf, 8-in.
1 oz. Genoa salami, thinly sliced
1 oz. provolone, thinly sliced
1 oz. mortadella, thinly sliced
1 oz. smoked ham, thinly sliced
1 oz. mozzarella, thinly sliced
2 oz. Olive Dressing (page 161)

Method

1. Slice the bread in half crosswise about 1 inch from the bottom.
2. Remove about ½ inch of the bread from inside the top and bottom of the loaf.
3. Fold over the salami, provolone, mortadella, ham, and mozzarella and layer them in the middle of the sandwich.
4. Add the olive dressing to the top of the sandwich and place the top of the loaf on all the other ingredients.
5. Impale with four large frilled toothpicks. Slice into quarters and serve.

Olive Dressing

INGREDIENTS

12 oz. Greek or Italian olives, mixed, diced
12 oz. Spanish green olives with pimentos, diced
6 oz. pickled pearl onions, diced
6 oz. Giardiniera, diced
1 tsp. basil
1 tsp. oregano
1 tbsp. minced garlic
¼ c. extra virgin olive oil
3 tbsp. balsamic vinegar

Method

1. Mix all ingredients.
2. Place in a nonreactive container (stainless or glass) and permit to stand a few hours in the refrigerator.

Wild Rice

Wild rice is technically not "rice." It is a grass or a grain. There are two varieties of wild rice out there for consumers. You are much more likely to see the Native American variety, though. Manchurian wild rice is a slightly smaller variety and not in common supply in the West. It's good, though. Try it should you run across it.

Yield: 6 to 8 portions

INGREDIENTS

3 c. wild rice
¼ c. clarified butter
1 c. minced onion
¼ c. minced celery
1 tbsp. minced garlic
7 c. stock
2 bay leaves
1 tsp. whole thyme
1 tsp. salt
black pepper, to taste

Method

1. Wash rice thoroughly—this may take several rinses.
2. Sweat rice in a casserole in the clarified butter for 2 or 3 minutes.
3. Add onion and celery and continue to sweat until the onion is soft. Add garlic.
4. Add stock and all spices.
5. Bring to a boil, cover, and reduce to a simmer. Simmer 45 minutes. Check for moisture content. Simmer uncovered while stirring with a fork if the rice seems too wet.

Potato Dishes

We humans have been eating potatoes for over 2,000 years. The Spanish "discovered" them in the Andes in the middle of the 16th century and took them back to Europe. They were a hard sell in Europe because they are related to the nightshade plants, which Europeans knew to be poisonous. In fact, all parts of the potato plant except the tuber we eat are mildly poisonous. Americans eat about 140 pounds each of potatoes per year. Sound like a lot of potatoes? Europeans eat twice as many as we do.

In the United States, we have three basic types of potatoes: starchy, waxy, and somewhere between those two. What we think of as a "baking potato" or Idaho potato is a Burbank potato, developed by Luther Burbank in 1872 in an attempt to improve the Irish potato to make it more resistant to the blight that caused the Potato Famine. This is the starchy potato, good for baking, frying, and smashing. The White and Red Rose potatoes are waxy and good for salads and boiling. In between these two extremes are several varieties of which the Yukon Gold is typical. Neither starchy nor waxy, they are good for gratins because they hold their shape well.

Mashed Potatoes

The thick-skinned Burbank-type (Idaho) potatoes are best for making this traditional American dish. I call them "mashed," although technically they are "milled." It seems to be trendy to make lumpy mashed potatoes nowadays. Perhaps some chefs are just trying to prove they are using fresh potatoes. I like them smooth and lump free.

Yield: 8 portions

INGREDIENTS

boiling water, to cover
6 baking potatoes, peeled and cut into large pieces
salt, to taste
white pepper, to taste
1½ c. milk
2 tbsp. butter

Method

1. Place potatoes in boiling water with 1 teaspoon of salt.
2. Boil until potatoes are just tender.
3. Put potatoes through food mill. Add salt and pepper.
4. Add milk and thoroughly combine with a whip or a wooden spoon.
5. Add butter and thoroughly incorporate.

Purée of Garlic Potatoes

The thick-skinned Burbank-type (Idaho) potatoes are best for making this more or less traditional American dish. I usually pipe these in the center of the plate and present grilled or sautéed meats or poultry on top of them.

INGREDIENTS

boiling water, to cover
6 baking potatoes, peeled and cut into large pieces
1 tbsp. finely minced garlic
salt, to taste
white pepper, to taste
1½ c. milk
2 tbsp. butter

Method

1. Place potatoes in boiling water with 1 teaspoon of salt.
2. Boil until potatoes are just tender.
3. Sweat the garlic in a little of the butter. Do not allow the garlic to brown. Add to potatoes.
4. Put potatoes and garlic through food mill. Add salt and pepper.
5. Add milk and thoroughly combine with a whip or a wooden spoon.
6. Add the rest of butter and thoroughly incorporate.
7. Place in a large pastry bag equipped with a large star tube and pipe onto plates.

Gnocchi di Patate

This is the most straightforward and easiest gnocchi to make.
    Yield: 6 to 8 portions

INGREDIENTS

3 lb. potatoes
2 c. flour
1 c. parmesan

Method

1. Boil potatoes in jackets.
2. Peel and put them through a food mill as soon as they are soft.
3. Add flour a little at a time and knead into potatoes until mixture is soft, smooth, and still a little sticky.
4. Shape into long cylinders about ¾-inch thick.
5. Cut cylinders into pieces about ¾-inch long.
6. Press each gnocchi with your finger into the tines of a fork.
7. Pop off onto counter. Make sure you have plenty of flour on everything while you are doing this.
8. Drop the gnocchi into boiling, salted water and cook until they rise to the surface.
9. Cook an additional 10 seconds.
10. Remove gnocchi with a slotted spoon to a warm platter.
11. Toss with the parmesan and serve with a Bolognese (page 269), pesto (page 39), or a tomato sauce (page 294).

The gnocchi leads us naturally into a few boiled pasta dishes.

Pastas and Their Sauces

Although the origins of pasta are somewhat murky, we know one thing for sure: Marco Polo did not introduce it to Italy. Ancient Greeks and Romans ate a noodle dough they called *laganon*. It was not boiled, though; it was baked. Boiled noodles are not mentioned until the fifth century. There is good evidence that the first fried pasta was probably sold in Palermo. When the Spanish brought the tomato back from the New World in the 16th century, pasta really took off. Incidentally, pasta had been eaten with fingers until sauces came along. The fork was most likely invented to eat pasta with sauce (tomato sauce). The dried pasta traveled well, and the Italian explorers took it all over the world.

    Pastas are made from several different types of flour. The dried pasta typical of southern Italy is made with a durum-wheat semolina flour, a fairly coarse flour best for dried pasta. For fresh egg pasta, you may use all-purpose flour or bread flour or a combination of the two.

Pasta all'Uovo

This is the fresh egg pasta of northern Italy.
Yield: About 12 portions of noodles

INGREDIENTS

4 c. flour
4 eggs
4 tbsp. extra virgin olive oil
2 tsp. salt
water, as needed

Method

1. Place flour and salt in a mixer with a dough hook.
2. Add eggs, one at a time, while mixing on slow speed.
3. Add olive oil in a stream.
4. Add a little water only if the dough seems too dry.
5. Wrap the dough in plastic wrap and keep the dough tightly wrapped unless you are making noodles immediately.

Fettuccine Alfredo

Undoubtedly, the best known of all Roman pasta dishes, it may be traced to a restaurant called *Alfredo alla Scrofa* in the 1920s. This may well be the richest of all pasta dishes. Very simple and quick to make.

Yield: The following is for 1 portion of pasta (3 ounces). I try not to cook more than 3 portions at one time.

INGREDIENTS

boiling water, several quarts
1–2 tbsp. kosher salt
3 oz. fresh fettuccine noodles
6 oz. heavy cream
1 tsp. minced garlic
3 oz. parmesan
1 tsp. butter, softened (optional)
nutmeg, pinch
black pepper, to taste

Method

1. Add salt to water and reduce water to simmer.
2. Place cream in a sauté or fry pan over medium heat. Use a nonreactive pan.
3. Add garlic to cream and simmer until cream is reduced by one-half and slightly thickened. About this time, the cream will begin to froth and attempt to escape from the pan.
4. Add parmesan to cream and thoroughly incorporate (add optional butter).
5. Add noodles to simmering water. Stir noodles using a fork or tongs. Cook noodles about 60 seconds.
6. Drain noodles and add to cream in sauté pan. Stir or toss to thoroughly mix cream and noodles.
7. If the sauce seems a little thin, add a little more cheese.
8. Grind black pepper over the pasta. Serve in a flat-rimmed soup bowl.

Tortellini

Here is a stuffed pasta dish from the Emilia-Romagna area of Italy.

Yield: 8 to 10 portions

Note: When making pasta, the cooks in Emilia-Romagna do not add oil. Omit the oil from the recipe.

INGREDIENTS

1 recipe pasta (page 165)
¼ c. finely minced parsley
1 c. parmesan
1½ c. ricotta
1 egg yolk
½ tsp. salt
nutmeg, pinch

Method

1. Make the pasta.
2. Combine the parsley, parmesan, ricotta, egg yolk, salt, and nutmeg in a bowl.
3. Roll the pasta out with a pasta machine to the next to last number—quite thin.
4. Cut out 2 ½-inch circles with a cookie cutter.
5. Place approximately 1 teaspoon of the filling in the center of the dough.
6. Fold the dough over, with the top not quite reaching out as far as the bottom. Press firmly to seal.
7. Hold the dumpling in your hand and wrap the points around the tip of your left index finger, forming a circle. Allow it to fall down and around your finger. Press the tips together to close the circle.
8. Place in rapidly boiling water and, once the water has returned to a boil, boil for 5 minutes. Drain.
9. Serve with a heavy cream, butter, and parmesan reduction or with a tomato sauce.
10. Serve with Sugo di Pomodoro e Panna (see page 300). (This tomato-cream sauce comes to us from Emilia-Romagna and is often served with tortellini.)

What You Need to Know

When do we use dry pasta and when do we use fresh pasta? I like them both. This is largely a matter of personal preference, although some foods naturally lend themselves to one or the other. Both the dry pasta and the most of the tomato sauces are products of southern Italy and make a very natural pairing. The cream sauces marry better with the fresh noodles of the more northerly Italian climes—that's where the cows were/are, folks. Seafoods swing both ways. The two pastas cook very differently. Fresh pasta must be served very soon after cooking; dried pasta can be held in olive oil for a spell after one stops the cooking. The best fresh egg pastas can be made with the American variety of all-purpose flour. Dried pastas are made from a durum, semolina flour. They will store for quite a long period.

Red Clam Sauce for Pasta

I particularly like the canned baby clams for this dish. The sauce is very quick to make, and it will probably take longer to cook your dried linguine noodles. You can have this dish on the table in literally 15 to 20 minutes.

Yield: 6 to 8 portions

INGREDIENTS

1½ c. littleneck clams, fresh or canned
½ c. finely minced onions
1 tbsp. finely minced garlic
¼ c. extra virgin olive oil
2 c. chopped canned Italian tomatoes
¼ c. clam broth (from clams)
2 tbsp. tomato purée
1 tsp. whole oregano
2 tbsp. minced parsley
salt, to taste
black pepper, to taste

Method

1. If clams are fresh, thoroughly scrub them and place them in a pot with about 1 inch of water. Steam them until they open. Reserve two or three in the shell to garnish the pasta bowls with. Remove the rest from the shell and

chop roughly. If you are using canned clams, strain them but reserve the juice to add later.

2. Place the oil in a fry pan and heat over high heat.

3. Add onions and sauté for a minute or two. Add garlic.

4. Add tomatoes, clams, oregano, parsley, salt, and pepper and simmer for 5 minutes. Serve tossed with thin pasta.

Garnish with the reserved, steamed clams, chopped parsley, and freshly grated parmesan cheese. Many Italians do not like cheeses with their seafood pastas. This is a personal preference of mine.

What You Need to Know

Here's just a little clam lore. In the eastern part of the United States, the clams most readily available commercially are quahogs (pronounced "cohogs"). When you hear clams referred to as "cherrystones" or "littlenecks," this is that clam. Littlenecks are the smallest and, to me, the tastiest; cherrystones are a little larger, and the largest you will want to steam. Larger clams are best left for chowders. While there are soft-shell clams available on both coasts, I rarely see them offered today. The Pacific Northwest has a large clam called the goeduck ("gooeyduck"). The other principal edible clam is the United States is the razor clam. These, too, will not be seen in the markets. Maybe you can convince someone to take you clam digging.

Ravioli

There are many ways to form the ravioli. My method here works just fine if you have not already stumbled on one you like better.

Yield: 6–8 portions

INGREDIENTS

¼ c. finely minced yellow onion

1 c. ground veal

¼ c. clarified butter

1 c. spinach, cooked, drained, squeezed, and chopped

salt, to taste

black pepper, to taste

nutmeg, pinch

½ c. parmesan

1 c. ricotta cheese
2 eggs, lightly beaten
1 recipe Pasta all'Uovo (page 165)

Method

1. Sweat onions and veal in clarified butter until onions are soft.
2. Add spinach, salt, pepper, and nutmeg. Sweat briefly and cool.
3. Combine cheeses in a mixing bowl.
4. Add eggs to cheeses and thoroughly incorporate.
5. Add veal mixture to cheeses and combine.
6. Roll pasta out with machine until it is quite thin.
7. Cut pasta into two uniform rectangular sheets of the same size.
8. Place 1 teaspoon of the veal mixture about every 2 inches on one of the sheets of pasta.
9. Using a small pastry brush, paint between the mounds of filling with a little cold water.
10. Place the other sheet of pasta on the filling and the bottom sheet and press into place. Try to prevent air pockets from forming and ensure the top sheet is firmly pressed into the bottom sheet.
11. Using a ravioli wheel, cut into individual raviolis.
12. Boil in lots of salted water for about 7 to 8 minutes.
13. Serve with a tomato or cream sauce or even with a ragu such as Ragu alla Bolognese (page 269).

Vinaigrette and Mayonnaise

These are two of the principal bases for salads containing cooked ingredients, and you will require either vinaigrette dressing or mayonnaise for several of the following potato salad recipes and the coleslaw (page 175).

Vinaigrette

This is the basic dressing for salads of mixed greens. You will occasionally see a recipe for vinaigrette in which you are enjoined to beat the oil slowly into the vinegar to form an emulsion. This procedure is totally unnecessary since no true emulsion is, in fact, formed. Just beat it all together with a wire whip. When it comes apart, which it will, beat it again. This recipe will make about 2 cups. It stores well. You may add just about any herbs, spices, or condiments you enjoy to the basic vinaigrette. There is a classic French recipe in which the vinaigrette is "bound" with "pounded calf's brain."

INGREDIENTS

1½ c. extra virgin olive oil (or a mixture of olive oil and peanut oil)
½ c. red wine vinegar
1 tbsp. Dijon mustard
salt, to taste
black pepper, to taste

EGGS AND VEGETABLES

What You Need to Know

Time for a short disclaimer here. Several of the recipes in this chapter contain raw eggs. About 1 in 20,000 eggs produced in the United States has been demonstrated to contain salmonella. Heat invariably kills salmonella. So you are always safe from this scourge if you cook your eggs. All my recipes here that contain raw eggs also contain two acids: acetic (vinegar) and citric (lemon juice). Poultry producers frequently add these acids (and lactic acid) to the drinking water they give their fowl to kill salmonella. I am not saying this is foolproof, but I will say that I have been making these recipes for others and myself for at least 35 years, and I have never had food poisoning, nor have those who've eaten my dishes made with raw eggs. If you are worried, don't eat raw eggs.

You also need to know how to make mayonnaise.

Mayonnaise

All mayonnaises are an emulsion of eggs, or egg yolks, and oil with a variety of spices, herbs, seasonings, and even vegetables. There are two interesting speculations as to the origin of the word "mayonnaise." Carême, a well-known French chef, believed that the verb *manie* ("to stir") is the genesis of the word, and he would have this cold sauce spelled "magnonaise." I think he has already lost the battle on this one. There is an Old French word *moyeunais*, which means "egg yolk." Mayonnaise, classically, in France, is made with egg yolks. Our lighter (but not by much) mayonnaise is made with whole eggs. I think you will like this much better than anything available in the supermarket, and its preparation is simplicity itself.

INGREDIENTS

3 eggs
2 tbsp. lemon juice
2 tbsp. white vinegar
1 tsp. dry mustard
salt, to taste
white pepper, to taste
3 c. peanut oil

[Method]

1. Place all ingredients, except the peanut oil, in a food processor or blender. Pulse until smooth.
2. Add oil, very slowly, in a stream until the desired consistency is obtained. Refrigerate until needed.

What You Need to Know

You may make the emulsion as thick as you like, depending on the use you have in mind for the sauce. The more oil you add, the thicker the mayonnaise will be, up to a point. A large egg will easily absorb 1 cup of oil, though.

The following is the classic handmade French mayonnaise.

INGREDIENTS

2 egg yolks, room temperature
½ tsp. dry mustard
½ tsp. salt
cayenne pepper, dash
1 tsp. lemon juice
1 tbsp. wine vinegar
1–1¼ c. extra virgin olive oil

> **Method**

1. Place the egg yolks in a clean, dry, medium-sized bowl. Beat with a wire whisk until lemon colored.
2. Beat in the mustard, salt, cayenne pepper, sugar, and ½ teaspoon of the lemon juice.
3. Continue beating and begin to add the olive oil *very* slowly, about a tablespoon at a time. The mixture will begin to thicken and emulsify. Continue until all the oil is incorporated.

What You Need to Know

Before we get into making salads: Don't just plop a glop of dressing on top of a salad the way they do in greasy-spoon eateries! Toss the ingredients with the dressing! This procedure ensures all the leaves/ingredients are well coated. Even on a composed salad where you have a multitude of topping ingredients in addition to the greens, toss the greens with the dressing before you top the salad with the remaining ingredients.

Several of the following potato salads also call for hard-cooked eggs. Here's my technique.

Hard-Cooked Eggs

Ever boiled an egg and found you had a lovely green halo around the yolk when you cut or bit into it? No? Well, just skip this section then.

Those of you who are still with us here, please note that I did not title this section "Hard-Boiled Eggs." If you are able to free your forebrain of the notion of boiling, this egg thing will make sense. While you boil the eggs a little, the residual heat remaining after you remove the eggs from the heat does most of the cooking. The reason your yolk was encased in its green sheath was that you overcooked it. Period. As little as 10 or 15 percent will do it.

Place the eggs in a pot or pan with cold water to cover (no salt required). Place the pot on the heat and bring it to a boil. Boil the eggs for 3 minutes, place a lid on the pot, and remove it from the heat. Set your timer for 15 minutes. When the timer beckons, pour off the hot water and immediately cool the eggs under cold running water. Peel immediately. The sooner you peel the eggs, the easier that procedure will be.

My method for peeling hard-cooked eggs works quite well. If you don't have a favorite, successful procedure, you might try mine. If I'm cooking a dozen or fewer eggs, I do them in a saucepan with a handle. Empty all the water from the pan first. Holding the pan by the handle, shake it vigorously back and forth in a horizontal plane. This will cause the eggs to bash about and career off each other and the sides of the pan, creating hundreds of tiny cracks in the shells. They will readily surrender their shells. Rinse them under cold running water and refrigerate.

German Potato Salad

This recipe is a tribute to my Great Aunt Dora, my mother's aunt. She made a hot, German-style potato salad that everyone raved about. Of course, she never showed anyone how she made it. Having eaten it on many occasions, I am re-creating an approximation.

Yield: 8 portions

INGREDIENTS

½ lb. bacon, lardons, blanched and sautéed
1 yellow onion, thinly sliced
3 or 4 ribs celery, thinly sliced
3 lb. potatoes, Red Rose, boiled and thinly sliced
4 hard-cooked eggs, sliced or chopped
1 c. vinaigrette dressing
½ c. brown or chicken stock (pages 285 and 286)
1 tbsp. dry mustard
1 tbsp. sugar
salt, to taste
black pepper, to taste
¼ c. chopped parsley

Method

1. Discard all but 1 or 2 tablespoons of the bacon fat remaining from sautéing the bacon.
2. Sweat the onion and celery in the bacon fat until just soft.
3. Add the celery and onion to the potatoes in a bowl and incorporate thoroughly.
4. Add the eggs to the bowl and thoroughly incorporate.
5. Place the vinaigrette in a skillet with remaining ingredients and heat.
6. Pour this mixture over the potatoes in the bowl and, again, thoroughly incorporate.

7. Serve warm immediately or chill. When completely chilled, add 2 cups of mayonnaise to the salad. This would be good for a picnic, but please keep it cold until you eat it.

Deviled Potato Salad

This is my version of the standard American potato salad. I think the Dijon mustard is what makes it. This is the one I serve with barbecue.

Yield: 8 portions

INGREDIENTS

¼ c. Dijon mustard
2 c. mayonnaise
1 c. thinly sliced yellow onion
1 c. diced celery
2 tbsp. cider vinegar
1 tbsp. sugar
8 c. cooked, peeled, and cubed potatoes
4 eggs, hard-cooked, peeled, and sliced
salt, to taste
black pepper, to taste

Method

1. In large bowl, combine Dijon, mayonnaise, onion, celery, vinegar, sugar, and salt.
2. Add potatoes and eggs and toss gently to coat.
3. Cover and chill at least 1 hour.

While we're at it, although there is no cooking involved in this dish, let me give you my recipe for my other traditional side dish with barbecue.

Coleslaw

"Coleslaw" most likely derives form the Dutch *koosla*, which means "cabbage salad." It has been present in the United States since before the turn of the 19th century. Served as a traditional side in delicatessens and with barbecue, it is truly a versatile adjunct to many different cuisines. I serve this with the Deviled Potato Salad (above) and with the Barbecued Baby Back Ribs (page 11).

Yield: 8 portions

INGREDIENTS

6 c. shredded white cabbage
2 c. shredded red cabbage
¾ c. shredded carrots
2 bunches green onions, finely minced
1 or 2 bell peppers, finely minced
chiles, jalapeño or serrano, to taste (optional)

Dressing

INGREDIENTS

2 c. mayonnaise (page 171)
2 tbsp. catsup
2 tbsp. vinegar
1 tsp. sugar
Tabasco, to taste
2 dashes Worcestershire sauce
salt, to taste
black pepper, to taste

Method

1. Combine vegetables and dressing.
2. Chill for several hours.

Italian Potato Salad

This is a very hearty potato salad.
    Yield: 8 portions

INGREDIENTS

3 lb. potatoes, Red Rose, B-size
1 c. vinaigrette (page 170)
2 bell peppers, diced
¼ lb. Genoa salami, thinly julienned
3 stalks celery, diced
1 bunch green onions (both green and white parts), chopped
4 hard-cooked eggs, marinated
16 Italian, Calamata, or Niçoise olives
1 c. pickled pepperoncini

Method

1. Wash the potatoes well and boil them in their jackets until just tender. Test with a paring knife periodically.
2. Slice the potatoes thinly, toss gently with the vinaigrette, and marinate them, covered, for several hours or overnight in the refrigerator.
3. Toss the potatoes with the salami, celery, and green onions.
4. Garnish with the eggs, olives, and pepperoncini. Seal and chill well.

What You Need to Know

For the Anise Vinaigrette, simply make your favorite vinaigrette dressing. Mine is on page 170. If you are able to find *Finocchio* for the Insalata Mista, mince about a tablespoon of the leaves and add them to the dressing. Anise, fennel, and Finocchio are virtually identical. If you use dried herbs, add about 2 teaspoons of fennel.

Salade Niçoise

Here is the southern French potato salad. *Niçoise* means "in the manner of Nice." We are "boiling" three items in this cold salad.

Yield: 8 to 10 portions

INGREDIENTS

1 or 2 heads Bibb or Boston lettuce
1 c. vinaigrette (page 170)
4 tomatoes, quartered
3 c. thinly sliced potatoes, Red Rose, boiled
3 c. blanched green beans
¼ c. Niçoise or Calamata olives
1 c. fresh-grilled tuna, canned in water or oil
4 hard-cooked eggs, quartered
6 anchovies
salt, to taste
black pepper, to taste

Note: This classic salad from the south of France is terrific with fresh-grilled yellowtail tuna. But have no qualms about making it with an oil or water-pack canned tuna. It's still quite good.

Method

1. Wash and core the lettuce. Separate the leaves but do not tear them. Dry.
2. Pour half a cup of the vinaigrette over the tomatoes, potatoes, and green beans.
3. Toss tuna with a little of the vinaigrette.
4. Arrange the lettuce leaves around a salad bowl.
5. Place the potatoes on the bottom of the bowl.
6. Arrange all the other ingredients, except olives and anchovies, in an aesthetically pleasing fashion over the potatoes.
7. Add salt and pepper.
8. Garnish with the olives and anchovies.
9. Pour the rest of the vinaigrette over all, chill, and serve.

Fagiolini Verdi in Insalata

This is a classic Italian green bean salad.
   Yield: 6 to 8 portions

INGREDIENTS

1 lb. green beans
3 or 4 roasted red peppers
1 onion
1 c. vinaigrette (page 170)
salt, to taste
black pepper, to taste
1–2 tbsp. lemon juice

Method

1. Trim, wash, and blanch the green beans until they are just tender. Cut into 2-inch pieces on the bias.
2. If using fresh peppers, roast and peel; if they are canned, drain and julienne.
3. Julienne the onion.
4. Gently toss all ingredients with the vinaigrette and the lemon juice. Refrigerate until chilled.

Cooking Eggs in a Liquid

We began to explore the egg in the mayonnaise and potato salad recipes. Now we are going to cook eggs in a liquid to several degrees of doneness, starting with a coddled egg or two.

Caesar Salad

No, this salad is named not for the noted Roman but rather for its inventor, an Italian restaurateur in Tijuana, Mexico, Caesar Cardini. There are various stories about when it was invented, but all take place in the 1920s.

Yield: 8 portions

INGREDIENTS

1 tbsp. minced garlic
1 c. olive oil (or ½ olive oil and ½ peanut oil)
2 small heads romaine lettuce
2 c. croutons
2 tsp. Dijon mustard
3 tbsp. lemon juice (approx. 2 lemons)
salt, to taste
black pepper, to taste
Worcestershire sauce, dash
Tabasco, dash
2 oz. anchovies
2 eggs
¾ c. parmesan

(Method)

1. Place the garlic in the oil and allow them to marinate for several hours or overnight.
2. Core, wash, and dry the romaine. You may tear it into bite-sized pieces now or just before you assemble the salad. Refrigerate, covered.
3. To make the croutons, cut a loaf of French bread into cubes approximately ¾ inch on a side. For the best croutons, trim off the crust.
4. Strain the garlic from the olive oil. Sauté the croutons until golden brown in ¼ cup of the garlic oil. Drain.
5. Beat together with a wire whisk the remaining oil, Dijon mustard, lemon juice, pepper, salt, Worcestershire, and Tabasco. This is the dressing.

6. Cook the eggs in boiling water for 1 minute. Cool under cold running water. Break the eggs into the dressing and combine thoroughly.

7. In a large salad bowl, toss the romaine with the dressing. Add the croutons and toss again. Add the parmesan and toss again. Garnish with the anchovies. Serve on chilled plates.

Cobb Salad

This salad is among the heartiest. It was created by Bob Cobb, proprietor of the distinctive Brown Derby, a restaurant that opened in Hollywood in 1926.

The restaurant was shaped like the hat of the same name. The restaurant was not much more than a diner, really, but it had a reputation for good, "honest" food and cleanliness, and celebrities flocked to it. The salad, created in 1926, includes ingredients from all along the food chain and actually employs three of the five techniques: hot air, fat, and liquid.

INGREDIENTS

6–8 handfuls mixed salad greens (lettuces, fresh herbs)
1½ c. vinaigrette (page 170)
6–8 oz. bacon, minced and cooked
6–8 oz. Roquefort cheese, crumbled
6–8 oz. finely chopped hard-cooked egg
6–8 oz. chicken breast, grilled and diced
3 c. diced tomato
2–3 Hass avocados, diced

Method

1. You may either make this salad on a large platter for a buffet-style presentation or choose to present it on individual, chilled salad plates. Whichever method you select, the color contrast and presentation are central to the making of this salad.

2. Toss the lettuces with about ¾ cup of the dressing and then choose one of the two previously listed methods.

3. Place the lettuce on the plate and distribute evenly with a slight mounding at the center.

4. Place the avocado in a mound in the center of the platter (plate).

5. Arrange the bacon, Roquefort cheese, hard-cooked egg, and chicken breast on the lettuces in wedge-shaped spokes radiating out from the avocado. Do not completely cover the lettuces.

6. Outline the wedges on either side with the diced tomato. Again, do not cover all the lettuce, or you will lose your green background.

7. Serve the remaining dressing in a ramekin on the side.

The bacon: My method of dealing with the bacon is to mince it in a food processor and cook it in the oven on a sheet pan. I then drain the fat through a sieve and place the "bacon bits" on toweling until I am ready for them.

What You Need to Know

Peeling an avocado: Use a sharp knife and cut around the pit, allowing the knife blade to rest against the pit as the blade circumnavigates the avocado. Set the knife down. Twist the two halves apart with your hands. Again, using your sharp knife, tap the blade into the pit and twist; the pit will be impaled on the blade of your knife. Use a large kitchen spoon to remove the fruit from the skin. If you are not assembling the salad immediately, squeeze a little lemon juice over the avocado to prevent it from oxidizing. As a matter of fact, it's a good idea to squeeze a little lemon over the avocado even if assembly is imminent.

Poaching Eggs

A properly poached egg should have a firm white and a yolk that is still runny. With a little practice, you should be able to poach six to eight eggs at one time. The water in which you poach must be acidulated, in this instance with *vinegar*, not *lemon juice*. The vinegar will cause the white to draw in. Lemon juice, unfortunately, will cause the white to dissipate.

What You Need to Know

Poaching is best done in a low-rimmed pan, such as a *sautoir*, sauté pan, or fry pan. Pour 2 inches of water into the pan and add 1 teaspoon of white vinegar for every 2 cups of water. Bring the water to a boil and reduce to a simmer. Crack the egg on the side of the pan and gently open the shell right on top of the water. Proceed around the pan until you have six to eight eggs in the water. When the first egg appears done, gently lift it with a slotted spoon or a skimmer. Probe the white with your finger. If it is firm, the egg is cooked. Drain the egg over a cloth towel with which you also lightly daub the top side of the egg. Place the egg on the muffin, toast, or plate.

Eggs Hussarde

This is a New Orleans brunch dish. Make the marchand de vin sauce ahead and the hollandaise at the last minute.

Yield: 6 to 8 portions

INGREDIENTS

12–16 English muffins
12–16 tomato slices (about ¼ in. thick)
12–16 slices Canadian bacon (¼ in. thick)
24–32 oz. marchand de vin sauce (page 299)
12–16 eggs, poached
12–16 oz. hollandaise sauce (page 295)

Method

1. Toast English muffins.
2. Grill tomato slices.
3. Grill Canadian bacon.
4. Place Canadian bacon on muffin.
5. Place tomato on bacon.
6. Ladle 2 ounces of the marchand de vin sauce over the tomato.
7. Place poached egg on marchand de vin sauce.
8. Ladle hollandaise over poached egg.

Eggs Benedict

Probably the best-known poached egg dish, it is a true American classic—from New York.

INGREDIENTS

12–16 English muffins
12–16 slices Canadian bacon
12–16 eggs, poached (page 181)
12–16 oz. hollandaise sauce (page 295)

Method

1. Toast English muffins.
2. Grill Canadian bacon.

3. Place Canadian bacon on English muffin.
4. Place one poached egg on each slice of Canadian bacon.
5. Ladle the hollandaise sauce over the poached egg.

Eggs Sardou

Here is another New Orleans brunch dish, from Antoine's restaurant.

INGREDIENTS

½ c. butter
2 lb. baby spinach leaves, washed
salt and pepper, to taste
3–4 c. heavy cream
2 oz. Gruyère cheese, grated
12–16 artichoke bottoms, fresh or canned
3 in. simmering water
1 tbsp. white vinegar
12–16 eggs
2–3 c. hollandaise sauce (page 295)
¼ c. minced parsley
paprika, sprinkle

[**Method**]

1. In a pan large enough to hold all the spinach, melt the butter. Add the spinach, a handful at a time.
2. Cook the spinach until it is wilted. Add salt and pepper. You will have a considerable quantity of water in the pan. Drain off all the water through a colander. Reserve spinach.
3. Place cream in pan and reduce ⅓ over medium heat.
4. Add cheese and melt.
5. Add drained spinach to this mixture and thoroughly incorporate. Set aside and keep warm.
6. Add vinegar to water. Break eggs over water and follow the egg-poaching procedure on page 181. Continue until all eggs are poached.
7. While the eggs are poaching, spoon some of the spinach mixture into each of the artichoke bottoms.
8. Drain eggs and place one on top of the spinach mixture on each artichoke.
9. Nap with the hollandaise sauce. I use a 1-ounce ladle.
10. Sprinkle parsley and paprika over all.

> ### What You Need to Know
>
> This dish is best with fresh artichokes, but I realize you cannot always obtain them. If you use canned artichoke bottoms, all you will need to do is drain and warm them. They are not quite as large as the fresh you will be able to buy, but they will suffice.
>
> Here is the procedure for fresh artichokes: Using a serrated knife, cut off all but about 1½ inches of the bottom of the artichoke. Cut off the stem. Immediately rub all cut surfaces with lemon. Cut remaining leaves off bottom with a paring knife. Remove choke with a spoon or baller. Rub lemon over all again. Bring salted water to a boil. Add artichoke bottoms and poach until a paring knife slips easily into the middle, about 15 minutes. Drain.

Cooking Vegetables in a Liquid

Steaming or boiling is an excellent manner in which to cook most vegetables. The harder winter squashes will need to be baked (page 84), and vegetables such as spinach with an extremely high water content do not require any water to cook.

Asparagus

These next two recipes show you how to deal with the harder vegetables in a two-step process that involves first blanching in water and then finishing in fat. I include them here because all the cooking is done with liquid—the finishing in the hot fat is just to flavor and bring the vegetables up to serving temperature. These vegetables include asparagus, green beans, broccoli, Brussels sprouts, cauliflower, and any other vegetable that, if sautéed in its raw state, would burn on the outside and remain raw inside. The softer vegetables, like the summer squashes, zucchini, and yellow crookneck squashes, may be sautéed raw and are featured in part III (pages 214–217). The *very* young asparagus we call "grass" may be sautéed from scratch.

Bear in mind anything that may be boiled may also be steamed. More caution is needed when steaming, as it is very easy to overcook the food.

Yield: I allow ¼ lb. per person. I like asparagus. 8 portions

Ingredients

2 lb. asparagus
2 qt. boiling water
1 tbsp. kosher salt
¼ c. clarified butter or olive oil

kosher salt, to taste
black pepper, to taste
1 tbsp. minced garlic

Method

1. Wash the asparagus under cold running water.
2. If you have large asparagus, peel it. Then bend each stalk gently between the thumb and forefinger of both hands until the tough, woody end snaps off. No need to force this. After breaking, I usually trim off the ends to make the spears all the same length.
3. Discard the end pieces.
4. Immerse in boiling water to which you have added the salt.
5. Blanch for approximately 10 minutes, depending on the thickness of the spears, or until just tender.
6. Drain and set aside until ready to finish the dish.
7. Heat butter or oil in a sauté pan on medium heat.
8. Add asparagus and salt and pepper.
9. When asparagus is heated through, add garlic. I love the asparagus with the hollandaise sauce (page 295).

Note: Do not cook asparagus in an iron pot or pan. There will be a chemical reaction.

Haricot Verts

Yes, green beans. If you are able to lay your hands on some of the real, small French *haricot verts*, you may, if they are young enough, sauté them without the initial steaming or boiling step. The two types of beans you are most likely to find in your market are the Blue Lake type (rounder and a deeper green) and the Kentucky Wonder types (flatter and paler.) The latter are also called "string beans."

Yield: About 8 portions

INGREDIENTS
3 lb. green beans (Blue Lake or Kentucky Wonder)
2 gal. rapidly boiling water
2 tbsp. salt
4 tbsp. butter
salt, to taste
black pepper, to taste

Method

1. Tip and, if necessary, string the beans. Cut into diagonal pieces about 1 inch long. You will not have to do this with the true French *haricot verts*, as they are fairly short to begin with.
2. Place beans in boiling, salted water and simmer until just tender—not soft (about 5 or 6 minutes). Remove a bean and bite it.
3. Drain beans and shock under cold running water.
4. Dry beans.
5. Melt butter in a pan large enough to hold all the beans.
6. Place beans in pan with butter, then toss and heat through. You may also add some minced garlic or minced fresh herbs.
7. Add salt and pepper.

Stuffed Artichoke

My daddy would stop on his way home from work in New Orleans and pick up a dish very much like this one at Manale's.
Yield: Ahem, 6 portions

INGREDIENTS

6 artichokes, trimmed and choke removed
3 c. French bread crumbs
1½ c. parmesan
1¾ oz. anchovies, finely minced
¼ c. finely minced parsley
1 tsp. cayenne pepper
1 tbsp. whole thyme
6 oz. extra virgin olive oil
2 tbsp. lemon juice
salt, to taste
black pepper, to taste

Method

1. Rub artichokes with a cut lemon and hold in water acidulated with lemon juice until ready to cook.
2. Combine all other ingredients except olive oil and lemon juice in a bowl.
3. Add half the olive oil to the bread crumb mixture and work in thoroughly.
4. Drain artichokes and loosely stuff the leaves and center with the bread crumb mixture.
5. Squeeze lemon juice over artichokes and drizzle remaining olive oil over them.
6. Pack artichokes close together in a brazier and pour in about 1 inch of the acidulated water.
7. Bring to boil, reduce to simmer, and cook, covered, for 30 to 40 minutes or until a knife inserted in the base goes in smoothly.

What You Need to Know

Acidulated water is water to which you have added some acid. Almost invariably, this will be either lemon juice or vinegar, although other fruit juices have acidity, too. In the case of the artichoke, you use lemon juice, about a tablespoon for each quart of liquid. Just about all vegetables have an enzyme in them called polyphenoloxidase; this is what causes them to discolor. With some vegetables—potatoes, for example—water alone is enough to prevent discoloration. Others need acids—artichokes are a good example of the latter.

Boiled Artichokes

Artichokes are right at the top of my favorite vegetable list. Yes, they are a little work to eat but well worth it. For those of you not yet completely confident in your culinary skills, artichokes contain a compound that makes everything you eat after the artichoke taste better. Serve them as an appetizer. Always cook artichokes in lots of water in an open, nonreactive pot. There are carotenes in artichokes that cause them to darken in a closed pot or when boiled with too little liquid. Lots of water dilutes the carotene, and the open pot allows them to evaporate.

Yield: 6 to 8 portions

INGREDIENTS

6–8 artichokes
2 gal. boiling water
1 tbsp. salt
1 lemon

(**Method**)

1. Using scissors, cut the sharp points off the tips of the artichoke's leaves. Rub all cut areas immediately with a half lemon to prevent oxidation.
2. Place salt in boiling water.
3. Gently pry the artichoke open to expose the small leaves in the center. Pull them out.
4. Using either a strong spoon or a melon baller, cut the choke out of the center of the artichoke. Squeeze lemon down inside the artichoke.
5. If you are not ready to cook immediately, hold the artichokes in acidulated water in which you have squeezed the juice of a couple of lemons, enough to cover.
6. Place the artichokes in boiling water. Squeeze the remaining juice from the lemon and place it in the water with the artichokes. Cover them with either a cloth kitchen towel or cheesecloth that you have dipped in the lemon water.
7. Boil until a knife inserted in the base of the artichoke goes in easily. For most artichokes, this boiling period will last 25 to 40 minutes.

Note: If serving the artichokes hot, we like them with either a lemon butter or hollandaise sauce (page 295). If served cold, we accompany them with a seasoned mayonnaise.

We will finish up our section on cooking with liquids with a couple of popular sweet steamed items. One is cooked on top of the stove and the other in the oven.

DESSERTS

Crème Caramel

I have served this steamed dessert in many restaurants, as it has always been very popular. Lately, though, I see it has been largely replaced by a trendier version called crème brulée. The difference? With the crème caramel, the caramel is on the bottom when the dish is cooked and then inverted when served.

INGREDIENTS

1½ pt. milk or half-and-half
½ c. sugar
3 eggs
3 egg yolks
1 tsp. vanilla extract
caramel (page 190)

Method

1. Bring milk or half-and-half to simmer.
2. Beat sugar in a bowl into eggs and yolks.
3. Gradually pour hot milk into egg and sugar mixture, beating constantly.
4. Add vanilla.
5. Strain mixture through sieve into ramekins into which you have poured the caramel.
6. Place ramekins in a pan into which you have poured 1½ inches of hot water. Bake approximately 40 minutes at 375°. Insert a toothpick to check doneness.

Caramel

INGREDIENTS

⅔ c. sugar
⅓ c. water

Method

1. Place sugar and water in saucepan.
2. Dissolve sugar over medium heat, stirring often. Brush the sides of the pan with a pastry brush dipped in hot water to prevent crystallization.
3. Cook until the sugar attains a light hazelnut color. Remove from heat and use as soon as possible.

Don't Toil When You Boil

Relax. There is very little to remember for success with this technique. For large pieces of meat or poultry, bring the liquid to a rolling boil initially so you can *see* the temperature: 212°. Then reduce the liquid to a simmer for the remainder of the cooking time. For the more delicate seafoods and eggs, stick with the tiny-bubble routine.

I know an old story about a father who boils eggs, carrots, and coffee for his child. The moral of the story is that each reacts differently to the boiling process. If you remember that, you will be fine.

PART III

The Third Technique
Cooking with Fat

Of the two types of cooking with fat, one will be found in the best restaurants and the other in just about every fast-food restaurant on the planet. Fat is flavor, and we love it.

Yet both types of cooking in fat have their places. I have no problem whatsoever with properly fried foods. They have a legitimate place in our diet. In the fast-food joints, I question only the fat they choose with which to fry foods and, in those without automatic temperature gauges, the temperature at which they fry. I use peanut oil exclusively for deep-fried and pan-fried foods. Fry at the proper temperatures in quality oils, and fried foods will be a welcome addition to your diet.

Sautéing

There are two subtechniques to cook with fat: sauté and fry. Frying requires a much larger quantity of fat than sautéing. For both cooking methods, the food must first be dried. The food is completely (deep frying) or partially (pan frying) immersed in hot fat. You then try to remove most of the fat from the outside of the food before you serve it. When you *sauté*, you cook the food in a small quantity of high-quality fat, which is usually then incorporated in the finished dish as a part of the sauce.

Successful Sautéing

1. Use a high-quality sauté pan or wok with a thick bottom. Use a pan with a nonreactive surface. By that, I mean a pan with a surface that will not react with acids (frequent ingredients in sautés). Poor choices of pans in which to sauté would be cast iron (with the exception of the stir-fry, which usually has no or few acids), aluminum, or unlined copper. The best choices would be aluminum lined with stainless steel or tinned copper (or stainless-lined copper). Some of the (black) anodized aluminum pans will work quite well. An enameled iron or steel pan would be an excellent choice. You might also use some of the nonstick pans as well. Of the available choices, the lined copper and aluminum pans are the best choices, as those two metals are quite efficient heat conductors. High heat is very important for successful sautéing.

2. Get the pan and, consequently, the fat quite hot. Do not be afraid of high heat!

3. Use the smallest possible quantity of fat to keep the food from burning. Usually, ½ to 1 ounce per person is quite adequate for most dishes.

4. Dry the food to be sautéed, even if you are going to dredge it in a starch.

5. Don't attempt too many portions at once. If you try to do too much at once, the temperature in the pan will drop considerably below the temperature required for successful sautéing. This mistake and too low an initial temperature are probably the two most common errors of the aspiring chef.

6. Use a *quality* fat. Do not attempt to sauté with whole butter because the milk-fat solids in it will burn. Use clarified butter instead (page 290).

What to Sauté

Any tender meat, fish, shellfish, poultry, or vegetable may be sautéed. Take special note of the word *tender*. The sauté station in a quality restaurant is the pivotal point on the cooking line. I usually put my best cook on this station or worked it myself.

MEATS

One of the best choices here is tenderloin of beef. Of course, it is also expensive. If you roast a tenderloin periodically, you might reserve the tail while still raw and freeze it for a future sauté. This piece becomes "Tenderloin Tips Whatever" on a restaurant menu. Flank steak, if sliced very thinly on the bias, is a good option for a stir-fry.

Other portions of the beef loin are also acceptable if thinly sliced. Thin slices (scallops) from the veal loin or leg—you're going to have to whomp on these a little—make wonderful sautés, such as *Marsala* (page 199) and *Piccata* (page 198).

Pork chops and boneless pork chops from the loin are good sauté items. The fatter shoulder chops are much better braised.

POULTRY

Unquestionably, the most versatile bird for the sauté is the chicken. The French have hundreds of chicken sautés, but the technique remains the same on all of them. I'll give you a "master" recipe for the chicken sauté. Because, however, chicken pieces are thicker than is advisable for the usual sauté, they must be "finished" in the oven. I'll talk about this in the recipe. Small, split quail sauté well, as do duck and pheasant breast.

FISH AND SHELLFISH

Shrimp, scallops, crab legs, squid, clams, scampi, lobster, oysters, and, in fact, just about all shellfish lend themselves wonderfully to this cooking technique.

Thinner fillets of fish sauté well, as do whole smaller fish, such as trout. The thicker fish, filets or whole, must, like the chicken sautés, be finished in a hot oven.

Several types of "sole" are available in the United States. The word "sole" is in quotes because there are no true sole indigenous to North American waters; the fish called sole are all members of the flounder family. Some of these are lemon sole, Dover sole, English sole, and our favorites, sand dabs, rex sole, and petrale sole. The latter three are most available in northern California, but I have seen them elsewhere.

VEGETABLES

All the softer summer and spring vegetables, such as zucchini, spinach, yellow squash, peas, and snow peas, may go straight into the sauté pan. Mushrooms sauté well. The harder vegetables associated with the cooler seasons, such as carrots, celery, onions, and cabbage, will work quite successfully with this technique if they are sliced thinly enough.

Broccoli, cauliflower, and Brussels sprouts are best when steamed or boiled before sautéing. All types of mature green beans should be boiled briefly before sautéing. Asparagus works well when boiled or steamed briefly.

STARCHES

If diced, "balled," shredded, or minced, potatoes are an excellent choice for this technique. They must be *very* dry, though. For all pilafs and risottos, the rice should be briefly cooked in hot fat before any liquid is added, but this distinction rightly belongs to part IV of this book.

THE ORIGINAL SAUTÉ DISH: THE STIR-FRY

What I have created here is a truly "generic" recipe for the stir-fry. It is expandable and contractible, limited only by the size of your cooking equipment. The emphasis here is truly on technique and not so much on individual ingredients. Add or subtract whatever you enjoy or dislike. Remember that all the food in a stir-fry is designed to be eaten with chopsticks—so the pieces should be cut with that in mind.

INGREDIENTS

¼ c. peanut oil

8–12 oz. meat (beef loin, pork loin, chicken breast or even leg of lamb are acceptable), very thinly sliced

or

8–12 oz. shellfish (shrimp, lobster, or scallops), very thinly sliced

2 medium carrots, thinly sliced at a 45° angle

1 medium onion, thinly sliced vertically

3–4 stalks celery, thinly sliced at a 45° angle

1 tbsp. finely minced garlic

1 tbsp. finely minced fresh ginger

3 tbsp. soy or tamari sauce

1 tsp. chili oil

1½ c. cold stock (beef, chicken or shellfish)

Note: These constitute our basic generic stir-fry ingredients. You may also add asparagus, broccoli, cabbage (Chinese or green), mushrooms, water chestnuts, bamboo shoots, bok choy, snow peas, or whatever vegetables you personally enjoy.

[**Method**]

1. Heat peanut oil in a wok or pan until it is quite hot—even smoking. Keep the heat high during the entire cooking procedure. In the unlikely event your pan gets too hot, add a little more oil; this will cool it sufficiently.
2. Add meat or shellfish and sear on the outside while tossing and turning all the while, for about 1 minute.
3. Begin adding the harder vegetables, carrots first. Sauté each vegetable until it begins to soften before adding the next.

4. When all the vegetables appear cooked, add the garlic and ginger. If added earlier, they will burn. Sauté for about 30 seconds.
5. Add the soy or tamari sauce.
6. Thoroughly combine the cornstarch with the stock—a wire whisk works well for this.
7. Add stock mixture to the pan and thoroughly incorporate. Cook until sauce clears and is translucent. Check the seasoning. If the sauce is too thick, add a little stock. If too thin, mix a little more cornstarch with a little cold stock and add it to the pan.
8. Serve over rice or noodles.

Other Options

For additional flavor, you may add a little rice wine, sake, or plum wine to the stir-fry. If you have one of the proprietary spice or sauce mixes you enjoy, such as hoisin or oyster, add it as well.

SAUTÉING MEATS

Beef Stroganoff

There are as many stories about the origin of this dish as there are versions of it. None of them can actually be substantiated, of course. My version is fairly traditional, incorporating the usual beef tenderloin, mushrooms, and sour cream.

Yield: 6 portions

INGREDIENTS

1½ lb. beef tenderloin, thinly sliced
½ c. flour
½ c. clarified butter
½ onion, finely diced
1 tsp. minced garlic
8 oz. sliced mushrooms
1 tsp. whole thyme
½ c. dry red or white wine
¼ c. tomato purée
½ c. beef stock
½ c. sour cream
salt, to taste
black pepper, to taste

Method

1. Divide the flour in half. Thoroughly dry the tenderloin and dredge it in half the flour. Shake off excess.
2. Make a brown roux with half the clarified butter and the other half of the flour.
3. Brown the tenderloin in the remaining clarified butter over high heat. Add salt and pepper.
4. Add onions and garlic to tenderloin and sauté briefly.
5. Add thyme.
6. Deglaze with wine.
7. Add purée.
8. Add stock.
9. Bring to a simmer and incorporate the roux.
10. Add sour cream.
11. Check seasoning.
12. Serve with either a fresh fettuccine noodle (page 165) or a rice pilaf (page 156).

Veal Piccata

Great dish. I have often wondered about the origin of the dish title, though. I can find only two words in Italian that are close: "piccato," which means "larded," and "piccarsi," which means "to prick oneself." Your choice.

INGREDIENTS

3 oz. veal, leg or loin, thinly sliced
flour, seasoned with salt and white pepper, to coat
2 tbsp. clarified butter
1 tsp. capers
½ oz. lemon juice
1 oz. dry white wine

Method

1. Pound the veal slices until they are wafer thin. Thoroughly dry the slices of veal and dredge them in the seasoned flour. Shake off excess.
2. Heat clarified butter in sauté pan until quite hot.
3. Sauté veal on both sides, about 15 seconds per side in the clarified butter.
4. Add the capers. Warm through.
5. Add lemon juice and deglaze with the white wine.
6. Toss the veal about in the pan and cook until the liquids reduce slightly and thicken.

I usually serve the Piccata with the Risotto Milanese (page 158) and a fresh sautéed vegetable, such as broccoli or zucchini.

Veal Scaloppini Marsala

Many years ago, I began adding the dry white wine to this dish because I found it too cloying with just the Marsala.

Yield: 6 portions

INGREDIENTS

12 veal scallops, 2 oz. each
salt, to taste
white pepper, to taste
1 c. flour
½ c. clarified butter
2 c. sliced mushrooms
4 oz. Marsala
4 oz. dry white wine
2 oz. lemon juice
2 oz. veal or chicken stock

(Method)

1. Thoroughly dry veal pieces, then salt and pepper them and dredge in flour. Shake off excess.
2. Heat clarified butter in sauté or fry pan until quite hot.
3. Sauté veal pieces approximately 1½ minutes or until browned. Remove.
4. Add mushrooms to pan and sauté approximately 1 minute.
5. Deglaze pan with Marsala, white wine, and lemon juice. Check seasoning.
6. Return veal to pan and heat through. Add stock. Reduce. Place on plate and sprinkle with chopped parsley. Serve with Risotto Milanese (page 158).

Steak au Poivre

In many of the restaurants where I was chef, this dish became more popular than the grilled steak. The pepper coating is not nearly as hot as you might suspect.

Yield: 6 to 8 portions

INGREDIENTS

6–8 steak, New York, 12 oz., or filet, 8 oz.
6 tbsp. black pepper, coarsely ground
4 tbsp. clarified butter
¼ c. brandy
2 tbsp. minced parsley
2 tbsp. minced chives
1 c. beef stock (optional)
1 c. heavy cream (optional)

Method

1. Thoroughly dry the steaks.
2. Place the pepper in a shallow dish or on a plate.
3. Dredge the steaks in the pepper, being sure you thoroughly coat both sides of the steak with the pepper.
4. Heat the clarified butter over high heat in a fry or sauté pan large enough to hold all the steaks.
5. Cook the steaks until you achieve the desired degree of doneness.
6. Remove the pan from the fire and deglaze with the brandy. Place the pan back on the heat and flame.
7. Remove the steaks from the pan, reduce the heat, and add the parsley and chives. If you wish to add the optional stock and cream, remove the steak to a warm platter; deglaze with the stock, incorporating all the fonds into it as you go; and reduce by half. Then add the heavy cream and reduce by half. Serve over the steak.

When I was in Paris, I was introduced to a little place that specialized in steaks. I was hanging out with some reporters from Le Monde, and they regularly ate lunch there. This was where I first had the butter/pan juice/herb mixture on the steak—without the stock and cream. One could get a grilled or sautéed steak and pommes frites and a salad, and that was about it.

Tournedos Sautés aux Champignons

Tournedos are the ultimate trimmed beef filet. No fat, no sinew, nothing but lean meat. Do not overcook them, as they have no protective fat. They are not a meteorological phenomenon. Pronounce the word with the emphasis on the first syllable and a short "e."

Yield: 6 to 8 portions

INGREDIENTS

6–8 tournedos
6–8 tbsp. clarified butter
salt, to taste
black pepper, to taste
6 tbsp. butter, whole
½–¾ lb. mushrooms
1 tsp. minced garlic
½–¾ c. dry white wine
2–3 c. demi-glace or Sauce Espagnole
1 tbsp. butter, softened

Method

1. Thoroughly dry the tournedos.
2. Heat clarified butter in a sauté pan.
3. Salt and pepper tournedos.
4. Sauté tournedos in butter until rare to medium rare.
5. Remove tournedos from pan and keep warm.
6. Wash, dry, and quarter all mushrooms except those for garnish.
7. Add unsalted butter to pan and melt.
8. Sauté mushrooms over medium heat until just softened. Add garlic.
9. Deglaze with the white wine.
10. Thoroughly incorporate the demi-glace or Espagnole (page 292).

You may serve on fried croutons with the sautéed mushrooms for a garnish in the middle of the platter. Garnish with chopped parsley. You may flute some mushrooms for additional garnish if you choose.

Sautéing Poultry

The same principles apply here as when we roasted the turkey and the chicken—both birds consist of both dark and light meats. Of course, one way to eliminate this problem is to purchase only the breast of chicken. I provide several recipes for just the breast. These two kinds of meats—dark and light—do not require the same amount of time to cook. Escoffier mentioned this fact himself when referring to the cooking of the Poulet Sauté. His solution to the two different cooking times was to begin sautéing the dark and light meat at the same time and to remove the light meat (the wings and breasts), and, consequently, have to keep them warm (7–8 minutes) before he removed the dark

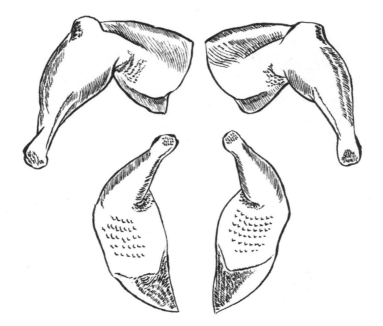

meat. Our solution is to cook the two different types of meat in two different pans so that both can be ready at the same time.

Chicken in the United States is inexpensive, and just about everyone enjoys it. It was not always so. In an old Creole cookbook I was perusing one day, the author allowed as how, in one recipe, if the family could not afford a chicken, a roast beef might be substituted. It seems that cooks are always looking for a novel manner in which to prepare this dish. Once you master the following Poulet Sauté, you will have literally hundreds of different dishes available to you.

Poulet Sauté

This is the basis for several dozen classic French sauté dishes. Once you master this technique, all the other dishes fall right into place. There are well over a hundred already-named chicken sautés in France. Only the garnishes vary. I love the color of the chicken and the crispness of the skin when cooked in this manner.

INGREDIENTS
2 chickens, fryer or broiler, about 2½ lb. each
½ c. clarified butter
1 c. flour
1 tsp. salt
½ tsp. black pepper

Method

Do not buy a cut-up chicken! American butchers do not cut up a chicken for sautés. Place your chicken, breast side up, on the counter in front of you. Take a *sharp* boning knife and cut off the thigh and leg—in one piece—at the hip joint. Set aside. Tuck the wings up under the remaining carcass to help stabilize the carcass as you bone the breast. The chicken should now resemble a toad, if you squint. Make a cut down the keel bone, the bone in the middle of the breast, scraping against the bone to remove the flesh. Stop short of the wing. Look for the joint where the wing bone meets the breast. Cut on the breast side of this joint. Remove the breast and wing in one piece. Do it again on the other side. You're almost finished. Remove the thigh bone from the leg/thigh section by scraping around the bone down toward the leg until you can see the joint. Cut the bone out. Cut off the two joints farthest from the breast on the wings. You're done. If it looks like the illustration on page 202, you were successful. Congratulations.

1. Disjoint chickens, using the method above.
2. Thoroughly dry the chicken before dredging the pieces in the flour to which you have added the salt and pepper. Shake off excess flour.
3. Heat 2 ounces of the clarified butter to about 360° in one sauté pan.
4. Place chicken thighs and legs in the sauté pan and sauté on both sides until golden brown.
5. Place the pan in a 450° oven. Set a timer for 15 minutes.
6. Heat the remaining 2 ounces of clarified butter in the other sauté pan to about 360°.
7. Place the breasts in the pan and sauté on both sides until golden brown. Place the pan in the oven.
8. Remove both pans from the oven when the timer beckons.
9. Before deglazing, remove all but 1 or 2 tablespoons of the fat from one of the pans. Only one pan will be needed to finish your sauce or garnish.

Variations

Poulet Sauté Creole: Deglaze with creole sauce (page 299).

Poulet Sauté au Vin: Deglaze with any wine you prefer (red or white), reduce, and add brown sauce. Call the dish by the name of the wine.

Pollo alla Cacciatoria (page 272): Briefly sauté a few mushrooms and peppers in the fat and deglaze with tomato sauce. Place the chicken on a bed of cooked pasta and pour the sauce over all.

Poulet au Currie: Deglaze with a velouté (page 291) to which you have added "curry" spices (page 210). Serve with rice and chutney.

Poulet Sauté à la Forestiere: Add quartered mushrooms and minced shallots to the fat and sauté for a few seconds. Deglaze with a little white wine and add a chicken velouté to the pan. Heat through and serve over the chicken.

Poulet Sauté à la Bourguignonne: I actually prefer this to the Coq au Vin Rouge you'll encounter in part IV because the chickens we have available in this country do not require any tenderizing. Sauté ¼ pound of previously blanched bacon in the fat until brown. Add 6 to 8 boiling onions and sauté until brown. Add two dozen button mushrooms and sauté briefly. Deglaze with dry red wine and 1 cup of chicken stock. Simmer, covered, for 15 minutes. Remove bacon, onions, and mushrooms from pan and thicken with 1 or 2 tablespoons of brown roux. Arrange vegetables and chicken on a platter and pour the sauce over all.

Poulet Sauté with Wild Mushrooms

If you have a very large skillet, you may be able to sauté this dish in one pan. Most folks don't have one large enough, though. You will probably require three 10-inch sauté or fry pans or two 14-inch fry pans. As with nearly all sautés, your pan must be of solid metal (no wooden handles) so that you may place the pan in the oven.

Yield: 6 to 8 portions

INGREDIENTS
3–4 chickens, about 2½ lb. each, quartered
1 c. flour
salt, to taste
white pepper, to taste
¾–1 c. clarified butter
12–16 oz. dry white wine
3–4 tbsp. lemon juice
1½ c. chicken velouté (page 291)
1–1½ c. heavy cream
4–6 oz. wild mushrooms (shiitake, shimeji, etc.)

(**Method**)

1. Disjoint the chickens. Trim off the last two wing joints.
2. Thoroughly dry the chickens and dredge the pieces in the flour to which you have added the salt and pepper to taste.
3. Heat the butter in the pans and follow the basic procedure for Poulet Sauté.

4. When the chicken is about 5 minutes from being finished, add the white wine and the lemon juice to the pan(s) and replace the pans in the oven.

5. Remove the pans from the oven and remove the chicken from the pans.

6. Stew the mushrooms in the butter, wine, and lemon juice mixture. Reduce the liquid by half on top of the stove. Add the heavy cream.

7. Check the seasoning and serve.

Boneless Breast of Lemon Chicken

This very simple sauté has always been one of my most popular in restaurants. The simplicity of the dish illustrates just how important technique is and what can be done with a few quality ingredients in a short time. This is one of the few times you will catch me using the skinless chicken breasts. I like the flavor of the skin, and the skin also keeps the breast from drying out. Here I cook the breasts quickly and also immediately add the wine so they do not have an opportunity to dry out.

Yield: I make this with small breasts and allow 2 per person; 6 to 8 portions

INGREDIENTS

12–16 chicken breasts, boneless, flattened slightly
1 c. flour
½ c. clarified butter
½ tsp. salt
white pepper, to taste
2 c. dry white wine
¼ c. lemon juice

What You Need to Know

Buy a couple of inexpensive aluminum dredges, the metal "shakers" you will see in cookware stores, and keep them handy in your kitchen. Fill each three-quarters of the way full with salt. In one of the two, fill the other one-quarter of the space with ground black pepper. Mix well. Fill the space in the other dredge with ground white pepper. Mix well. When you have a lot of seasoning to do, this saves a great deal of time. The results may not be quite as satisfactory as using kosher salt and freshly ground pepper, but in many instances they will suffice.

(**Method**)

1. Thoroughly dry the chicken breasts with towels.
2. Place the flour in a bowl and thoroughly dredge the breasts in it. Shake off excess.
3. Place a fry or sauté pan containing the clarified butter on high heat.
4. When the butter has reached a temperature of about 350°, add the breasts to the pan, placing the smooth, that is, the presentation, side down.
5. Sauté for about 2 minutes on this first side. Turn.
6. Add salt and pepper to the breasts. Cook for about 2 minutes. Do not brown.
7. Deglaze with the white wine, swishing the breasts around in the pan.
8. Add the lemon juice. Incorporate.
9. Place the pan in a 450° oven for about 5 to 6 minutes. The flour coating on the breasts will combine with the liquids to make a sauce. It is important that you do not use too much butter, as the ratio between the butter and the flour is what will cause the sauce to thicken.
10. Remove the breasts from the pan and pour the sauce over them.

SAUTÉING SEAFOODS

Batter-Sautéed Salmon with Braised Lettuce and Bacon

This recipe is adapted from a dish served at Lutèce in New York City. A very talented chef named Andre Soltner founded the restaurant. This recipe, though considerably simplified, is "after" his.

Yield: 6 to 8 portions

INGREDIENTS

½ lb. smoked salmon, sliced into small pieces
1 c. milk
2–3 garlic cloves
½ c. bread crumbs
½ c. flour
2 eggs
salt, to taste
white pepper, to taste
½ tsp. fresh thyme
2–3 heads Bibb or Boston lettuce
2 carrots, peeled and sliced
1 onion, peeled and sliced

8 slices bacon, blanched

2–3 c. chicken stock

2½ lb. salmon, filleted, skinned, and cut into 1- by 2- by 1-in. pieces

2 c. butter

Method

1. Sweat smoked salmon in a warm pan until it releases its oil.
2. Add milk and simmer 3 or 4 minutes. Place salmon in processor.
3. Blanch garlic in simmering water for about 8 minutes. Place garlic in processor and begin to process. Add bread crumbs and flour to processor while running.
4. Beat eggs, milk, salt, pepper, and thyme together. Add to processor.
5. Blanch lettuce heads in simmering water until wilted. Core.
6. Strew carrots and onions in a casserole dish. Roll lettuce leaves into tight oval bundles. Wrap bundles in a half slice of bacon and place on vegetables. Carefully pour in stock, cover with buttered parchment paper, and simmer for 20 minutes.
7. Remove bundles, strain stock, and reduce until you have 2 or 3 tablespoons.
8. Make Beurre Blanc (page 298) with the reduction and the butter.
9. Dry the salmon pieces, dredge in flour, dip in the batter, and sauté until golden brown on both sides. Serve all on a platter.

Sole Meunière

This classic French recipe for small fish filets has been around for at least 200 years. Literally translated, it means "in the manner of the miller's wife," who, presumably, always had flour on her hands.

Yield: 6 to 8 portions

INGREDIENTS

6 tbsp. clarified butter

6–8 sole filets, about 6 oz. each

4 oz. milk

salt, to taste

white pepper, to taste

1 c. flour

1 tbsp. butter

1 lemon lemon juice

1 tbsp. chopped parsley

Method

1. Heat clarified butter in a skillet.
2. Dry sole and dip it in the milk and then in the flour that you have seasoned with the salt and pepper.
3. Place the filet with the rounded side (presentation side) down in the skillet and sauté until golden brown on both sides.
4. Remove the sole to a platter and add the whole butter to the skillet. Cook until slightly browned.
5. Add lemon juice to skillet.
6. Add chopped parsley to skillet and pour over fish.

Seafood Sauté

You will notice the next four recipes are for one portion. I have deviated from my normal portions here because I want you to see just how easily and quickly you may prepare these sautés for just one or two folks. They are the fastest of all cooked foods to produce.

This was one of the most popular sautés I prepared in several restaurants in the San Francisco Bay Area. One of the most decadent and best-selling versions was at the original Scott's Seafood Grill and Bar at Scott and Lombard in San Francisco. I sautéed shrimp, sea scallops, and Dungeness crab legs in clarified butter with garlic and lemon and mushrooms, deglazed with white wine and heavy cream, then placed this mixture in a premade, fish-shaped puff pastry crust and topped the dish with hollandaise sauce (page 295).

INGREDIENTS

2 tbsp. clarified butter
flour, to coat
3–4 shrimp, medium to large, peeled and deveined
3–4 sea scallops
3–4 crab legs
¼ c. sliced mushrooms
1 tsp. minced garlic
salt, to taste
white pepper, to taste
2 oz. dry white wine
1 tbsp. lemon juice
1 oz. heavy cream
1 tbsp. minced parsley

Method

1. Heat clarified butter in a sauté or fry pan until quite hot.
2. Dredge shrimp and scallops in flour; shake off excess.
3. Cook shrimp and scallops in butter, tossing all the while until just beginning to brown.
4. Add crab legs.
5. Add mushrooms, garlic, salt, and pepper and continue to cook for about 30 seconds.
6. Deglaze with white wine and add lemon.
7. Add heavy cream and parsley and cook for an additional 30 seconds.

Most of the seafood sautés I do are presented very simply with a rice pilaf (page 156), a simple sautéed vegetable, and a lemon garnish.

The following three shrimp sautés are an excellent example of the universality of technique. All three are prepared exactly the same, with variations only in ingredients/garnishes. Each of the three is for one person only. This is the form in which I give recipes to line cooks in a restaurant. The flour coating in each makes a mini-roux and thickens the dish slightly, giving it body.

Shrimp Creole

I prepare this just like a stir-fry.

INGREDIENTS
2 tbsp. clarified butter
flour, to coat
6–8 shrimp, medium to large, peeled and deveined
2 oz. dry white wine
6 oz. creole sauce

Method

1. Heat clarified butter in a sauté or fry pan until very hot.
2. Dredge shrimp in flour; shake off excess.
3. Sauté shrimp until colored and crisped, tossing the pan all the while.
4. Deglaze with white wine.
5. Add creole sauce (page 299) and toss until all shrimp are thoroughly coated.
6. Serve with a rice pilaf.

Shrimp Curry

_____

What You Need to Know

You may, if you wish, purchase that stuff in the supermarket called "curry powder." However, I prefer to make my own blend. It will serve you well. Here it is:

1 tbsp. ground ginger
1 tbsp. turmeric
1 tsp. coriander
1 tsp. cardamom, decorticated
1 tsp. cloves
½ tsp. cinnamon
1 tsp. cayenne pepper
1 tsp. cumin

_____

INGREDIENTS

2 tbsp. clarified butter
flour, to coat
6–8 shrimp, medium to large, peeled and deveined
2 oz. dry white wine
1 tsp. finely minced fresh ginger
1 tsp. finely minced yellow onion
1 tsp. finely minced garlic
1 tbsp. curry powder
3 oz. béchamel or velouté
salt, to taste
white pepper, to taste

Method

1. Heat clarified butter in a sauté or fry pan over high heat.
2. Dredge shrimp in flour; shake off excess.
3. Stir or shake pan constantly until shrimp are colored and crisped.
4. Deglaze with white wine.
5. Add ginger, onion, and garlic. Toss.
6. Add curry powder. Toss.
7. Add béchamel (page 292) or velouté sauce (page 291). Toss again.
8. Serve with chutney and a rice pilaf (page 156).

Shrimp, Scampi-Style

In the seafood classes I have taught over the years, this simple sauté may well be the single most popular item.

INGREDIENTS

2 tbsp. clarified butter
flour, to coat
6–8 shrimp, medium to large, peeled and deveined
1 tsp. minced garlic
salt, to taste
white pepper, to taste
2 oz. dry white wine
½ oz. lemon juice
1 tbsp. minced parsley

(Method)

1. Heat butter in a sauté or fry pan over high heat.
2. Dredge shrimp in flour; shake off excess.
3. Sauté shrimp until colored and crisped.
4. Add garlic, salt, and pepper, tossing all the while.
5. Deglaze with the white wine and lemon.
6. Cook until the sauce thickens slightly.
7. Add parsley and toss to coat the shrimp with the sauce and parsley. Good with the Risotto Milanese (page 158).

Sole Doré

This is my personal favorite sautéed fish, provided the sole is impeccably fresh and the texture is firm. This was a big seller during the period I was night chef at Scott's Seafood Grill and Bar in San Francisco. If you are able to get fresh petrale, do so—you won't regret it. The word "*doré*" in French means "gilded" or "golden-colored." The piece of fish will look like an omelet when properly prepared. Serve it with the Beurre Blanc (page 298). Try this method with farm-raised catfish too.

INGREDIENTS

6–8 filet of sole, 5–6 oz. each
1 c. flour
1 tsp. finely ground white pepper
½ tsp. finely ground cayenne pepper
1 tsp. salt
6 eggs, lightly beaten
6 tbsp. clarified butter

Method

1. Thoroughly dry the filets and dredge them in the flour in which you have mixed the peppers and the salt.
2. Place them in the eggs in a bowl. You may do this ahead and refrigerate the fish.
3. Melt the clarified butter over medium-high heat in a sauté pan.
4. Lift the filets from the eggs and lay them in the clarified butter.
5. Cook until golden brown on the presentation side, the side next to the bone when the fish was fileted. Turn and cook until done. This should only take 3 or 4 minutes of total cooking time.
6. Serve with Beurre Blanc (page 298).

Crab Cakes

In the eastern United States, the crabmeat you are most likely to find will be blue crab "lump" meat. It may be purchased fresh or pasteurized. Either will work. Do *not* buy canned crabmeat! In the western United States, Dungeness crabmeat with or without claw meat will be what you're likely to use.

Yield: 8 comfortable portions

INGREDIENTS

1 lb. lump crabmeat, picked and cleaned
2 red bell peppers, diced
1 c. minced yellow onion
½ c. butter
1 c. bread crumbs
1–2 eggs
1 tbsp. prepared mustard

1 tbsp. Worcestershire sauce
1 tbsp. crushed red chiles
¼ c. minced parsley
¾ c. mayonnaise
1 tsp. salt
1 tsp. black pepper
½ c. clarified butter

Method

1. Set crabmeat aside in a stainless bowl.
2. Sweat bell pepper and onion in the butter until soft.
3. In a separate bowl, combine bread crumbs, egg, mustard, chiles, parsley, mayonnaise, salt, and pepper.
4. Cool pepper and onion mixture and combine with all other ingredients.
5. Gently toss crab with other ingredients. Form into 2- to 3-inch patties, 1 inch thick.
6. Sauté patties in clarified butter until browned on both sides.
7. Serve with the Roasted Red Pepper Coulis (below).

Roasted Red Pepper Coulis

What is a *coulis*? This word has become very trendy. Originally a word used to describe meat juices, it has become a catchall expression for nearly any type of purée.

Yield: About 2 cups

INGREDIENTS

6 large red bell peppers
1 c. extra virgin olive oil
1 jalapeño pepper
¼ c. green onion (or shallots), white part only
1 tbsp. minced garlic
½ c. chicken stock
2 tbsp. balsamic vinegar
salt, to taste
black pepper, to taste

Method

1. Roast, peel, and deseed all peppers.
2. Dice peppers and sweat briefly in oil.
3. Add onion or shallot and sweat a minute or two more.
4. Add garlic.
5. Deglaze with stock and balsamic vinegar.
6. Purée all in food processor.

Note: You may add more stock if the coulis seems too thick.

Sautéing Vegetables and Starches

Cooking vegetables in fat involves one step for the softer vegetables, just sautéing, and two steps for the harder ones, blanching and sautéing.

By "softer," I mean those vegetables that profit in terms of both texture and nutrition from being cooked in a little hot fat without first blanching or steaming them. In this group are zucchini, summer squash, crookneck squash, spinach, small green peas, mushrooms, onions, and even potatoes if they are dealt with in the manner detailed here. I slice the squashes ½ to ¾ inch thick and sauté them quickly in a little clarified butter or extra virgin olive oil. Just add salt and pepper, maybe a little minced garlic, and some of your favorite fresh herbs.

Among the "harder" vegetables are artichokes, larger asparagus, broccoli, Brussels sprouts, carrots, cauliflower, and the various green beans. I find it better to bake instead of blanch some of the harder vegetables, such as eggplant and the winter squashes, like butternut and acorn.

Of course, lately, grilled vegetables are becoming quite trendy as well. This is a procedure for the cook who has some grilling skills, though. I find that most folks burn them on the outside and leave them raw inside. Again, consider blanching the harder vegetables before you place them on the grill.

Sautéing the Summer Squashes

The following technique appears deceptively simple. Well, actually, it is simple, but it is one of the best ways to cook fresh summer vegetables—the maxim "a little is a lot" applies here or, if you prefer, the K.I.S.S. principle.

Yield: 6 to 8 portions

Ingredients

1½ lb. zucchini or crookneck or summer squash
½ c. clarified butter or extra virgin olive oil
salt, to taste
black pepper, to taste
1 tbsp. finely minced garlic

Method

1. Rinse the squash and slice them thinly, but not too thinly—it is quite easy to overcook squash—about ½ inch is good.
2. Place the clarified butter or oil in a large sauté pan (if you don't have a 14-inch pan, use two 10-inch pans) or a fry pan over a hot fire. Allow the fat to heat for a minute.
3. Add the squash all at once and toss or stir constantly. Salt and pepper the squash. Thirty seconds of cooking will probably be ample.
4. Add garlic and thoroughly incorporate.
5. Get the pan off the fire! Get the squash out of the pan! This is the point at which you may add whatever fresh herbs you enjoy.

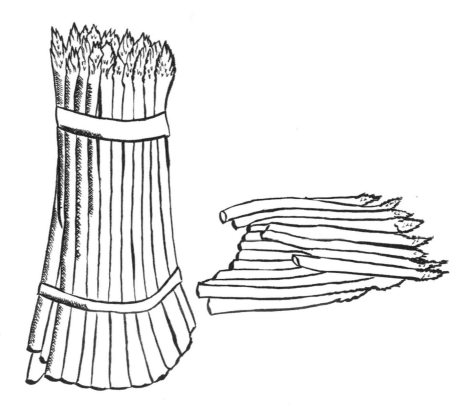

Italian Spinach

The following recipe is for one person. If you plan to do several portions at once you will need a large pan since the spinach will shrink to about ⅕ of its original volume.

Yield: 1 Portion. Yes, it takes one bunch of spinach to feed one person!

INGREDIENTS

4 tbsp. extra virgin olive oil
1 tsp. butter
1 bunch spinach, washed and stems removed
salt, to taste
black pepper, to taste
1 tsp. minced garlic
1 tbsp. parmesan

Method

1. Place olive oil in a sauté or fry pan over medium heat.
2. Add butter.
3. Add spinach and continue to cook over medium heat, turning the spinach constantly with a set of tongs.
4. When the spinach has wilted, add the salt, pepper, and garlic. Toss and incorporate thoroughly. Drain excess water.
5. Add parmesan and toss again. Serve immediately.

Carrots Vichy

Carrots add instant color to any presentation, but this is not the only reason I feature them often during the winter months, when fresh, local vegetables are in short supply. They are very high in sugar content and add sweetness to the savory plate.

Yield: 6 to 8 servings

INGREDIENTS

3 c. baby carrots
½ c. butter
¼ c. brown sugar
½ tsp. salt
black pepper, to taste

Method

1. Carrots should be peeled and washed before slicing. Blanch them for about 5 minutes in salted, boiling water. Drain and dry.
2. Heat butter in a skillet.
3. Add carrots, sugar, and salt to skillet. Toss well.
4. Place a lid on the skillet, reduce the heat, and sweat for 4 to 5 minutes.
5. Remove lid, raise heat, toss, and sauté for 3 to 4 more minutes. Check for firmness.
6. Add pepper.

You may add any fresh herbs to this dish for variations. Dill is commonly used.

Pommes de Terre Parisiennes

This French classic was once common in French restaurants. That was during the era of unpaid apprenticeships. It is a *very* labor-intensive dish. I consider it a nifty dish, though, and you might consider it for special occasions. You will be left with a potato that looks like a blitzkrieg aftermath. Cover these remnants with water until you make soup or mashed potatoes with them.

Yield: 6 to 8 portions

INGREDIENTS

6–8 potatoes, Russet type
4 tbsp. clarified butter
salt, to taste
black pepper, to taste
4 tbsp. finely minced parsley

Method

1. Peel the potatoes and, using a melon baller, scoop out perfectly round (right!) balls of potato. Use the small end of the baller.
2. Heat the clarified butter over medium-high heat.
3. Thoroughly dry the potatoes and add them to the clarified butter. (Do this in several loads—don't attempt to sauté too many at once.)
4. Keep the potatoes in constant motion by shaking the pan so the potatoes are always rolling around. When they begin to brown, add salt and pepper.
5. Cook the potatoes until they are light brown all over.
6. Place the pan in a 450° oven for 15 minutes. You might want to open the oven once or twice and give them a shake.
7. Remove from the oven, toss with the parsley, and serve.

I like these best with beef, pork, or lamb roasts.

Some Sautéed Egg Dishes

These first two are scrambled egg dishes.

Joe's Special

There are many restaurants in the San Francisco Bay Area with the word "Joe's" in their name. This dish originated at Original Joe's. It is a good buffet dish for a brunch. We call these dishes that do not need to be made to order "dish up" dishes. It is always handy to have a few of them on your menu for a large group. They can save you both time and grief. This is a spiffy scrambled egg dish.

Yield: 6 portions

INGREDIENTS

4 tbsp. butter
1 lb. lean ground beef, 10% fat
1 c. minced onion
1 tsp. minced garlic
1 c. thinly sliced mushrooms
2 c. spinach, washed, dried, and julienned
salt, to taste
black pepper, to taste
1 dozen eggs, lightly beaten

(**Method**)

1. Melt butter in a skillet large enough to contain all ingredients.
2. Add ground beef and sauté until browned.
3. Add onions and cook until soft.
4. Add garlic and mushrooms. Drain through a sieve, squeezing out fat. Return mixture to pan.
5. Add spinach and cook until wilted. Allow most of the water to boil away. Or you may cook the spinach separately and add it at this point.
6. Add salt and pepper.
7. Add eggs, all at one time, and cook, stirring constantly, until eggs are just set.

> **What You Need to Know**
>
> The principal flavors in nearly every savory dish are fat and salt. In dishes where I want the flavor of the fat but wish to eliminate any excess fat, I cook the ingredient containing the fat, add the other ingredients, *then* drain the fat.

Hangtown Fry

This dish was supposedly invented during the gold rush in California in a town called Placerville in the Sierra foothills. A judge in the town had a very tough reputation and was noted for his stiff sentences. Hence, Placerville came to be called "Hangtown." A condemned man, when asked what he would like for his final meal, selected items that were quite scarce and expensive, among them oysters, spinach, and eggs. By the time all the ingredients arrived, a pardon from the governor had also arrived, and the sheriff ended up eating the dish.

INGREDIENTS
½ c. butter
12–16 oysters
1 c. flour
salt, to taste
black pepper, to taste
½ lb. bacon lardons, cooked and drained
2 c. spinach, washed, dried, and julienned
1 dozen eggs, lightly beaten
6–8 oz. sharp cheddar cheese, grated

Method

1. Melt butter in a skillet large enough to hold all ingredients.
2. Dry oysters with a towel. Dredge oysters in flour and shake off excess.
3. Add oysters to skillet and sauté until you are sure the flour is cooked.
4. Add bacon and spinach and sauté until the spinach has wilted.
5. Add eggs and cook until the eggs are just set, stirring constantly.
6. Add cheese to top of dish and melt either under a salamander or place a lid on the sauté pan and lower the heat as if for an omelet.

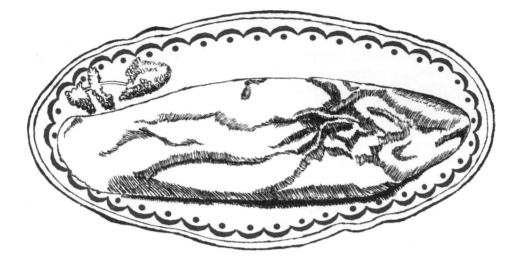

The Omelet

> "*On ne saurait faire une omelette sans casser des oeufs.*"
> "To make an omelet, you're going to have to break some eggs."

The preceding peripatetic homily issues, most often I have noticed, from the mouth of someone who is about to break your eggs, not his. The word *omelet* derives from a medieval French word for the "thin, flat shape of the blade of a sword or knife." *Alumelle* first appears as a culinary term in the 14th century, and the first omelet mentioned was a sweet one: "*Alumelle frite au sucre.*"

The making of an omelet is yet another of these very simple procedures that, for some reason, has become shrouded with an aura of unnecessary complexity. This recipe is designed to feed one person. If you are feeding six to eight, do it six to eight times. This is a "filled" omelet. Some chefs cook the ingredients for the omelet right in the pan and then add the eggs. This will distribute the ingredients throughout the omelet. This is a matter of preference. I prefer a filling. After you've made a few hundred of these, you'll probably be able to make them by flipping the eggs like the guys you've seen do it on the tube.

Yield: The following is for *one* omelet. There are just some recipes that won't work for six to eight persons.

INGREDIENTS

3 eggs
1 tsp. cold water
1 tbsp. butter
salt, to taste
black pepper, to taste

Method

1. Beat the eggs in a bowl with the cold water. The water helps to lighten the omelet as it steams out.
2. Heat the butter, over medium-high heat, in a well-seasoned fry pan. I prefer a 10-inch stainless-lined, cast aluminum pan. Use whatever you have. The butter should be just beginning to brown.
3. Add the eggs all at once and agitate vigorously with a fork, spatula, or rubber scraper.
4. When the eggs are nearly set, with only a thin film of "liquid" remaining on the top, add any filling you desire. Place the filling across the center of the omelet, directly in line with the pan's handle.
5. Reduce the heat to very low and place a snugly fitting lid on the pan. Cook for approximately 60 seconds.
6. Remove the lid from the pan and attempt to move the omelet. If it will not slide freely, nudge it around the edges with your fork or scraper until it will.
7. Remove the pan from the heat and, with your rubber scraper or metal spatula, fold the rear one-third of the omelet over the filling (if any). Slide the omelet to the front of the pan, holding it all the while with the rubber scraper pressing down on the one-third you have folded over; tip the pan so the omelet rolls out; and release your hold on the omelet. The rear one-third you were holding will fall across the front one-third and present you with a neat trifold omelet. The omelet should be nicely streaked with brown highlights.

What You Need to Know

You may fill the omelet with any *cooked* food you prefer. Notice I stressed cooked food. All foods contain some water. You want to eliminate the water before you cook the omelet. Also, the temperature inside an omelet never gets high enough to cook most foods. I sometimes garnish the top with a little sour cream. For a sweet omelet, you might choose one of the flavored yogurts.

I like to serve the scrambled egg dishes and omelets for brunch or lunch accompanied by a simple green salad or fruit salad. Of course, you can't go wrong with the Pommes Frites (page 248) either.

Cold Spinach Salad

Make sure you *thoroughly* wash the spinach! Then dry it, of course.
Yield: 6 to 8 portions ("bunch" size will vary)

INGREDIENTS

2 bunches spinach leaves, destemmed, washed, and dried
2 hard-cooked eggs, grated
¼ lb. bacon, diced and cooked
6–8 mushrooms, washed and thinly sliced
salt, to taste
black pepper, to taste
3 oz. vinaigrette dressing (page 170)

Method

You may either place all the ingredients in a bowl and toss or toss just the
spinach with the dressing and arrange the other ingredients decoratively on top
of the spinach on a platter.

Insalata Mista

This is the Italian version of the mixed salad. One of the main differences
between the French or American salad and the Italian is the mixing of the salad
dressing. The Italians do not mix it ahead.

INGREDIENTS

1 large cucumber, shredded
1 bell pepper, julienned
1 head green leaf Boston or Bibb lettuce
1 bunch lamb's lettuce (if available)
1 bunch arugula (if available)
(Mesclun may be substituted for the above three greens.)
6–8 artichoke hearts
1 bulb finocchio (if available), thinly sliced
1 heart of celery, from one head
1 lemon
6–8 green onions, thinly sliced
2 large tomatoes

salt, to taste

¾ c. extra virgin olive oil

¼ c. red wine vinegar or balsamic vinegar

Method

1. Combine cucumber and bell pepper.
2. Wash and dry lettuces. Tear into bite-sized pieces.
3. Drain artichoke hearts if canned.
4. Slice finocchio (fennel) into thin rings.
5. Wash, dry, and slice celery into thin pieces.
6. Combine all the previous ingredients and squeeze lemon over all.
7. Add green onions and tomatoes.
8. Add salt. Add olive oil and vinegar and toss well.

Mixed Green Salad

I have been making variations of this salad for over 20 years and have never, until now, written down a recipe for it. It has always seemed simplicity itself.

Yield: 8 to 10 portions

INGREDIENTS

2 heads salad greens, torn into bite-sized pieces

¾ c. raspberry vinaigrette dressing

½ c. fresh herb leaves (mint or basil)

12–16 sun-dried tomatoes

6–8 garlic croutons (see page 68)

½ oz. mushrooms (enoki if available)

¼ c. slivered almonds

Method

1. Wash, dry, and tear the lettuces.
2. Pluck the leaves from the herbs and rinse, if necessary.
3. Toss the lettuces with the vinaigrette until the leaves are just coated.
4. Lightly retoss the salad with the fresh herb leaves.
5. Arrange the greens on chilled salad plates.
6. Garnish the salad with the sun-dried tomatoes and the garlic croutons.
7. Sprinkle the mushrooms and almonds over the salad. Serve immediately.

I like a mix of romaine and butter lettuce, with some of the smaller, more tender greens, such as lamb's lettuce and/or arugula, thrown in, if available. Shredded red cabbage, shredded carrots, fresh tomatoes, or whatever may also be added.

Waldorf Salad

This makes an excellent side for an omelet or quiche or for stuffed, savory crêpes.
    Yield: 6 to 8 portions

INGREDIENTS
2 c. celery, cut into large (¾-in.) dice
2 c. apples, mixture of red and green, cut into large dice
2 tbsp. lemon juice
½ c. walnuts
1 c. mayonnaise
salt, to taste

(**Method**)

1. Combine celery, apples, and lemon juice.
2. Add walnuts, mayonnaise, and salt and toss together.
3. Chill and serve on a bed of lettuces.

Making Crêpes

Here are the two basic crêpe batters, one sweet and one savory.

Pâte à Crêpes

The word *pâte*, without an accent over the "e," in French most often refers to a batter of a consistency somewhat thinner than a "dough." This is the French "pancake" batter. The crêpe differs from the pancake in that it is lighter, thinner, and unleavened. Rarely, if ever, is it served alone. It is nearly always filled with something or dredged in a sauce. There are recipes for folded, rolled, and even stacked crêpes. The dessert crêpe preceded the savory crêpe, just as it does in the recipes.

    There is one oddity involved here. While we wish to heat and season the pan with clarified butter, we wish only a miniscule quantity to remain in the pan for the actual crêpe making. Allowing fat to remain in the pan will prevent the batter from adhering to the pan, which, in this instance, we devoutly desire. If the batter does not adhere, you will make something resembling a spiral nebula instead of a crêpe.

Yield: 12 to 16 10-inch crêpes

INGREDIENTS

1½ c. flour
¼ tsp. salt
4 tbsp. butter, melted
1½ c. cold milk
1 tbsp. sugar
3 tbsp. brandy
3 eggs

Method

1. Place all ingredients in a blender or food processor. Blend until all ingredients are thoroughly intermingled.
2. Refrigerate for 2 to 3 hours. This will allow the gluten to relax so you will be able to make very delicate crêpes.

Pâte à Crêpes, Salées

This is the *savory* crêpe, the one you will want to use for appetizers and main courses. I find crêpes quite handy for using up leftovers of just about anything. I make a béchamel (page 292) or velouté (page 291), add a little grated cheese, and bind the ingredients with the sauce. Mushrooms, spinach seafoods, chicken, and pork all work well this way.

INGREDIENTS

2 c. sifted flour
½ tsp. salt
4 tbsp. butter, melted
2 c. cold milk
2 eggs

Method

1. Place all ingredients in a food processor or blender. Process until all ingredients are completely combined.
2. Refrigerate for 2 to 3 hours.

What You Need to Know

Crêpes may be made in just about any size or pan. The two most common formats are the 6-inch and 10-inch crêpes, made, as you might suspect, in a 6-inch or 10-inch pan. They cook very quickly indeed, and if you use one of the previously mentioned formats, they will weigh between 1 and 2 ounces each. The best pans for making crêpes are thin-iron, well-seasoned, or stainless-lined aluminum pans. You may, of course, use any nonstick pan you have lying around. Do observe the "resting period" in the refrigerator, though, to allow the gluten to relax. The crêpe will be more delicate.

Method

1. Place the pan on medium-high heat.
2. Place a 1- or 2-ounce ladle in the crêpe batter, depending on which size of crêpe is desired.
3. Cover the bottom of the pan with clarified butter.
4. After 30 or 40 seconds, pour the butter out of the pan.
5. Gently beat the batter with a wire whisk to compensate for any settling that may have occurred in the refrigerator.
6. Ladle batter into pan. Tilt and twist pan with your wrist until the entire bottom of the pan is covered with the batter.
7. Return pan to fire.
8. Cook crêpe until a very light, slight rim of brown appears around the edge of the crêpe, maybe 30 seconds. Do not overcook, as the edges will tend to crack when you fold, spindle, and mutilate the crêpe.
9. Turn crêpe, using a rubber scraper or metal spatula and your fingers. Cook just 15 to 20 seconds on the second side.
10. Slide the crêpe out of the pan and onto a plate. You may make these a day or two in advance of when you plan to serve them.

Crêpes Suzette

This classic French "pancake" dish is somewhat shrouded in mystery. Several chefs claim to have conceived it. Whoever Suzette was, she must have been quite a dish herself. A very simple dish to prepare, this is probably the one French dessert best known planet-wide.

Yield: 6 portions

INGREDIENTS

2 oranges
¼ c. sugar
1 c. butter, softened
¼ c. cognac
¼ c. Grand Marnier
12–16 sweet crêpes, 10-in.

Method

1. Zest the two oranges. A microplane is good for this—or a zester, of course.
2. Juice the two oranges.
3. Cream the orange zest, sugar, and butter together.
4. Beat in the orange juice and one half of the Cognac and Grand Marnier.
5. Melt the orange butter in a pan large enough to hold the crêpes over medium heat.
6. Dip the inside of the crêpe in the orange butter and then turn it with the presentation side down.
7. Fold the crêpe in quarters and place it against the side of the pan. It should look like an equilateral triangle with an arc for a base.
8. Repeat step 7 until you have done all the crêpes.
9. With the pan still on the heat, flame with remaining Cognac and Grand Marnier.
10. Serve two to each guest, preferably while the crepes are still flaming. You may sprinkle a little powdered sugar over them and/or the plates.

And finally, here's a quick sautéed dessert.

Bananas Foster

This dish is the most popular dessert at Brennan's restaurant in New Orleans. This is my version.

Yield: 6 portions

INGREDIENTS

4 tbsp. clarified butter
¼ c. brown sugar
6 ripe bananas
1 tsp. cinnamon
1 oz. banana liqueur
2 oz. white rum

Method

1. Heat butter in fry pan, sauté pan, or chafing dish.
2. Add brown sugar and thoroughly incorporate.
3. Peel bananas and slice lengthwise.
4. Sauté bananas briefly.
5. Add the cinnamon and incorporate thoroughly.
6. Add banana liqueur and rum, heat through, and ignite. Shake or stir pan until all the alcohol has burned away.

Serve with vanilla ice cream (page 124).

② Frying

What is the difference between sautéing and frying? When you sauté, you employ a small quantity of high-quality fat. Most often the fat is going to be incorporated into a pan-made sauce for the sauté.

When you fry, you cook in a much larger quantity of fat. If the food is completely submerged in the fat, this method is "deep frying." If the food is only partially submerged in the fat, you are "pan frying."

As a rule you are going to remove as much fat as possible from the food after you cook it.

For both methods of cooking in fat, the food must be tender because this technique does not cook the food long enough to have any tenderizing effect. Many of the foods you fry will have a coating on them. Most often this coating will be some form of breading or batter.

Fried food has a reputation as unhealthy food in the United States. To my mind, fried food need not be any more unhealthy than food prepared with any of the other techniques—if consumed in moderation. The only two fats in which I fry are peanut oil and extra virgin olive oil. Both are low in saturated fats; they are monounsaturated fats. Everyone needs some fat in their diet. These are the good fats to eat. Neither is cheap, and many eating establishments choose to fry in less expensive, more saturated fats. This is the reason I try to restrict most of my fried-food eating to foods I fry myself. I think if you do the same, you will find a place for fried foods in your diet.

Frazzle-Free Frying

1. Ensure that all the pieces of food to be fried at one time are of a uniform size. They will all cook in the same time frame.
2. Thoroughly dry the pieces of food, even if you are going to coat them with a breading or batter. If you are frying a food without a coating—potatoes, for instance—this will prevent spattering and assist caramelization. If, on the other hand, you are frying a coated food, the coating will adhere better if the food is dry.
3. Never overload the cooking oil with too much food. The temperature will drop below the acceptable temperature, and the food will become saturated with the fat.
4. Ensure the fat is up to temperature. Most food will be deep fried at 350° to 360°. As a rule of thumb, larger pieces of food at lower temperatures and smaller at higher temperatures. Never allow the temperature to rise above 375° or to fall below 325°.
5. If you are using a basket in your fryer, never fill it more than half full.
6. Always drain and season the food immediately after cooking.
7. Never attempt to fry too large a piece of food. A chicken segment is just about the largest piece of food I fry. The deep-fried turkey is an exception, but it requires very special handling.
8. You may reuse your cooking oil. But, as both batter and crumbs leave some residue in your oil, you must strain it as soon as it cools. Also, do not fry seafoods with other fried food, as they tend to flavor the oil. When your oil begins to darken, it is time to toss it.

9. Never put your fried food directly on a plate or platter. Always arrange a drain area of some sort. A wire rack over a pan is good as is toweling—not terry, though, as it tends to lead to fuzzy food.

Let's begin with two fried breads from two very different cultures.

Beignets

These are New Orleans "doughnuts." They are *unholy* and cut into squares or diamonds and dusted with powdered sugar. They were for many years a staple at the Morning Call before it moved to Metairie. The popular spot now is Café Du Monde.

INGREDIENTS

2 c. milk, scalded
¼ c. shortening
¾ c. sugar
2 oz. dry yeast
5–6 c. flour
2 tsp. salt
2 eggs
peanut oil, as needed in deep fryer
powdered sugar, as needed

Method

1. Pour milk over shortening and sugar in a stainless bowl.
2. Cool to about 125° and add yeast. Place in mixer bowl.
3. Run mixer slowly and add about one-half of the flour.
4. Add eggs, one at a time, and salt.
5. Add remaining flour. Allow to rise in an oiled bowl covered with plastic wrap until doubled.
6. Turn out onto a floured board and roll to a thickness of about ¼ inch.
7. Cut into squares or diamonds and place in a floured hotel pan and allow to double again.
8. Carefully drop into 350° peanut oil and cook until golden brown, turning once.
9. Drain on toweling and sift powered sugar over them.

Poori

This Indian bread is the only fried bread I have included in the book. Indians make many wonderful breads, nearly all flat.

Yield: Approximately 18 6-inch Poori

INGREDIENTS

1½ c. flour
1½ c. whole-wheat flour
1 tsp. sea salt or kosher salt
¼ c. peanut oil
1 c. warm water
peanut oil, as needed in fryer

Method

1. Place flours and salt in the mixer.
2. Add oil with mixer running.
3. Add water. Allow the dough hook to knead the dough for a minute or two.
4. Cover dough in an oiled bowl and permit to rest for about a half hour.
5. Place some flour on the bench. Divide dough in half.
6. With your hands, roll each piece into a rope and cut each rope into eight equal pieces.
7. Form pieces into balls. Roll balls into 5-inch circles. Just as with pasta, keep the pieces you are not working on covered so they will not dry out.
8. Heat peanut oil to 350° to 360°. Fry bread for about 15 seconds on each side. Lightly tap the bread while it is frying. This will cause it to puff. Drain on toweling and serve. Goes well with the Indian Ginger Chicken (page 136).

What You Need to Know

Battering and Breading

When do you *batter*? When do you *bread*? Good question. Largely, it's a matter of personal choice. Breading provides a lighter, thinner coating than battering. The main advantage of breading is that it doesn't have to be done at the last second as does battering. The crumb coatings will adhere to the food for a few hours without becoming soggy. The batter will run off the food immediately if you set it anywhere besides the hot fat in which you are going to cook the food.

Many of the foods I fry are coated with either breading—which isn't necessarily *bread* but could be ground nuts, cornmeal, or even coconut—or a batter. These coatings do double duty. They provide a shield between the hot fat and the food so the food does not absorb the fat as well as an attractive, crispy crunch when you bite into the fried food. Although a wide variety of batters exists, these next two are the ones I use most for savory dishes.

Beer Batter

The lighter beers will work best in this savory all-purpose batter. I use this mostly for vegetables such as onions, zucchini, cauliflower, mushrooms, chiles, and seafoods.

Yield: Enough batter for a couple of dozen pieces of food

Ingredients
2 c. flour
1 tsp. salt
½ tsp. sugar
2 tsp. paprika
12 oz. warm beer
1 tsp. dry yeast
2 egg yolks

Method

1. Sift flour, salt, sugar, and paprika together.
2. Combine beer and yeast. Allow mixture to work a few minutes.
3. Add beer mixture to flour and beat until there are no lumps.
4. Thoroughly incorporate egg yolks.
5. Allow dough to rise in a warm place for an hour or so. Punch it down and add more warm beer if it has gotten too thick.
6. Refrigerate, covered, or use.

Tempura Batter

This is the very simple batter used in most sushi bars. You must use *cold* water to prevent the batter from becoming too sticky. When you add the flour, whisk quickly just to mix it in evenly. The sticky batter will cause the tempura to be fatty.

Yield: Enough for two dozen shrimp or pieces of vegetable

INGREDIENTS

1 egg, lightly beaten
1 c. cold water
2 tbsp. dry white wine
1 c. flour

(Method)

Combine all ingredients and mix thoroughly. Do this quickly and use immediately. Use this batter with vegetables and seafoods.

Fruit Fritter Batter

This is a third batter that I often use. While the other two are savory, this one is sweet and employed most often with fresh fruit.

Yield: Enough for a couple of pounds of fresh fruit pieces

INGREDIENTS

1 c. flour
1 tsp. baking powder
1 tbsp. sugar
½ tsp. salt
½ c. milk
2 eggs, separated

(Method)

1. Combine all ingredients except egg whites.
2. Whip egg white and fold into batter.

Breading

Many of the students with whom I have spoken over the years have been confused about the marching orders on breading foods to be fried. For consistent, quality results, there is a proper procedure:

1. Dry the food. Season the food.
2. Dredge the food in flour. Coat the food completely and shake off the excess.
3. Dredge the food in beaten eggs. Cover completely.
4. Roll the food in the coating (bread crumbs, ground nuts, coconut, cornmeal, etc.). Cover completely.

5. Place the pieces of coated food in a pan or on a plate, not touching each other, in one layer. If not to be cooked immediately, refrigerate.
6. Fry the coated food within several hours.

What You Need to Know

The food must be dry for the flour to adhere successfully. The eggs will cling to the flour more readily than they will cling to the food. The bread crumbs will seal the food from the frying fat much more effectively with the underlayment of eggs. If the pieces of coated food are permitted to touch or are stacked, bits of the coating will rub off, leaving an opening for the fat to penetrate. The best bread crumbs are those without any crust since the crust has already been cooked once.

Onion Rings

I have seen breaded onion rings, but I really prefer a batter here. Notice I cut the onion slices wider than most fast-food establishments.

Yield: 6 to 8 portions

INGREDIENTS
2 yellow or red onions (the sweeter the better)
1 c. flour
½ tsp. salt
½ tsp. white pepper
¼ tsp. cayenne pepper
1 recipe beer batter
1 gal. cooking oil

Method

1. Peel the onions and slice them into ¾- to 1-inch disks. Place the onions in a bowl of ice water. Separate the layers into individual rings.
2. Sift the flour, salt, and pepper together.
3. Dry the onion slices and dredge them in the flour. Coat completely.
4. Dip the rings in the beer batter (page 233) and gently lower them into the 350° cooking oil.
5. Fry until golden brown. Remove with a skimmer, drain, and serve immediately on a napkin or as a garnish for grilled meats.

Wiener Schnitzel

This is the traditional breaded veal cutlet from Vienna (*Wien* is German for Vienna). Oddly enough, though, most Austrians and Germans prefer breaded pork cutlets to the veal. I don't consider it that odd myself. My mother was from southern Indiana, where there is a large German presence, and I went to high school there. The quality of the food in my high school cafeteria was somewhat suspect (at least I suspected it). I always sneaked off campus—I hope the statute of limitations has run out—to a little diner around the corner that offered "breaded pork tenderloin" sandwiches. This sandwich was a pork tenderloin pounded very thin, breaded and deep fried, about 8 or 9 inches across. Although the bun was quite large, the meat stuck out from the bun about 2 inches all the way around. The garnish on the sandwich was chopped lettuce and tomatoes with mustard. I was addicted to them. I make this at home and have passed this on to my sons. They love it, too.

Yield: 6 to 8 *very* healthy portions

INGREDIENTS

6–8 veal scallops, thinly sliced and pounded (3–4 oz. per person)
salt, to taste
black pepper, to taste
1 c. flour
4 eggs, lightly beaten
1½ c. bread crumbs
vegetable oil, to cover
6–8 lemon wedges
6–8 anchovy filets (or ¼ c. capers)

Method

1. Thoroughly dry the veal and salt and pepper the pieces.
2. Dredge the veal in the flour, coat completely, and shake off the excess.
3. Dredge the veal in the eggs and shake off excess.
4. Dredge the veal pieces in the bread crumbs. Once again, coat completely but shake off excess.
5. Fry the veal in 350° vegetable oil until golden brown.
6. Drain off fat on toweling.
7. Serve garnished with the lemon wedges and anchovies (or capers).

Southwestern Boneless Loin of Pork Rouladen, Rellenos

This combination of the Old World *Rouladen* and the New World *Chiles Rellenos* is one of my favorites. I find it goes well with both a salsa and Dijon mustard.

INGREDIENTS

12 boneless pork loin chops
salt, to taste
black pepper, to taste
4 tbsp. Dijon mustard
12 green chiles
12 oz. Queso Blanco or Monterey Jack cheese, grated
2 c. cooking oil

Method

1. Cut away any visible fat on the chops.
2. Pound the chops with the side of a meat tenderizer or a veal pounder until they are about ⅛ of an inch thick. Do not tear. When finished, the cutlets should be about 6 inches long and 4 inches wide.
3. Thoroughly dry the cutlets. Salt and pepper them.
4. Using a rubber scraper, spread the mustard over one side of each cutlet, covering completely.
5. Slit a whole green chile down one side and open it flat on the mustard. Lay one chile on each cutlet.
6. Spread the cheese evenly over the chile.
7. Fold two opposing sides of the cutlet over the chile and cheese. Roll the cutlet into a cylinder and secure with toothpicks. Repeat until all are done.

Supremes de Volaille à la Kiev

This is a French, not a Russian, dish. French culture held sway for many years at the Russian court, and there are a number of dishes with Russian names that were devised by French chefs.

Yield: 6 to 8 portions

INGREDIENTS

6–8 boneless, skinless chicken breasts
6–8 tbsp. butter, quite cold
salt, to taste
white pepper, to taste
2 tbsp. minced chives
1 tsp. minced tarragon
1 c. flour
2 eggs, lightly beaten
2 c. bread crumbs, no crusts
2 c. peanut oil

Method

1. Dry the breasts and flatten them.
2. Cut the butter into pieces 1-inch long and ½-inch square.
3. Salt and pepper the breasts on both sides.
4. Roll the butter in the chives and tarragon. Place the butter on the "rough" side of the breast (across the width of the breast).
5. Roll the sides of the breast in over the butter, then roll the breast lengthwise. Secure with one or two toothpicks.
6. Heat the peanut oil to 360°.
7. Dredge the breasts consecutively in the flour, egg, then bread crumbs.
8. Fry the breasts until golden brown on all sides. Drain and serve garnished with lemon wedges.

Boneless Breast of Chicken Schnitzel

Just in case you would like to try it, this is the exact same procedure for making the wiener schnitzel I mention on page 236—but it is much cheaper to make.

Yield: 6 to 8 portions

INGREDIENTS

6–8 boneless chicken breasts, pounded thinly
salt, to taste
white pepper, to taste
1 c. flour
2 eggs, lightly beaten
2 c. bread crumbs, no crust
2 c. peanut oil
12–16 lemon slices or wedges
12–16 anchovies, rolled

Method

1. Thoroughly dry the breasts and salt and pepper them.
2. Dredge the breasts consecutively in the flour, eggs, and bread crumbs.
3. Heat peanut oil to 350°.
4. Fry the breasts until they are golden brown. Drain.
5. Serve garnished with the lemon and anchovies.

Pollo Parmigiana

And here is the Italian claim to the breaded cutlet. Make it with veal too.
Yield: 6 to 8 portions

INGREDIENTS

6–8 boneless chicken breasts, flattened
salt, to taste
black pepper, to taste
1 c. flour
2–3 eggs, lightly beaten
2 c. bread crumbs, fine, no crust
1 c. parmesan
5 oz. olive or peanut oil (or half-and-half blend)
½ c. dry white wine
2½ c. tomato sauce (page 294)
6–8 mozzarella slices

Method

1. Dry breasts thoroughly, season with the salt and pepper, and dredge consecutively in the flour, egg, and the bread crumb and parmesan mixture.
2. Heat the oil(s) in a fry pan over medium heat and add the chicken breasts.
3. Cook the breasts until golden brown on both sides, turning only once.
4. Remove breasts to a serving platter or a casserole dish. Keep them warm.
5. Deglaze the pan with the white wine.
6. Add tomato sauce and warm through.
7. Pour sauce over breasts.
8. Top each breast with a slice of the mozzarella cheese.
9. Melt the cheese in a 350° oven. Serve.

Cajun Barbecue Chicken Wings

I don't do much Cajun cooking. My New Orleans style is definitely Creole. The dry rub I use for barbecue has a certain Cajun bent to it, though, hence the name of the recipe. I have an appetizer list of about 30 items I do with my students for parties. This is one of the most popular items. They are addictive—and messy.

Yield: 10 to 12 servings

INGREDIENTS

2½–3 lb. chicken wings
¾ c. dry rub (page 9)
1 c. butter
1 c. Tabasco
2 c. barbecue sauce (page 10)
2 qt. peanut oil
2 c. flour
2 c. Gorgonzola dressing (page 241)
12 radishes
12 celery sticks
12 green onions

[**Method**]

1. Cut the "drumette" away from the other two joints of the wing. Thoroughly dry the wings.
2. Place wings in a large nonreactive bowl and sprinkle with the dry rub. Toss to coat completely. Cover and refrigerate while you make the sauce.
3. Melt butter in a saucepan and add Tabasco.
4. Add barbecue sauce, incorporate well and heat through. This sauce is done.
5. Heat peanut oil to 360°.
6. Toss wings in the flour. The best way I have found to get rid of the excess flour is to then place the wings in a sieve and shake off the extra flour before adding the wings to the oil.
7. Fry the wings, a few at a time, in the 360° oil for 10 minutes. Drain.
8. Toss the wings with the sauce and put them in an ovenproof dish. Place the dish in a 500° oven for 10 minutes.
9. Serve with Gorgonzola dressing (see the next recipe), celery sticks, radishes, and green onions. Also serve a good, crusty bread and butter.

Creamy Gorgonzola Dressing

This is the "creamy" version of this dressing. You may make a vinaigrette-based version as well.

INGREDIENTS

1 recipe mayonnaise (page 171)
¼–½ lb. good Italian Gorgonzola
¼ c. white vinegar
1 tsp. Worcestershire sauce
Tabasco, to taste
1 c. heavy cream
½ c. sour cream
salt, to taste
white pepper, to taste

Method

1. Crumble all the Gorgonzola and reserve half of it.
2. Combine all ingredients except reserved Gorgonzola in a food processor or blender. Blend until smooth.
3. Place dressing in a nonreactive bowl and add remaining Gorgonzola. If the dressing is too thick for your taste, thin out with half-and-half. Chill.

Southern Fried Chicken

You heard me, Southern Fried Chicken. During the few brief weeks my professional students are with me, I try to impart the fact to them that good cooking done by home cooks can be wonderful food. Many of the best home cooks have terrific instincts and follow the five techniques intuitively. I use a few typical American meals to illustrate this point. The Thanksgiving meal (page 13) is one. This is another. Why buttermilk as a marinade? Buttermilk actually does make the chicken more tender. This dish will be best begun the day before you wish to fry the chicken. Most of the food I fry is deep fried. This is the only pan-fried dish in the book.

Yield: 6 to 8 portions (depending on how hungry folks are)

INGREDIENTS

3 chickens, fryers cut into serving pieces
3 tbsp. salt
3 c. buttermilk

4 c. flour
1 tbsp. kosher salt
2 tsp. garlic powder
2 tsp. thyme
1 tbsp. dry rub (page 9)
1 tbsp. paprika
2 tsp. black pepper
6 eggs, lightly beaten with 1 tbsp. cold water
1 qt. peanut oil

Method

1. Rinse and dry the chicken. Toss with the salt. Place the chicken in a nonre-active bowl with the buttermilk. Allow the chicken to rest several hours or overnight, covered, in the refrigerator.
2. Mix the flour and all the seasonings together.
3. Heat the peanut oil to 350°.
4. Set up a breading sequence in two bowls. Dry the chicken and dredge it in the flour, shaking off the excess. Then dip the chicken pieces in the eggs. Go back into the flour with the chicken pieces. This procedure will give you a coating impervious to penetration by the oil. It will also be very crispy.
5. Now you're ready to go straight into the oil. Use a pan large enough so that you have between 1 and 2 inches of oil in the pan.
6. Fry the chicken a few pieces at a time, turning about 10 minutes into the cooking time. Total cooking time will be about 20 minutes. The dark-meat pieces will take a little longer than the white. Drain.

Serve with the Southern Milk Gravy (below), Mashed Potatoes (page 162), and Buttermilk Biscuits (page 103). Vegetable optional with this meal.

Southern Milk Gravy

This gravy is actually a combination of two of our classic sauces—velouté (page 291) and béchamel (page 292)—with the addition of fat from frying the chicken. That's what makes this a "gravy" instead of a "sauce."

Yield: About 1½ quarts

INGREDIENTS
½ c. fat from the pan in which you fried the chicken
2 tbsp. butter
¼ c. minced onion

4 oz. flour
salt, to taste
black pepper, to taste
3 c. chicken stock (page 286)
3 c. milk

Method

1. Place fat and butter in a saucepan over medium heat.
2. Add minced onion and sweat until soft.
3. Add flour, incorporate thoroughly with the fats, and cook until the flour has a "cooked" aroma. Do not color. Add salt and pepper.
4. Add hot stock and incorporate completely with a wire whisk.
5. Add milk and incorporate with a wire whisk.

La Mèdiatrice

The name *La Mèdiatrice*, "the female mediator," was apparently coined by 19th-century New Orleans husbands as the name for this useful and delectable dish. The gentlemen, arriving home at various hours and in varying states of sobriety, did not wish to appear on the stoop empty-handed to face the wrath of an irate spouse. A stop on the way was mandated to pick up this oyster loaf.

Yield: 6 to 8 portions

INGREDIENTS

6–8 French bread, 2 baguettes or individual loaves
24–36 oysters, shucked
¼ c. Pernod
1 tsp. salt
1 tsp. black pepper
½ tsp. cayenne pepper
½ tsp. cumin
1½ c. yellow cornmeal
1 c. flour
3–4 eggs, lightly beaten
1–2 qt. peanut oil
1 c. aioli (page 244)
2 c. shredded romaine lettuce

Method

1. Using a bread knife, slice the loaf (or loaves) lengthwise about two-thirds of the way up the side of the loaf. Use your fingers to hollow out the bottom section.
2. Marinate the oysters in the Pernod for an hour or so.
3. In a bowl, combine the salt, peppers, cumin, and cornmeal.
4. Dry the oysters thoroughly.
5. Dredge the oysters in the flour, then the egg, then the cornmeal.
6. Heat the peanut oil to 350°.
7. Toast the bottom of the loaf in a hot oven.
8. Slather the aioli all along the inside of the toasted loaf.
9. Arrange the lettuce down inside the loaf.
10. Fry the oysters until golden brown. Drain.
11. Arrange the oysters on the bed of lettuce.

Note: We like to serve the sandwich with lemon wedges and Tabasco sauce.

Aioli

In the south of France, this cold sauce is most often made with raw garlic. We have found, for us anyway, the taste is immeasurably improved by sweating the garlic briefly in a little butter or oil. In Provence, this sauce is used with seafood and vegetables, in soups, and as a bread spread. In New Orleans, we use it on the Médiatrice.

INGREDIENTS
2 tbsp. finely minced garlic
1 tbsp. clarified butter
½ tsp. white pepper
¼ tsp. cayenne pepper
½ tsp. salt
1 lemon lemon juice
2 eggs
2 c. peanut oil
½ c. extra virgin olive oil

Method

1. Sweat garlic in clarified butter over medium heat until soft.
2. Add peppers, salt, and lemon juice. Cool slightly.
3. Place eggs in food processor or blender and pulse to beat.

4. Add garlic mixture to processor and pulse a few times.
5. While processor is running, slowly add oils in a stream.
6. When the proper mayonnaise-like consistency has been reached, remove from processor and chill until needed.

Note: Since you will only require about a cup for the Médiatrice loaf (page 243), keep the remainder in the refrigerator to use on sandwiches, in salads, and so on. It should remain fresh and wholesome for about a week.

Fried Calamari

Another favorite deep-fried Italian food. Note this is a slight variation on the Beer Batter (page 233).
Yield: 6 to 8 portions

INGREDIENTS
1½–2 lb. small fresh squid
1¼ c. flour
1 egg yolk
¼ tsp. salt
black pepper, to taste
2 tbsp. vegetable oil
1 c. light beer
2 egg whites, lightly beaten
2 qt. peanut oil
6–8 parsley sprigs
6–8 lemon wedges

Method

1. Rinse squid well under running water. Cut away tentacles and reserve in one piece. Discard beak, clear "quill" and ink sac. Peel away skin and cut body of squid into ¾-inch rings. Drain and dry all pieces well.
2. Sift flour into wide bowl. Mix in salt, pepper, egg, oil, and enough beer to make a smooth but flowing batter. Stir until all lumps have disappeared.
3. Let batter stand for 1 hour, then beat one egg white until stiff peaks form and fold into batter.
4. Heat oil to 350° for deep frying. Dredge squid pieces in flour, then batter, place in hot oil, and fry until crisp and golden, 4 to 5 minutes, turning frequently. Remove and drain. Garnish with parsley and lemon wedges and serve. We also serve this dish with the cocktail sauce (see the next recipe).

Cocktail Sauce

INGREDIENTSS

24 oz. catsup or chili sauce
freshly grated horseradish, to taste
1 tsp. Worcestershire sauce
Tabasco, to taste
lemon juice from ¼ lemon
½ c. minced green onions
¼ c. minced parsley

Method

1. Mix all ingredients together and refrigerate until use.

Beer Batter Fried Soft-Shell Crabs

The method for this recipe is a very traditional manner in which to cook soft-shell crabs. I think my beer batter is an improvement on the batters used by many New Orleans restaurants. This batter seals in all the succulence of the crab. This recipe is for a main course-size portion. Halve it for an appetizer.

INGREDIENTS

1 recipe beer batter (page 233)
1 gal. peanut oil
2 c. flour
1 tbsp. sea salt
2 tsp. white pepper
2 tsp. cayenne pepper
12–16 jumbo soft-shell crabs

Method

1. Make the beer batter and allow it to rest for an hour.
2. Preheat peanut oil to 350°.
3. Combine flour, salt, pepper, and cayenne pepper in a bowl.
4. Thoroughly dry the crabs, then dredge them in the flour. Shake off excess flour.
5. Fry the crabs, a few at a time, in the oil until they are golden brown. This will probably take 5 to 6 minutes.
6. Drain them on paper towels.

Note: I like to serve the crabs on folded white linen napkins. You may serve the crabs with either the béarnaise (page 297), beurre blanc (page 298), rémoulade (page 151), or cocktail sauce (page 246). And garnish them with lemon twists or crowns and a sprig of fresh parsley.

Egg Rolls
(Spring Rolls)

This has long been a popular item in Chinese and Vietnamese restaurants. I am also beginning to see many variants on this basic theme in eclectic American restaurants.

INGREDIENTS

¼ c. peanut oil
1 tbsp. sake or rice wine
1 tsp. cornstarch
½ lb. ground pork
½ lb. shrimp, peeled, deveined, and chopped
½ head Chinese (Napa) cabbage, shredded
1 bunch green onions, thinly sliced
1 c. bean sprouts
2 ribs celery, thinly sliced
2 tsp. minced garlic
1 tsp. salt
1 tbsp. sugar

Method

1. Heat oil in wok.
2. Combine sake, cornstarch, pork, and shrimp. Sauté until pork is cooked in oil.
3. Add vegetables, salt, and sugar and sauté briefly; vegetables should remain crisp.
4. Drain for 15 minutes in colander.
5. Make a paste of 2 tablespoons of water and 1 tablespoon of flour. Place the egg roll wrapper with one of the points toward you. Place about 3 tablespoons of the filling in the center of the wrapper. Brush left and right corners with the paste. Fold bottom point over filling. Fold left and right points over filling and bottom point. Brush top point with paste, roll, and seal. Fry in 4 or 5 cups of 360° peanut oil until golden brown. Drain.

Serve with reconstituted dry mustard. Mix a little cold water with dry mustard until you have a paste-like consistency.

What You Need to Know

You should continually turn the egg rolls or, if you have a fryer with a basket, place the egg rolls in the fryer without the basket and then place the basket on top of them. This will keep them submerged for even browning. A variation you might want to try is the Vietnamese version with "rice paper" rolls.

And here is our version of the most popular fried item in the United Sates. If there is one food that is responsible for the success of McDonald's, it is their "French fries." They look suspiciously like Pommes Frites Allumettes.

Pommes Frites Allumettes

It is difficult to conceive today, but until the Spanish stumbled over the potato in the West Indies around the year 1500, European vegetable staples were cabbage, carrots, onions, and "pease." The potato first encountered was more like what you know today as the sweet potato. Not until 30 or 40 years later was that tuberous ancestor of all our other potato varieties discovered in Ecuador. It didn't exactly take England by storm, either, when it was introduced by Sir John Hawkins in 1563. Sir Francis Drake reintroduced it in 1586, and it fared somewhat better. The Irish can thank Sir Walter Raleigh for first growing the potato in Ireland. It is, I think, just the least little bit ironic that when Parmentier first extolled the virtues of the potato in 1771, he suggested it might be consumed in times of food shortage.

Now, of course, in all those countries where rice is not the basic dietary starch, the potato is eaten almost daily. Whether they are called pommes frites, chips, or French fries, fried potatoes are beloved throughout the Western world but are not often prepared in the home—mainly (I am told) because the results are less than satisfactory and partially because so much fried food is consumed away from home. I may be of some assistance with the former; with the latter, you're on your own.

One of the main differences between restaurant-fried potatoes and home-fried potatoes is that in the restaurant, we fry them twice. The first frying reduces the moisture content of the potato and readies it for the crisping and caramelizing process of the second frying. The two keys to avoiding fat-laden, "soggy" fried potatoes are the temperature of the oil and the second frying.

Allumettes means "matchsticks," but the potatoes are not actually cut quite that small. "Allumette" and "omelet" both come from the same root.

INGREDIENTS
2–3 lb. potatoes, Russet type
1 gal. cooking oil
salt, to taste

Method

1. Peel the potatoes and place them in a bowl of cold water. You may add a little sugar if you wish, as this helps with the caramelization.
2. Square off the ends of the potatoes.
3. Cut the potatoes into thin pieces approximately ⅛ to ¼ inch on a side. Return them to the bowl of water as you work.
4. Heat the cooking oil to 350°. Use a candy or deep-fry thermometer to ascertain the temperature.
5. Remove the potatoes from the water and dry thoroughly.
6. It is important not to attempt to fry too many potatoes at once since the more food one places in the oil, the lower the temperature becomes. Never fill the basket more than half full. This is also the reason I recommend frying in the large quantity of oil listed here. The higher the temperature you are able to maintain, the better the result. Cook the potatoes in batches.
7. Cook the potatoes for 4 or 5 minutes. The actual time will depend on the temperature of the oil and the size you have cut the potatoes. The potatoes should be just on the verge of browning when you remove them—with brown highlights around the edges. They will be soft enough to mash between your thumb and forefinger.
8. Remove the potatoes from the oil, using a skimmer (or the basket if you are frying in a deep fryer), and place them on some toweling. Spread them out.
9. You may now hold the potatoes for several hours should you choose.
10. Heat the oil to 360° just a few minutes before you are ready to serve the potatoes.
11. Fry the potatoes—a small batch at a time—until they crisp and are nicely browned. This should take only 2 to 3 minutes.
12. Drain and salt immediately.

Cottage Fried Potatoes

This dish comes to us from Ireland. It was made in homes in iron pans with the potatoes arrayed in one layer.

Yield: 6 to 8 portions

INGREDIENTS

2 qt. peanut oil
3 lb. Russet potatoes, peeled
salt, to taste

(**Method**)

1. Heat peanut oil in a thick-walled pot to 350°.
2. Using a slicing machine, slice potatoes to a thickness of ⅛ inch. Place in cold water until ready to fry.
3. Thoroughly dry potatoes and fry in the oil for 1 to 2 minutes. Drain.
4. You may now set the potatoes aside until just before you are ready to serve, as the second frying should be quite brief.
5. Heat the oil again to 350° and fry the potatoes until they are golden brown and crisp.
6. Drain on toweling, then salt.

Fear of Frying

Don't be afraid of this technique. There is great hysteria out there today about the downside of fried foods. They are unhealthy. Americans eat too much fat. Blah. Blah. Blah. If you fry with proper technique at the right temperature, in quality fats, such as peanut oil and olive oil, you need have no health fears about including a little fried food in your diet.

PART IV

The Fourth Technique
Braising—Cooking with Fat and Liquid Combined

BRAISED MEAT DISHES

BRAISING POULTRY

BRAISING SEAFOOD

MANY OF THE foods cooked with this method would fall under the heading "comfort foods." The Sunday pot roast with which many of us grew up is cooked by this method. Beef stew is an old favorite.

This method of cooking was disappearing from the fine dining scene for much of the middle of the 20th century. The "Swiss steak" survived this period intact in the diner and home-cooking-style establishments. It is, I am happy to see, making a strong comeback in the better restaurants.

The preponderance of foods cooked by this method are tougher than those foods sautéed, grilled, or roasted. Most of a steer, for instance, is composed of tough meat. As a general rule, the tender or "middle meats" make up only about one-third of the animal. What are you to do with the rest of the carcass? Why, you braise it!

The cuts suitable for braising on a steer come from the chuck primal or the round primal. The brisket is also suitable.

I divide this technique into three basic categories: stews (several pieces of food to make one portion), braised individual portions where a single piece of food makes up a portion (chicken pieces and Swiss steaks), and pot roasts (one piece of food contains several portions). All are cooked in precisely the same manner; only the time of cooking varies.

Braising Basics

1. As always, when you wish to caramelize (brown) a dish, you must first dry it thoroughly.
2. Season the meat while raw. For many dishes, the meat will be dredged in flour at this point.
3. Brown the meat in a fat with a high flash point, such as peanut oil, olive oil, or clarified butter. *Never* use whole butter because the high temperature will burn the milk-fat solids.
4. Get the fat very hot before adding the meat.
5. Brown the meat! Do not make the mistake of taking the meat out of the fat or adding the liquid too soon. This will result in an unattractive grayish coloration with very little eye appeal. This is a truly key point. It is one of the main differences between home cooks and professional chefs. We know just how much flavor results from caramelization! If you attempt to brown too many pieces of food at one time, the temperature in your pan will drop below the point where effective caramelization can take place. Just brown a few pieces at a time.
6. In certain dishes, flavorful vegetables will be added at this point. Generally, only the vegetables that are in the dish for flavor go in now. Any vegetables that are added as a visual and textural part of the dish will go in much later.
7. Add the liquid, bring the dish to the boil, and reduce to a simmer. And cook until done. Those dishes with the longest cooking time will be pot roast-type dishes. Stews will take less time and braised steaks the shortest time of all. You may have to check the liquid level in the pot periodically. Add more if necessary.

8. Add the garnish vegetables over the period of the cooking time with the hardest going in first.

BRAISED MEAT DISHES

This first dish has meat in it, but you are not actually braising the meat—you braise the dough. Very unique.

Pot Stickers

You may either buy the wonton wrappers, found in most supermarkets today, or make your own egg noodle dough for the following dish. The fresh pasta recipe on page 165 will work just dandy. My friend Bernard Chang's mother made the best pot stickers I've ever had. She formed the dough completely by hand.

Yield: About 4 dozen pot stickers. You need not eat them all at once—they freeze. I selected this quantity because about 50 wonton wrappers come in one package.

INGREDIENTS
1½ c. shredded Chinese or Napa cabbage
1 lb. lean ground pork
4 green onions, minced
1 tbsp. finely minced fresh ginger
1 egg, lightly beaten
2 tbsp. sake or dry sherry
2–3 tbsp. soy sauce (tamari)
1 tsp. salt
1 tsp. sesame oil
1 tsp. cornstarch
50 wonton wrappers, cut into 3-in. circles
2 egg whites, lightly beaten
peanut oil, to coat pan
3 c. chicken stock

Method

1. In a bowl, thoroughly combine the cabbage, pork, onions, ginger, egg, sake, soy sauce, salt, sesame oil, and cornstarch.
2. Use a large round cookie cutter to make round from the wonton squares. Select one that goes all the way to the edges of the wrapper.

3. Place a small teaspoon of this filling in the center of each wonton wrapper.
4. Paint the edges of the wrappers with the egg white and seal the dumpling. (You may crimp the edges with a fork to decorate should you choose.)
5. Heat the peanut oil in a pan until quite hot.
6. Place the pot stickers in the pan and sear on one side.
7. Add a little stock to the pan. You'll need to cook the pot stickers in several batches.
8. Place a lid on the pan, reduce heat to medium, and simmer for 5 to 6 minutes.
9. Remove from pan and serve with pepper oil or chili paste.

What You Need to Know

Here's how I make my pepper oil: Place 2 cups of peanut oil in a saucepan with ¼ cup of sesame oil and ½ cup of crushed red chiles. Bring this mixture to about 300° and allow to cool.

Grillades

This is a very flavorful New Orleans version of the basic "Swiss" or braised steak.
Yield: 6 to 8 portions

INGREDIENTS
¼ c. clarified butter or cooking oil
3–4 lb. beef, eye of round
1 tsp. black pepper
1 tsp. white pepper
1 tsp. cayenne pepper
1 tbsp. salt
1 c. flour
1½ c. diced yellow onion
1½ c. diced bell pepper
1½ c. diced celery
1 tbsp. minced garlic
3 c. canned Roma tomatoes
1 c. tomato purée
3 or 4 bay leaves
1 tbsp. whole thyme
1 qt. brown stock (page 285)
approx. ½ c. brown roux

Method

1. Slowly heat butter or oil in a large skillet.
2. While the oil is heating, slice the eye of round, across the grain, into ½-inch-thick slices.
3. Pound slices until they are between ⅛- and ¼-inch thick. Try not to tear them.
4. Combine black, white, and red peppers with salt and flour in a shallow bowl.
5. Thoroughly dry the beef and dredge both sides in the flour mixture.
6. Sauté the beef in the butter or oil until well browned on both sides. Remove.
7. Sauté onion, bell pepper, and celery until lightly browned. Add garlic.
8. Add tomatoes, tomato purée, bay leaves, and thyme.
9. Add stock.
10. Place mixture in a roasting pan or casserole with a cover, place beef in this mixture, and cover.
11. Cook in a 375° oven for approximately 45 minutes or until beef is tender enough to be cut with a fork.
12. Remove beef from sauce when done and incorporate just enough roux to thicken slightly. Return meat to sauce.
13. Serve with cheese grits (below) or boiled or steamed rice.

Cheese Grits

This is the grits dish I usually serve with Grillades (page 254). In the South, they traditionally accompany egg dishes in the mornings.

Yield: 8 to 10 portions

INGREDIENTS

6 c. skim milk
2 tsp. salt
1 tsp. white pepper
4 tbsp. butter
1¼ c. white grits
½ c. parmesan
½ c. grated provolone
½ cup grated sharp cheddar

Method

1. Over medium heat, in a saucepan bring the milk, salt, pepper, and butter to a boil. Watch the pot! It will boil over if you space out.
2. Slowly stir in the grits.
3. Add the cheeses a little at a time. Check seasoning.
4. Serve with any breakfast or brunch dish—always with Grillades (page 254).

Rouladen

To the French, *rouladen* (rolls) are usually veal or pork. This substantial Teutonic version is made with very lean beef round. The quality of this rouladen, clearly, will be determined by the quality of the pickles and mustard you elect to incorporate.

Yield: About 8 healthy portions

INGREDIENTS

3 lb. beef round (eye of round works well)
½ lb. bacon, diced
3 or 4 kosher dill pickles
2 tbsp. German prepared mustard
1 tsp. whole oregano
salt, to taste
black pepper, to taste
6 tbsp. clarified butter
3 c. beef stock
4 tbsp. flour

Method

1. Slice the eye of round into pieces approximately ½-inch thick. Pound the meat with a hammer or veal pounder until the pieces are about 4 by 6 inches.
2. Blanch the bacon in boiling water for about 5 minutes; cool. Sauté.
3. Slice the pickles lengthwise into either quarters or halves, depending on their size. You might need to trim the ends off the larger pickles so they will fit in the Rouladen.
4. Spread a little of the mustard on each piece of meat.

5. Sprinkle the oregano, salt, and pepper on the pieces of meat.
6. Strew the bacon over the meat.
7. Lay a slice of pickle on each slice of meat, across the shorter direction.
8. Roll the rouladen tightly and secure with toothpicks.
9. The meat may have wept somewhat at this point. If so, dry it before you brown it in hot clarified butter in a sauté or fry pan.
10. After you have browned all the rolls, place them in a casserole and pour in the brown stock.
11. You may either cook the rouladen in a 350° oven for approximately 2 hours or simmer the casserole on very low heat on top of the stove. They are done when a fork will cut the meat.
12. Make a brown roux with the remaining butter and flour.
13. Remove the rolls from the casserole and incorporate the roux, using a wire whip, into the stock.
14. Serve the sauce over the rouladen.

Note: Some Germans, Swiss, and Austrians stuff the rouladen with sauerkraut instead of the pickle. Serve with buttered noodles (see the Pasta all'Uovo recipe on page 165) or dumplings (page 139).

Carbonnades de Boeuf à la Flamande

The word *carbonnade* means, as you might suspect, "meat grilled on charcoal." "Carbonnades," an old word, now simply means "browned." *Flamande* means "Flemish," an epithet for those who inhabit Flanders, an area that today spans France and Belgium. These are the beer-drinking French and Belgians, a fact reflected in this unique and hearty stew. Also, note the meat for this dish is thin-sliced as opposed to "cubed." You may slice the pieces small or large, depending on whether you want a "stew" or a "Swiss steak."
    Yield: 6 to 8 portions

INGREDIENTS
3 lb. beef, round or chuck, sliced ¼-in. thick
¼ c. clarified butter
2 c. thinly sliced yellow onions
1 tbsp. minced garlic
3 bay leaves
1 tsp. whole thyme

salt, to taste
black pepper, to taste
2 tbsp. dark brown sugar
3 c. dark beer
1 c. brown stock
2 tbsp. strong vinegar, such as balsamic
2 tbsp. cornstarch or arrowroot

Method

1. Thoroughly dry the slices of meat.
2. In a casserole or brazier, heat the butter over high heat. Brown the beef, a few pieces at a time. Remove.
3. Lightly brown the onions in the butter.
4. Add the garlic, bay leaves, thyme, salt, pepper, and brown sugar and continue cooking for 3 or 4 minutes. Deglaze with beer.
5. Add half the brown stock and all the vinegar.
6. Return the meat to the casserole, put a lid on the pot, and place in a 350° oven. Bake for 2 to 2½ hours. Test the meat for doneness with a fork.
7. Combine starch and stock and add to the stew.

Boeuf à la Bourguignonne

This dish comes from the area of France known as Bourgogne (Burgundy), and the French themselves proclaim that the best foods and wines come from here. When you see "*à la Bourguignonne*" ("in the manner of Burgundy"), you know it means, when referring to meat, a method of braising a tougher cut of meat with boiling onions, mushrooms, bacon, and, of course, red burgundy wine. This appellation may be attached to a stew, a braised "steak," or a pot roast. You'll do a stew. Notice we make a roux within the context of the dish. Do not feel in the least that you are cheating if you don't pour a bottle of French burgundy in this dish. Burgundies have gotten so expensive that only a maniac would do so. Any decent dry red wine will do nicely. I like the very drinkable Shiraz's from Australia or the Grenaches from the Rhone Valley in France.

Yield: 6 to 8 portions

INGREDIENTS

½ lb. bacon, cut into ¾-in.-wide pieces
6 tbsp. clarified butter
3 lb. beef brisket, cut into 2-in. cubes
1 tbsp. salt
black pepper, to taste
2 c. thinly sliced yellow onion
1½ c. peeled and thinly sliced carrot
1 tbsp. finely minced garlic
4 tbsp. flour
24 oz. dry red wine
16 oz. brown stock (page 285)
1½ c. peeled, seeded, and chopped tomatoes
2 or 3 bay leaves
1 tsp. whole thyme
12–16 boiling onions, brown-braised
12–16 mushroom caps

Method

1. Sauté bacon in clarified butter until just browned.
2. Dry beef thoroughly, salt and pepper it, and brown in the fat. Remove beef.
3. Sauté the onion and carrot in the fat. Remove onion and carrot and discard half the fat.
4. Return the beef, bacon, onion, and carrot to the pot and sprinkle the flour over all.
5. Cook the flour through.
6. Deglaze with the red wine.
7. Add stock, tomatoes, garlic, bay leaves, and thyme. Bring to a simmer and cover.
8. Place in a 350° oven for 2 to 2½ hours.
9. Add boiling onions and mushrooms.
10. If sauce does not seem thick enough, you may reduce it slightly on high heat while stirring constantly. Serve with noodles or the Puree of Garlic Potatoes (page 163).

What You Need to Know

Brown-Braised Onions

This is actually a "braise-within-a-braise." After you have peeled the onions, sauté them in a little clarified butter until they begin to brown. Add about 1 cup of stock to the pan, cover, and simmer for about 10 minutes. Drain. Now they are ready to add to the dish.

Navarin of Lamb Printanier

On October 20, 1827, French, British, and Russian forces cornered and decimated the Turkish and Egyptian fleets in the harbor of Navarino (Pylos), Greece. This decisive Battle of Navarino turned the corner in the Greek War of Independence from the Ottoman Empire. The victors must have feasted heartily on lamb following the victory. There would be no other manner to feast on the following dish. The word *Navarin* is unique because it is used exclusively in French as the name for a hearty stew of mutton or lamb. The word *Printanier* indicates you will find "spring" vegetables in the dish.

Yield: 8 portions

INGREDIENTS
3 lb. lamb, shoulder or leg, cubed in 2-in. pieces
salt, to taste
black pepper, to taste

¼ c. extra virgin olive oil
1 tbsp. minced garlic
brown stock (or brown lamb stock), to cover (page 285)
1 c. peeled, seeded, and chopped tomatoes
½ c. tomato purée
2 bay leaves
2 tsp. whole thyme
2 tsp. whole oregano
6–8 boiling onions
12–16 pieces carrot, quartered and pared
12–16 pieces turnip, peeled and cut into small ovals
12–16 new potatoes, or very small "B"-size red potatoes
1 c. fresh peas
1 c. green beans, tipped and cut into 1-in. pieces
2–3 tbsp. flour

Method

1. Dry the lamb and salt and pepper it.
2. Heat 2 tablespoons of the olive oil over medium heat until quite hot. You will require a fairly large pot with a lid for this dish. Look at the ingredients!
3. Cook the pieces of lamb until they are browned on all sides.
4. Add the garlic. Cook just long enough to soften—but not brown—the garlic.
5. Add the stock, tomatoes, bay leaves, thyme, and oregano.
6. Cover and place in a 350° oven for about 60 minutes.
7. Prepare all your vegetables while the lamb is simmering in the oven.
8. Remove the lamb from the oven and skim off any visible fat. Add more stock if you need to.
9. Peel the onions, carrots, turnips, and potatoes, if you haven't already done so, and add them all to the pot. Be sure the stock covers all the ingredients. Cover the pot and place it back in the oven for an additional 35 to 40 minutes.
10. Test the vegetables for doneness.
11. Remove the pot from the oven and add the peas and beans. You may now finish the simmering, if you choose, on top of the stove with the pot covered. Simmer for 10 minutes.
12. Make a brown roux with the remaining olive oil and the flour.
13. Remove all the solids from the pot and, using a whip, incorporate the roux into the stock. Check the seasoning in the sauce. Return all the solids to the pot and heat through.

Braised Lamb Shanks

Lamb shanks are one of my favorite lamb dishes. They must be braised.
  Yield: Serves 6

INGREDIENTS

6 garlic cloves
6 lamb shanks
kosher salt, to taste
black pepper, to taste
1 c. flour
½ c. extra virgin olive oil
3 carrots, large dice
2 onions, peeled and quartered
4 stalks celery, large dice
2 c. dry red wine
1 tbsp. fresh thyme
1 tbsp. minced fresh basil
1 28-oz. can Roma tomatoes with juice
1½ c. beef or chicken stock

Method

1. Slice the garlic cloves vertically. With a paring knife, make small incisions in the meaty part of the shanks. Insert the garlic cloves in the incisions.
2. Dry the shanks and salt and pepper them. Dredge them in the flour and shake off the excess.
3. In a thick-bottomed pot, get the olive oil quite hot and brown the lamb shanks completely. Remove them from the pot and set aside.
4. Sauté the carrots, onions, and celery in the oil until light brown.
5. Deglaze with the red wine, scraping the bottom of the pot to incorporate all fonds.
6. Replace lamb shanks in pot. Add thyme, basil, tomatoes, and stock.
7. Cover and place in a 350° oven for 2 to 2½ hours, stirring occasionally.

Serve with the Risotto Milanese (page 158) or the Purée of Garlic Potatoes (page 163). Plain buttered noodles go well also.

Rippchen mit Kraut

This is my version of a traditional Teutonic braised dish in which I elect to use the tenderer baby back ribs as opposed to the country-style ribs. For the caramelization, I quickly deep-fry the ribs, in the Chinese style.

Yield: 6 to 8 portions

INGREDIENTS

1 or 2 baby back rib rack
2–3 qt. peanut oil
1 tbsp. kosher salt
2 tsp. black pepper
1 tbsp. smoked paprika
2 tbsp. clarified butter
4 slices bacon
1½ c. thinly sliced yellow onion
2 Granny Smith apples, thinly sliced
4 or 5 juniper berries
1–2 lb. sauerkraut, rinsed
3 c. sparkling apple cider, apple cider, or white wine
1 sprig fresh thyme
2 or 3 bay leaves

Method

1. Remove the membrane from the back of the ribs.
2. Dry the ribs. Segment the ribs into three- or four-rib portions. Mix the salt, pepper, and paprika.
3. Rub the ribs with the paprika mixture and set them aside while the peanut oil heats to 350°.
4. In a fry pan or sauté pan, heat the clarified butter until quite hot. Slice the bacon into lardons and add to the pan.
5. When the bacon has caramelized, remove about half the fat and add the onion to the pan.
6. Lightly brown the onion.
7. Add the apples and cook until soft.
8. Add juniper berries, sauerkraut, cider or wine, thyme, and bay leaves.
9. Place all in a large brazier.
10. Caramelize ribs in peanut oil for about 5 minutes, until quite brown.

11. Drain ribs and add to pot with sauerkraut mixture.
12. Distribute ribs throughout sauerkraut. Cover and cook in a 350° oven for 2 to 2½ hours.
13. Serve with potato dumplings.

Sauerbraten

There are many different styles of sauerbraten in the Rhineland. The traditional vinegar marinade is one; in Bavaria, beer is often used instead; and in northern Germany, you will run across a buttermilk marinade. This version is fairly traditional, substituting dry red wine for half the vinegar. The resultant dish is not quite so "sour."

Yield: 8 to 10 portions

INGREDIENTS

approx. 5 lb. beef, eye of round or rump
2 c. red wine vinegar
2 c. dry red wine
2 c. water
1 c. mirepoix
½ tsp. minced garlic
1 tbsp. juniper berries
8 whole cloves
1 tsp. black pepper
2 tsp. salt
¼ c. clarified butter
1 c. flour
1 c. raisins or currants
¼ c. brown roux
1 c. sour cream

Method

1. Place beef in a nonreactive bowl, stainless steel or glass.
2. In a saucepan, combine vinegar, wine, water, mirepoix, garlic, juniper berries, cloves, pepper, and salt. Bring to a boil. Cool.
3. Pour marinade over the beef and marinate for several hours or overnight. Turn occasionally.
4. Remove the beef from the marinade and dry thoroughly.

5. Heat the butter in a large casserole or Dutch oven. Spread the flour on a large plate and dredge the beef in the flour. Sear on all sides, including the ends.
6. Add marinade to casserole. Bring to boil. Reduce to a simmer and cook, covered, for approximately 2½ hours.
7. When the meat is tender but not shredding, remove the meat to a warm place while you make the sauce.
8. Strain the marinade and place it back in the casserole. Add the raisins or currants. Reduce until you have approximately 3 cups of liquid.
9. Using a wire whip, add the roux, a little at a time. Should you have too much, don't insist on incorporating all of it. The sauce should coat the back of a spoon.
10. Incorporate the sour cream with the whip. Check for salt and pepper.
11. Slice the beef into ¼-inch slices. Serve on a bed of the sauce and lightly nap the top of the beef as well.

Note: The accompanying starch is most often a potato dumpling. An egg noodle will serve nicely. You will occasionally see the Red Cabbage Allemande in Bavaria. A relish or preserves normally accompanies the meat.

What You Need to Know

When I am braising or boiling a large piece of meat, I check for doneness by plunging a large cook's fork into the center of the meat. If you can lift the piece of meat straight up and it clings to the fork, it is not done. If the meat slips off the fork and you must tip it to the side to gain leverage to lift the meat, it is done.

Spaetzle Noodles

This is the basic Teutonic "dumpling" dough. These spaetzle are served with many braised meat dishes.

INGREDIENTS
4 eggs, lightly beaten
3 c. flour, sifted
1 c. milk
1 tsp. salt
¼ tsp. baking powder

Method

1. Bring a pot of salted water to a boil, reduce the heat, and maintain a simmer.
2. In a bowl, stir all the ingredients together.
3. Place a colander over the pan, pour about one-quarter of the batter into the colander, and press through the holes with a rubber scraper or the back of a large spoon.
4. When the spaetzle starts to float to the surface, cover the pan and simmer until the spaetzle appears to puff slightly.
5. Remove the dumplings and repeat the procedure with the remaining batter.

Spaetzle Cheese Noodles

If you find plain boiled dumplings a little bland for your palate, give this variation a try.

Yield: 4 servings

INGREDIENTS

¼ c. butter
3 c. sliced yellow onions
6 oz. Emmenthaler cheese, grated
1 tbsp. dry mustard
4 c. spaetzle noodles (page 265)
2 tbsp. minced chives

Method

1. Heat butter in fry pan, add onions, and brown lightly.
2. Toss the Emmenthaler with the dry mustard.
3. Thoroughly combine onions, cheese, and spaetzle.
4. Bake in a buttered casserole at 350° for 25 to 30 minutes.
5. Sprinkle with chives just before service.

You might also try these potatoes with the sauerbraten.

Reibelkuchen
(Potato Pancakes)

This is just one of the many Teutonic variations on the "potato pancake" theme. I like it.

Yield: 6 to 8 portions

INGREDIENTS

4 potatoes, large, 80-count baker
¾ c. milk
1 c. minced onion
2 eggs
½ c. flour
salt, to taste
black pepper, to taste
½ c. clarified butter

(**Method**)

1. Using the large hole on the grater, grate the potatoes into the milk. Allow them to soak for 10 minutes.
2. Drain the potatoes and combine with the onion, eggs, flour, salt, and pepper. Squeeze out excess liquid and form into flat patties 4 or 5 inches across.
3. Cook in hot clarified butter until golden brown on the first side; turn and cook until golden brown on the second side.
4. Drain on toweling. Hold them in a warm oven while you prepare the rest.

Swiss Steak

Is there not a Swiss Defamation League? Just what *is* a "Swiss steak"? The Swiss steak is an individually braised piece of meat, most often beef—most often round, sometimes chuck—found nowadays in "family restaurants," schools, prisons, truck stops, and "three-vegetable plate" diners in the Midwest and the South. The reason? It's cheap. The Swiss steak can be a wonderful way to use the tougher cuts of beef. Grillades (page 254) is a spicy Swiss steak dish. This dish is generic and subject to almost infinite variation. Serve with egg noodles or boiled or mashed potatoes.

Yield: 6 to 8 portions

INGREDIENTS

6–8 beef round steaks, 5–6 oz. each
1 c. flour
salt, to taste
black pepper, to taste
½ c. clarified butter (or cooking oil)
½ c. finely minced onion
1 tsp. minced garlic
3 c. brown stock (page 285)
¼ c. tomato purée
2 bay leaves
1 tsp. whole thyme
¼ c. brown roux

Method

1. Lightly pound the steaks with a veal pounder or the side of a meat hammer. Dry.
2. Salt and pepper the steaks and dredge in the flour. Shake off excess.
3. In a large casserole or sauté pan, heat the butter or oil until quite hot.
4. Brown the steaks well on both sides and transfer to a casserole, brazier, or Dutch oven.
5. Brown the onions in the fat. Add garlic for final 30 seconds of browning. Add to meat.
6. Add brown stock, tomato purée, bay leaves, and thyme to the meat.
7. Cover and cook in a 350° oven for 1½ hours. Check for tenderness.
8. Remove meat and thoroughly incorporate roux.
9. Return meat to sauce and serve.

Feel free to add just about anything you like to this basic recipe. Red wine, peppers, chiles, celery, carrots, and even beer go well in the dish.

Try this cabbage as a side with the Swiss Steak.

Red Cabbage Allemande

This is the classic sweet/sour red cabbage dish served all over Europe.

Yield: 8 to 10 servings

INGREDIENTS

1 head red cabbage (2½–3 lb.)
½ c. red wine vinegar

3 tbsp. sugar
6–8 juniper berries
1 c. thinly sliced yellow onion
1 c. peeled and thinly sliced tart apples (Granny Smith or Pippin)
¼ c. butter
2 c. chicken or beef stock
salt, to taste
black pepper, to taste
½ c. dry red wine

Method

1. Shred cabbage and place it in a mixing bowl.
2. Combine vinegar and sugar.
3. Crush juniper berries with the flat of a knife and add to vinegar mixture.
4. Marinate cabbage in vinegar mixture while you prepare the rest of the ingredients.
5. Sweat onions and apples in butter in a large sauté pan until they are tender.
6. Add cabbage and marinade and raise heat to high. Simmer for 5 minutes.
7. Add stock, salt, pepper, and red wine and simmer, covered, for about another 20 minutes. Serve when most of the liquid has evaporated and the cabbage is tender.

Ragu alla Bolognese

You may find surprising that the following dish is not in the chapter on sauces. Look at the dish while you remember the parameters that define a braised dish. First you brown the meat, then you add liquid and cook until the meat is tender.

You are browning meat in hot fat (albeit *very* small pieces of meat), adding some vegetables and liquids and cooking until done: a good working definition of a braised dish.

The batch size is 20 servings—yes, 20 servings. You will want to keep this on hand. Freezing will not harm the texture of ground meat. In Bologna, they call this sauce a *ragu*. You may note the similarity between *ragu* and *ragout*, the French stew. Both are derived from a Latin word meaning to "excite the appetite." Technically, too, though the pieces of meat are quite small in the ragu (ground), both are made with the stewing or braising technique.

This recipe will feed more than the six to eight persons in most of the recipes in this book. My standard operating procedure includes giving you recipes for larger amounts when the preparation time for a given dish goes over a couple of hours.

INGREDIENTS

1 c. extra virgin olive oil
3 c. diced yellow onion
1½ c. finely diced carrot
1½ c. diced celery
4½ lb. ground chuck
1 lb. ground pork
¼ c. minced fresh basil
2 tbsp. oregano
2 tbsp. finely minced garlic
2 c. dry white wine
1½ c. half-and-half
nutmeg, pinch
1 #10 can Italian tomatoes with juice
1 qt. chicken or beef stock
2 c. tomato purée
2 tbsp. salt
1 tbsp. black pepper

You may also include ground veal in the meat mix. Pancetta is also added by some Bolognese. Chicken livers are a common addition as well.

Method

1. Sauté onion, carrot, and celery in olive oil until just tender.
2. Add ground beef to pan and sauté until lightly browned.
3. Add basil, oregano, and garlic and continue to sauté.
4. Deglaze with wine and simmer until wine evaporates.
5. Add half-and-half and nutmeg. Simmer until half-and-half disappears.
6. Add tomatoes, stock, purée, salt, and pepper. Simmer for about 3 hours, uncovered. Skim the fat periodically.

The sauce is traditionally served with tagliatelle and lasagne. Most Americans think of this sauce as "spaghetti" sauce.

BRAISING POULTRY

Most of the chickens, turkeys, and ducks available in this country do not require the braising technique. They are young and tender. Traditionally, braising has been reserved for tough old birds that were not producing anymore, whatever it was they were supposed to produce. You will occasionally see an old stewing bird in the supermarkets in this country.

There are, however, some dishes that you braise out of preference. Coq au Vin (page 272) is a good example, as is Chicken Cacciatoria (page 272). These are classic dishes that people have come to like over the centuries. All domestic turkeys in this country are slaughtered at a young, tender age. Older ducks and pheasants will require this technique.

Quail Braised with Sauerkraut and Champagne

I devised this dish using quail I obtained from a fine gentleman named Tommy Crook, who had the Gibson Bayou Quail farm in Arkansas. I also used Schramsberg Cremant, a slightly sweet sparkling wine. I prepared the dish for Jamie Davis of Schramsberg Winery in California. She asked permission to use it in a cookbook she was compiling for the winery.

INGREDIENTS

6–8 whole dressed quail
salt, to taste
black pepper, to taste
1 tbsp. fresh minced sage
1 c. flour
½ c. clarified butter
6–8 slices bacon, cut into lardons
1 c. diced onion
1½ lb. sauerkraut, drained and rinsed under cold water
½ c. peeled and grated potato (Red or White Rose)
6–8 fresh rosemary sprigs
12 oz. Cremant champagne or sparkling wine

Method

1. Dry the quail and salt and pepper it.
2. Rub the quail inside and out with the sage. Dredge the birds in the flour.
3. Brown the quail on all sides in hot clarified butter. Remove the quail.
4. Brown the bacon in the butter. Remove.
5. Sauté the onion in the bacon fat and butter. Remove.
6. Combine the bacon, onion, sauerkraut, and potato.
7. Place the sauerkraut mixture in a casserole and spread evenly.
8. Insert a sprig of rosemary in each quail. Place the quail on the sauerkraut mixture.
9. Pour the Cremant over all.
10. Cook in a 400° oven, covered, for 20 to 25 minutes.

Chicken Cacciatoria

Cacciatoria means "in the manner of the hunter." My guess? Hunters during the Middle Ages were wealthier people, and only they could afford to eat poultry on a regular basis. Also, when the hunters were in the woods, they would be surrounded by mushrooms.

Yield: 6 portions

INGREDIENTS

2–3 chickens
¼ c. extra virgin olive oil
2 oz. salt pork or blanched bacon, diced
¼ c. clarified butter or olive oil
1 c. thinly sliced onions
1 c. quartered mushrooms
1 tbsp. minced garlic
1 tbsp. whole oregano
1 tbsp. fresh minced basil
2 tbsp. minced parsley
6 c. canned Italian "Pear" tomatoes
3 c. beef or chicken stock
¼ c. tomato purée
salt, to taste
black pepper, to taste

(**Method**)

1. Disjoint chickens as for a Poulet Sauté (page 202). Thoroughly dry and salt and pepper the pieces.
2. Heat olive oil and add salt pork or bacon. Sauté until lightly browned.
3. Add chicken pieces and sauté until golden brown on both sides.
4. Add onions; cook until softened and they begin to brown.
5. Add mushrooms.
6. Add spices and tomatoes with juice. Add stock.
7. Add purée, salt, and pepper.
8. Cover and simmer for 20 to 25 minutes. Serve on a base of thin, cooked pasta. Pour sauce over all.

Coq au Vin (Rouge)

This is a very old braised dish, its origins somewhat shrouded by the haze of time. With the tender young chickens available today, there is no real necessity for braised chicken other than as a taste preference. This dish was most likely designed originally for either the old hen whose egg output had dropped drastically or the impotent rooster. The original pork in the dish was probably not bacon; it was, in all likelihood, fresh pork. Use any good, dry red wine that you would drink for the dish.

Yield: 8 portions

INGREDIENTS

8–12 strips bacon, diced into lardons (pieces ½ in. by 1 in.)
6 tbsp. clarified butter
salt, to taste
black pepper, to taste
2 chickens, disjointed as for a poulet sauté
1 tbsp. minced garlic
2 oz. brandy
12–16 boiling onions
12–16 mushrooms
4 c. dry red wine
2 c. chicken stock
½ c. peeled, seeded, and chopped tomatoes
2 bay leaves
1 tsp. whole thyme
¼ c. flour

Method

1. Brown the bacon in 2 tablespoons of the clarified butter. Remove bacon from pan and drain.
2. Remove excess fat from pan—leave just enough to sauté the chicken pieces.
3. Dry the chicken well; salt and pepper it and sauté it in the fat.
4. Add garlic to pan. Sauté briefly.
5. Deglaze with the brandy. When the flames have subsided, add the red wine.
6. Add tomatoes, bacon, bay leaves, and thyme to pot. Cover and simmer for about 25 minutes.
7. While the chicken is simmering, first brown the mushrooms, then the boiling onions, in 2 tablespoons of the clarified butter in a fry pan.
8. Remove the mushrooms from the pan, add ½ cup of the chicken stock, and place a lid on the pan. Reduce the heat and simmer the onions for about 10 minutes.
9. At the end of the 25-minute cooking period for the chicken, remove it from the pot and place it in a bowl or on a plate with the onions and mushrooms.

10. Make a brown roux with the remaining butter and the flour. Using a wire whip, incorporate this roux into the wine mixture in the pot.

11. Place chicken, onions, and mushrooms in the pot, cover, and simmer for an additional 5 minutes.

BRAISING SEAFOOD

Well, really, it's just not done. There is no need. Braising is useful primarily for tougher foods. Seafoods are tender foods by nature. The following French classic from Brittany is as close as you come to braising seafood. Be careful here; it is *very* easy to overcook the lobster.

Homard à l'Américaine

When you see the appendage *l'Américaine*, it probably comes originally from the Roman name for Brittany, which was *Amorica*. In point of fact, the expression most often implies that the dish contains tomatoes, white wine, tarragon, shallots, and brandy.

Yield: Allow one lobster for every two people you are serving

INGREDIENTS

3 Atlantic or Maine lobsters
4 tbsp. clarified butter
2 Brunoise carrots
1 Brunoise onion
1 tbsp. finely minced garlic
4 tbsp. finely minced shallot
¼ c. brandy
2 c. peeled, seeded, and diced tomatoes
1 c. chicken stock
1 c. dry white wine
1 tbsp. tarragon
6 tbsp. cold butter
salt, to taste
black pepper, to taste
3 tbsp. minced parsley

Method

1. Cut lobster into segments. I tell you how to commit *lobstercide* on page 49. Sauté in hot clarified butter *just* until shell reddens. Remove the lobster from the pan.

2. Sweat onion and carrot in the clarified butter for 3 or 4 minutes.
3. Add garlic and shallots and sweat an additional 2 or 3 minutes.
4. Deglaze with the brandy.
5. Add tomatoes, stock, wine, and tarragon to the pan. Simmer for 10 to 15 minutes to reduce by about one-third.
6. Slowly add the cold butter to the pan, incorporating a little at a time, either with a wire whip or by swirling the pan.
7. Return lobster to the pan and warm through. Do not boil.
8. Add salt, pepper, and parsley.

This is one of my very favorite southwestern meals. I think the meal as I serve it works well and is complete. So, here I will offer you the entire menu as I did with the Thanksgiving meal on page 13.

Carnitas

This is a word that simply derives from the Spanish word for "flesh." In fact, it is a tougher piece of meat cooked until it begins to shred, seasoned and spiced, and is meant to be mixed with one of the following sauces. Carnitas usually refers to beef. A very descriptive term was coined by my younger son, B.J.—when he was quite young—for meat cooked to this stage. He calls it "string meat." He liked it, primarily, initially, I think, because it is easy to eat.

There are several choices for the technique here. We have chosen "braising," for we feel it provides the best combination of flavor and texture.

Our two choices of meat here are among the "stringiest" available: the beef brisket for the Colorado and the pork shoulder or "Boston Butt" for the Verde. The techniques and seasonings for the two meats are the same.

INGREDIENTS

4–5 lb. boneless pork shoulder or beef brisket
½ c. peanut oil
3 tbsp. minced garlic
2 tbsp. black pepper
2 tbsp. cumin
2 tbsp. whole oregano
boiling water, to cover
1 tbsp. salt
1 tbsp. cinnamon
2 tsp. cayenne pepper

> **Method**

1. You may proceed for the initial caramelization in one of two manners. Either cut the meat into small chunks (2 by 2 inches) and sauté in the peanut oil in a sauté pan or dry and brown the whole piece of meat in the oven and then add the liquid. In either case, you will first caramelize the meat and then simmer it in the liquid. The sautéing will be quicker but if you have the time; 3 to 4 hours in the oven will work just as well.
2. Brown the meat by whichever method you choose and then combine the meat with the boiling water and all spices and herbs in a pot. Return the liquid to the boil on high heat, reduce to a simmer, and place the lid on the pot. Simmer for 2 to 2½ hours or until the meat begins to "string."
3. Remove meat from liquid and shred with either a knife or your fingers.
4. This is the unique step in this dish. First we caramelized the meat and then cook in it a liquid. Now we are going to sauté it to add some flavor and texture. Dry the meat and sauté it briefly in the oil with the cumin, cinnamon, cayenne pepper, salt, and pepper.
5. Bind the meat with either the Colorado (beef) or the Verde (pork) and heat. I serve the Carnitas with Chiles Rellenos (page 279), flour tortillas (page 281), rice and Frijoles Refritos (page 280), and Salsa Fresca (page 278).

Chili and Chiles

What is the difference between *chili* and *chile*? There shouldn't be any, in theory. But there is, in fact. Both words derive from the Spanish name for members of the capsicum family, a name they borrowed from the Aztecs. Both spellings are commonly used and may mean many different things. In this book, I use the "chile" spelling for the following sauces (and for the peppers themselves) and "chili" for the red meat (and, often, bean) soup/stew made all over the United States. I'll delve a little deeper into "chili" in my "Chili con Frijoles" recipe (page 325). These two sauces, Chile Colorado and Chile Verde, are the backbones of southwestern cuisine. Note that I use dried chiles for the red sauce and fresh chiles for the green.

Chile Colorado
(Red Chile Sauce)

INGREDIENTS

18 dried Ancho chiles
boiling water, to cover
¼ c. peanut oil

3 tbsp. flour
1 tsp. cumin
1 tsp. minced garlic
4 c. peeled, seeded, and chopped tomatoes
1 c. tomato purée
salt, to taste
1 tbsp. cayenne pepper (or other hot chile powder)

Method

1. Pick chiles over, remove stems, and cut in half.
2. Roast chiles in a heavy pan or skillet for 4 or 5 minutes—until skins blister.
3. Place chiles in a bowl and pour boiling water over them. Allow them to steep for 15 minutes or so.
4. Make a light brown roux with the oil, flour, and cumin. Add the garlic to this mixture.
5. Purée the chiles with about half the water in the food processor.
6. Push chiles through a sieve.
7. In a saucepan, combine chile mixture with roux and blend thoroughly. Add oregano and salt.
8. Add tomatoes and enough of the remaining liquid to achieve a sauce consistency. Add cayenne pepper. Simmer for 5 minutes.

Chile Verde
(Green Chile Sauce)

INGREDIENTS

3 tbsp. peanut oil
1 yellow onion, minced
1 tbsp. minced garlic
3 tbsp. flour
½ tsp. black pepper
½ tsp. cumin
2½ c. chicken stock or pork broth
12–16 green chiles, roasted and peeled
12–16 tomatillos, husked and pureed
2 or 3 jalapeños or serranos
½ tsp. whole oregano
salt, to taste

┌─────────────[**What You Need to Know**]─────────────┐

Roasting and peeling chiles: Go to your attic or basement or garage and rummage around until you find that old fondue set you have. You won't need the pot, just the forks. They are great to roast the chiles over open flame without roasting you. The little barbs cling well even as the chile roasts and softens. Impale the chile in the top next to the stem and set it over open flames on your stove. Thoroughly blacken the chile all over, rotating it as necessary, before you remove it from the fire. Roll loosely in plastic wrap and let it sweat for a few minutes before peeling.

└──┘

If you don't plan to stuff the chile (and I don't here), slice it in half vertically, flatten it, and scrape away all the black and remove the seeds. Some say rinse; some, don't. I hold with those who favor don't and usually won't, but if I had to cleanse it twice, rinsing's nice and will suffice.

[**Method**]

1. Heat the oil over medium-high heat.
2. Reduce heat and add onion and garlic and sweat for 4 to 5 minutes.
3. Add flour and cumin and thoroughly incorporate. Cook the roux for 3 or 4 minutes. Add pepper.
4. Add stock or broth and incorporate with a wire whip.
5. Mince chiles and jalapeños or serranos; add to pan. Add tomatillos.
6. Add salt and simmer for 25 to 30 minutes.

The following salsa is a very simple one that lends itself to many applications. I am sure my old friend Spencer Moore would approve of it. Although he has a restaurant in Cabo San Lucas, he is known as the "Salsa King" in Reno, Nevada. It's a long story; he'll have to tell you about it.

Salsa Fresca with Cilantro

INGREDIENTS

12 Roma tomatoes, finely chopped
1–2 bell peppers, minced
1–2 jalapeños, finely sliced
4 green onions, minced
1 tbsp. minced garlic

1 c. tomato or V8 juice
1 tbsp. fresh minced cilantro
1 tsp. cumin
salt, to taste
black pepper, to taste

If you desire the salsa hotter, you may add some crushed red pepper, serrano chiles, habañeros, or more jalapeños. Mango or papaya may also be added to the salsa.

Chiles Rellenos

I teach my students a few southwestern dishes and techniques. (See the Chile Colorado on page 276 and the Chile Verde on page 277.) This stuffed chile dish has a light batter that you may use with other fried foods. Look at the Chile Verde recipe on page 277 for tips on how to roast and peel chiles.
Yield: 6 to 8 portions

INGREDIENTS

6–8 green chiles, roasted and peeled
6–8 oz. Monterey Jack, goat cheese, or Queso Blanco
1 c. flour
1 recipe batter
2 c. peanut oil (for frying)

Batter for Chiles Rellenos

INGREDIENTS

3 eggs
1 c. milk
1 c. flour
1 tsp. salt
1½ tbsp. peanut oil or corn oil

Method

1. Separate the eggs.
2. Using a food processor, mix all the ingredients for the batter together, except the egg whites.
3. Allow the batter to relax for about 30 minutes.

4. Whip the egg whites until stiff and gently fold them into the batter with a rubber scraper.
5. Cut the cheese into pieces no larger than your little finger.
6. Stuff the chiles with the cheese.
7. Heat the peanut oil to approximately 360°.
8. Carefully dry the chiles, dredge them in the flour, and coat with the batter.
9. Fry the chiles in the peanut oil until golden brown on both sides, turning halfway through the cooking. This will take only about 2 minutes.
10. Drain on toweling and serve with a southwestern-style chile–tomato sauce, such as Chile Colorado (page 276).

Frijoles

Beans are an essential element in the cooking of the American Southwest and all of Central and South America. Served with rice, they are an inexpensive "filler" and are very nearly complete nutritionally.

Yield: 10 to 12 portions

INGREDIENTS

3 c. pinto beans, washed, boiled, and soaked
1 large yellow onion, minced
2 tbsp. minced garlic
¼ lb. salt pork or bacon, roughly chopped
2 tsp. cumin
2 tsp. oregano
salt, to taste
black pepper, to taste
water, to cover

Method

1. Place all ingredients in a pot and bring to a boil.
2. Reduce to a simmer and cook, covered, for approximately 3 hours. Be sure you have ample water—at least twice as much water as beans.

Frijoles Refritos

Heat about ¼ cup of high-quality oil or bacon fat in a skillet until quite hot. Add one minced onion to the fat and sauté. Add one minced onion to the fat and sauté until soft. Using a skimmer, add about 4 cups of beans to the fat and onion. Put a little of the bean liquid in with a ladle and mash them as you sauté them. I use a veal pounder for this procedure.

Flour Tortillas

INGREDIENTS

2 c. flour
1 tsp. baking powder
1 tsp. salt
6 tbsp. shortening
approx. ½ c. water

Method

1. Place all ingredients except water in food processor and process until thoroughly combined.
2. Add just enough water for the dough to form a ball in the processor bowl. Dough should be smooth—not "gummy" to the touch.
3. Wrap dough in plastic wrap and allow it to rest at room temperature for about 30 minutes.
4. Separate dough into 12 equal pieces.
5. Form dough into balls, flatten, and roll into 6- or 7-inch rounds.
6. Bake tortillas on a medium-hot griddle, approximately 1 minute per side. Twist the tortilla immediately after turning. This will cause it to rise somewhat.
7. Place on a plate and cover. You may reheat the tortillas in a warm oven, wrapped in foil, for about 5 minutes.

Braising: A Final Fillip or Two

If you take away with you from this chapter that braising is used principally as a method for making tougher pieces of food tender and tasty, without cooking them any longer than necessary, then you have grasped the basics of what braising is all about. Any dish that can be braised could be boiled, too. You braise because you like meats caramelized. The few poultry dishes that do not involve tough food that I have included are merely taste preferences or classic dishes. Wild game of unknown age is nearly always better braised than cooked with any of the other techniques. The Pot Stickers (page 253) are included because they are truly unique, and seafoods are far too tender to be braised; consequently, I have included just one dish. Vegetables, too, may be braised as a matter of taste.

PART V

The Fifth Technique
Extraction—Stocks, the Five Mother Sauces, Additional and Derivative Sauces, and Soups

STOCKS

THE FIVE MOTHER SAUCES

ADDITIONAL AND DERIVATIVE SAUCES

SOUPS

THIS LAST technique is quite different from the other four techniques. With all four of the previous techniques—dry heat, liquid heat, fat, and fat and liquid heat combined—the object was to keep the maximum flavor and nutrition in the solid food. All our efforts were directed to that end.

Here we are making liquid food, and our aim is to extract flavor and nutrition from solids and pull them into a liquid. Not every item in this section will involve the extraction technique, but dishes here all have one thing in common: they are all liquid food. That's why they are here with the extraction technique. I would say a full 90% of the soups contain stock, the essence of the extraction technique. One of the principal flavor-improving ingredients in all quality cookery is stock. The flavor basis of most soups, many sauces, and braised dishes is stock. There are two types of stock: brown and white. Each of these may be made with many different ingredients, but the technique is always the same.

Brown stocks are usually made from heavier, more robustly flavored meats or game—although, theoretically, you could make a brown stock from just about anything from which you would make a white stock. The main difference between the two stocks is first browning the ingredients in a hot oven. With a white stock, you place all the ingredients directly in cold water.

Beef is the meat most often used to make brown stock. Game would be a good choice here as well. You can make either a brown stock or a white stock from veal. Chicken, turkey, and fish and shellfish stocks are almost invariably white, as is vegetable stock.

Stock is an essential ingredient in two of the five mother sauces—Espagnole (page 292) and velouté (page 291)—and is frequently used in tomato sauces. Soups and all braised dishes benefit greatly from the inclusion of stock in their preparation.

STOCKS

Stock, water that has been infused with flavor from meat or fish and vegetables and herbs, is the basis of two of the mother sauces and an infinite variety of soups and, when reduced, an addition to many sauté dishes. You have to make a stock to make most sauces. There are now on the market some excellent "bases," such as fish base, beef base, and chicken base, to which you need only add water to create a stock. These bases are essences of the food mentioned, which come, usually, in the form of a paste. While they tend to be quite high in fat, they would be my first choice if stock were unavailable. There are also canned stocks—most are actually broths—available in nearly every supermarket in the country. I have found that most bouillon cubes make stocks that are too salty for my taste. I shun them.

Stocks Made Simple

Making your own stock, though, is incredibly simple and not at all time consuming. The chances are excellent that you already have most of the ingredients in your kitchen. Here are a very few simple rules for making stock of any kind:

1. Always begin with cold water. The cold water will extract both flavor and nutrition from the ingredients. Do not boil the stock. Bring it to a boil and then reduce to a simmer. For a clearer stock, skim the albumen that rises to the top.

2. Never salt stock. There are two reasons. If there is no salt in the water, the natural salts occurring in the foods (which carry much of the flavor) will migrate to the liquid, a desirable reaction. Also some stocks are reduced to 25 percent of their original volume. If the stock had the proper amount of salt at its full volume, it will be inedible when reduced.

3. Always roast the bones, trimmings, and vegetables for a brown stock.

4. The best stocks will result from a ratio of about 2 pounds of bones and trimmings for each gallon of water.

5. Leave the skins, leaves, and tops on vegetables to obtain the maximum flavor and nutrition from them.

6. You may freeze stock with absolutely no negative effect. Should you not have room in your freezer, you may also keep stock under refrigeration indefinitely if you bring it out of the refrigerator every 2 or 3 days and boil it for 20 minutes.

Brown Stock

I know this is a large quantity of liquid. Cut it in half if you don't have a large enough pot to make 5 gallons, but do make at least 2½ gallons. Take a gander at step 7 and note the simmering time required to extract flavor and nutrition from beef. It's very handy to have around and freezes with no problems whatsoever.

INGREDIENTS

10 lbs. beef and/or veal bones, scraps, oxtails, etc.
2 onions, roughly chopped
4 carrots, roughly chopped
6 ribs celery, roughly chopped
6 oz. tomato purée
4 garlic cloves, smashed
12 whole black peppercorns
1 tsp. whole thyme
6 cloves
6 bay leaves
2 or 3 sprigs parsley
5 gal. cold water

(**Method**)

1. Have the butcher or purveyor crack the bones with a cleaver or his saw. Reducing the size and opening the bones will increase the surface area exposure and enable you to extract the maximum flavor and nutrition from them.
2. Place the bones in a roasting pan large enough to hold the bones and vegetables and roast in a 450° oven for about 30 minutes or until the meat/bones are beginning to caramelize.
3. Add the vegetables and herbs and spices to the pan and continue to roast for an additional 30 minutes.
4. Place the bones and vegetables in a pot large enough to hold them and the water. Add the water. You may use a little of the water to deglaze the roasting pan and scrape off the fonds.
5. Bring the water to a boil; reduce to a simmer.
6. Skim the stock periodically.
7. Simmer for 6 to 10 hours.

The oxtails are a really significant contributor to body in this stock. They will gelatinize the stock as well.

White (Chicken) Stock

I've given you a smaller quantity for this stock because you can easily make it when you need it, and it will not take much of your time.

INGREDIENTS

4 lb. chicken bones, skin, etc.
1 or 2 onions
2 carrots
4 ribs celery
12 stems parsley
2 garlic cloves
4 bay leaves
1 tsp. whole thyme
8–12 whole black peppercorns
2 gal. cold water

[**Method**]

1. Place chicken in stockpot.
2. Wash and roughly chop onion, carrot, and celery. Do not peel vegetables. Include celery leaves. Add to chicken in stockpot.
3. Add parsley stems.
4. Smash garlic cloves with the side of your knife. Add.
5. Add spices.
6. Cover with cold water.
7. Bring to a boil, skim, and reduce heat to a simmer and cook for 2 hours.
8. Strain through a china cap. If you have the luxury of making the stock a day ahead and refrigerating it overnight, you will have a much easier time removing the fat.

In California, I was able to obtain chickens and ducks before they had been decapitated and had their feet amputated. The bills and feet, if you are able to get them, will gelatinize this stock.

What You Need to Know

Veal stock will take about 4 hours to extract the flavor and nutrition from the bones; vegetable, about 1. To make veal stock, follow the recipe for white (chicken) stock and simply substitute veal bones for the chicken.

Fish or shellfish stock requires only 30 to 45 minutes. Fish stock is made with fish bones and trimmings. Shellfish stock may be made with shrimp shells, lobster shells (cooked or uncooked), or the trimmings or shells of whatever shellfish may be involved in the dish. Vegetable stock takes about the same amount of time.

THE FIVE MOTHER SAUCES

Just as there are five cooking techniques to be mastered, there are five "mother sauces" to learn to cook like a professional. They are easily remembered by colors—two are white or off-white, one is yellow, one is brown, and one is red. The following five sauces are considered the mother sauces of classical European-inspired cookery. How did this matriarchal designation come about? The nomenclature is traceable to Antonin Carême, a French chef of the early 19th century, and was honed by Auguste Escoffier, a French chef of the first quarter of the 20th century. Both agree that if you know these five sauces, you will be able to make hundreds of derivative sauces. So now you have a total of 10 things to try to remember to cook like a pro.

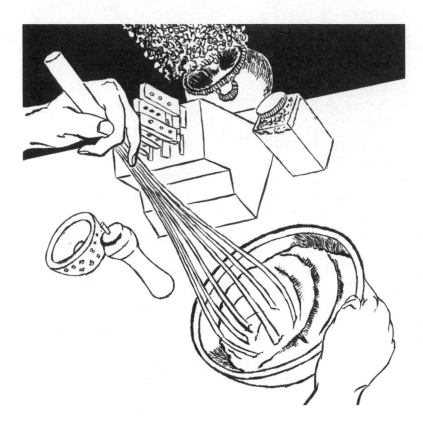

The Five Sauces: Velouté
Béchamel
Espagnole
Tomato
Hollandaise (and Mayonnaise)

Before I actually get into the five sauces, I want to say a few words about roux and clarified butter since a roux is required for the first three sauces and clarified butter for one of them.

A Few Words about Roux

Roux is a mixture of fat and flour, cooked together. Although you may use just about any fat generally recognized as safe, butter is the fat of preference in nearly all classical cookery. For certain applications, olive oil or peanut oil might be chosen.

Roux should be thought of in terms of shades. As long as you are making roux with butter, there is no true "white" roux. When chefs speak of white roux, we are talking about a roux in which the flour has not been allowed to color.

That white roux will actually be a pale blond color. The next gradation will be a medium blond, followed by a light brown, medium brown, and dark brown.

Roux, primarily used as a thickener, actually has three functions:

1. It is used to thicken sauces, soups, and stews.
2. It provides heartiness and depth of flavor in a given dish.
3. It may be a "binder." For example, certain soups, such as lentil or split pea, have a tendency to stratify in the pot with the heavier ingredients sinking to the bottom. A little roux added to the soup prevents this.

What You Need to Know

As long as your roux is to be a blond one, you may make it with whole butter. But if you wish to make a brown roux of any shade, you must use clarified butter or a cooking oil.

White or Blond Roux

Begin with equal parts of flour and fat in a saucepan, sauté pan, or fry pan with a thick bottom. The fat may be any your conscience allows. I use butter 90 percent of the time. Use a whisk or wooden spoon to stir the mixture over medium heat until the flour gives off a "cooked" smell. Remove from heat and cool immediately. This should only take 3 to 5 minutes.

Brown Roux

Again, you may use just about any fat you prefer with the single exception of whole butter. The milk-fat solids in whole butter will burn before the roux has browned. Most of my brown rouxs are made with clarified butter. But any cooking oil or pork fat or bacon fat will do, depending on your use for the roux. You will have a much longer cooking time here. And, as with the white roux, begin with equal parts of fat and flour. Begin with medium heat and lower it to low when you smell that "cooked" flour smell. Stir constantly, making sure you do not allow one part of the roux to get darker than the rest. I usually allow 15 to 20 minutes for a brown roux. Remove it from the heat before it attains the color you are looking for. The hot pan will continue to darken the roux. If it seems to be getting away from you, remove it from the pan. Do not touch the roux or get it on any part of your person you care about. It will burn you!

I gave you no specific quantities of fat and flour because how much you make doesn't matter as long as you make enough. I think roux has a half-life of

500 years. It will keep, possibly longer than you will, in the refrigerator. I will tell you what I tell my students when they ask me how much roux to make: "Make too much—always."

I know I told you previously to make your roux with a wooden spoon or whisk, but I usually don't. Roux has the proper consistency when it looks like a large, dense pancake. I nearly always make my rouxs in a fry pan with sloping sides and flip them as if I were doing a sauté. Here comes one of the most famous of caveats—don't try this at home! Roux will burn you! One of my assistants in my evening classes smelled a brown roux I was making and decided to stick his finger in it and taste it. Not a good idea. Naturally, he burned himself. (I don't administer IQ tests to potential assistants.) But, wait, he wasn't finished! He then stuck his finger in his mouth and burned it, too. I warned you.

Clarified Butter

There are two principal varieties of butter available across the United States: "unsalted" and "lightly salted." Chefs use only unsalted butter for cooking. Why? Butter is salted primarily for two reasons. Salted butter has a longer shelf life than unsalted butter, and salted butter retains more water than unsalted butter. It is difficult for me to see where either of these reasons is a benefit to you or me. Additionally, since I infinitely prefer the flavor of unsalted butter, I use it exclusively. If the butter producers were proud of the salt in their butter, why would they select the adverb "lightly"?

What You Need to Know

The principal difference between American and European butter is the butterfat content. American butters run about 80 percent butterfat, while European butters are in the 82 to 84 percent range. European butters are also allowed to "ripen" a little before sale. Of course, European butter aficionados also claim that *terroir*, the field or area where the cows were eating, plays a significant role in flavor, too.

Why "clarified" butter? Butter consists, primarily, of three visible constituents: water, butterfat, and milk-fat solids. When you melt the butter very slowly over low heat, it will separate into these three components, with the water rising to the top, the butterfat remaining in the center, and the heavier milk-fat solids falling to the bottom. If you have ever heated butter to a very high temperature, you have seen it turn first brown, then black. The water dissipates, and the solids burn. You clarify butter to eliminate this burning. Folks in India from whom we inherited clarified butter do it a little differently. They allow some caramelization of the milk-fat solids before they remove them—this is *ghee*. It has a stronger, more caramelized flavor than the Western version.

Attempting to clarify less than 1 pound of butter at a time is frustrating—and difficult. Two would provide even more satisfactory results. It lasts well in the refrigerator, and you'll have it when you need it.

Place the butter in a saucepan over very low heat. Students of mine have told me they achieved very satisfactory results performing this operation in a microwave oven. When the butter has completely melted, remove the water and the lighter milk-fat solids from the top with a shallow ladle or large spoon. The clear liquid lying below this layer is the clarified, or "drawn," butter. Carefully pour this middle layer off into another container. Remaining in the bottom of your pan will be a residue of the heavier milk-fat solids. You may use both the top and the bottom layers to enhance the flavor of cooked vegetables—or even popcorn.

Velouté

Let's begin with one of the two basic white sauces. You're now ready to make the velouté. There's no historical anecdote involved here. "Velouté" simply means "velvety" or smooth.

INGREDIENTS
½ c. butter
4 oz. flour
1 qt. hot white stock
salt, to taste
white pepper, to taste

Method

1. Melt the butter in a fry pan or a saucepan on medium heat.
2. Add the flour and incorporate thoroughly with a wire whip.
3. Simmer the roux until the flour has cooked and has just begun to color slightly.
4. Add the roux to the stock and thoroughly incorporate.
5. Add salt and white pepper to taste. Simmer 5 minutes.
6. Strain through a sieve or china cap.
7. If the sauce is not to be used immediately, dot the top with butter.

Béchamel

This second of the white sauces is named after Louis de Bechameil, Marquis de Nointel, who was Steward of the Royal Household under Louis XIV. Since a Marquis would not likely be out in the kitchen rattling pots and pans, the sauce was probably conceived in the royal kitchen and given the Marquis' name to glorify him. Although the sauce has undergone some small transformations since its conception in the 17th century, it is still nothing more than a mixture of roux and milk. The original béchamel was probably a mixture of the velouté and the béchamel as made today. This is somewhat ironic in that when making these sauces for restaurant use, we usually combine the two.

Yield: About 3 cups

INGREDIENTS

½ c. butter
6 oz. flour
2½ c. milk
salt, to taste
white pepper, to taste
nutmeg, pinch

Method

1. Combine the butter and flour in a saucepan. Cook over medium heat, whisking constantly with a wire whip, until the flour smells cooked and a light golden color is achieved. It will have virtually no smell until it is cooked. Remove from heat.
2. You just made a blond roux.
3. Bring the milk to a simmer in another saucepan.
4. Using the whip, thoroughly incorporate the roux into the milk.
5. Add salt, pepper, and nutmeg.
6. Strain the sauce to remove any little bits of flour that may not have been thoroughly incorporated.
7. Dot the top of the sauce with a little butter and set aside until needed.

Sauce Espagnole

The first great French chef, Marie-Antoine Carême, who plied his art during the first third of the 19th century, gives a complicated recipe for this sauce in his *Le Patissier Royal Parisien*. That volume is filled with Carême's outrage over all the cookbooks being published by those entirely ignorant of the art of cookery. I guess things don't change that much. At any rate, here is my somewhat simplified, modern version of this classic sauce.

Yield: About 2 quarts

INGREDIENTS

¼ c. diced carrot
¼ c. diced celery
¼ c. diced onion
¼ lb. bacon, blanched and diced
1 c. tomato purée
½ tsp. whole thyme
2 bay leaves
½ c. dry white wine
2 qt. hot brown stock
½ c. clarified butter
½ c. flour
1 tsp. salt
½ tsp. black pepper

Method

1. In a fry pan or sauté pan, cook the carrots, celery, and onion in a couple of tablespoons of the clarified butter over medium heat until just soft.
2. Add the blanched bacon and cook gently for 4 to 5 minutes.
3. Add thyme and bay leaves. Deglaze with white wine.
4. Add vegetable mixture to the hot stock in a saucepan.
5. Make a brown roux with the remaining butter and the flour.
6. Incorporate the roux into the stock and vegetable mixture with a wire whisk.
7. Incorporate the tomato purée and salt and pepper in the sauce.
8. Simmer for 2 hours, stirring occasionally.
9. Strain through a sieve or china cap.
10. Refrigerate until needed.

What You Need to Know

Very often in professional chef's recipes, you will see "demi-glace" as an ingredient. In order to make demi-glace, you will need to first make both the brown stock and the Espagnole. Sure you want to get into this?

Demi-Glace

Yield: 1 gallon

INGREDIENTS

1 gal. Espagnole sauce
1 gal. brown stock
1 bouquet garni

[**Method**]

1. In a stockpot, combine the Espagnole sauce, brown stock, and bouquet garni.
2. Place over medium-high heat. Bring up to a boil, reduce the heat to medium low, and simmer until the liquid reduces by half. This will probably take about 1½ hours.
3. Skim occasionally. Season with salt and pepper. Strain through a china cap.

For those of you with lives, there is a product on the market called "Demi-Glace Gold." Many fine dining restaurants use it. If you do have a life, I hope it is a rewarding one since this product will run you about $33.00 per pound.

Tomato Sauce or Salsa di Pomodori or Sauce Tomate au Maigre

The Roma tomato will make the best sauce. This is the tomato the Italians use. It has fewer seeds than most tomatoes and a better color and flavor than the other tomatoes available most of the year. If you are able to acquire fresh, home-grown, or fresh heirloom tomatoes, by all means use them.

Much of the year, though, you are better off using the canned Italian Roma tomatoes as opposed to the "fresh" tomatoes available in the supermarket or from wholesale produce dealers. These tomatoes, for the most part, are sold to the produce dealer green. They are then placed in a sealed chamber, and gases are added to ripen them. Of course, they never develop the flavor, or nutritional value, a vine-ripened tomato has.

Yield: About 1 quart

INGREDIENTS

1 onion, finely diced
1 carrot, finely diced
1 tsp. minced garlic
¼ c. extra virgin olive oil
12–16 Roma tomatoes, peeled and seeded

½ c. tomato purée
2 tbsp. fresh basil
½ tsp. salt
black pepper, to taste

Method

1. Cook onion, carrot, and garlic in olive oil over low heat in a sauce pan until just softened, about 5 minutes. Do not brown.
2. Add tomatoes, puree, basil, salt, and pepper.
3. Simmer, covered, for about 45 minutes.
4. Pass the sauce through a food mill or process in the food processor. The food mill is better because it will rid the tomatoes of their seeds.
5. Use or refrigerate.

What You Need to Know

For fresh tomatoes, place a pot of water on the stove and bring it to a boil. With a paring knife, make an X-shaped slit in the bottom of each tomato. Immerse the tomatoes in the water to which you have added salt and boil until the skin begins to pull away from the pulp. Remove. Peel back the skin with the paring knife. Cut the tomato in half lengthwise and remove the seeds.

Hollandaise Sauce

This last of the five mother sauces might properly be placed in the chapter with eggs instead of here because it is an egg emulsion sauce. It has virtually nothing in common with the other mother sauces. The technique for making the sauce is completely different. I include it here because it is one of the five classic mother sauces and one you must know how to make. I don't want it to get lost in another chapter.

The other four mother sauces lend themselves to almost infinite variations—that's why they are called mother sauces. Hollandaise has only three or four logical wrinkles, the best known of which is béarnaise. Hollandaise is the mother sauce of the *warm* egg emulsion sauces. Mayonnaise, the mother sauce of the cold group of egg emulsion sauces, has many offspring. It is the versatile player here, and I have several versions throughout the book.

The egg emulsion group of sauces consists of any sauce that is a combination of eggs and fat. Notice we make these warm egg emulsion sauces on direct heat. Do not be afraid—you can do it!

However, the warm egg emulsion sauces do not like a *lot* of heat, or the eggs will scramble. They do not favor cold, or they will separate. These sauces must be kept *warm* while holding for service.

This egg emulsion sauce gives rise to the fewest derivative sauces, probably because it is so good as it is. A 19th-century French sauce, it has a much newer name. The original name was probably *Sauce Isigny* from the name of a village in Normandy famous for its butter. During World War I, France had to import much of its butter from Holland. This gave birth to hollandaise sauce. This is the mother sauce of the *warm* egg emulsion group of sauces.

INGREDIENTS

4 egg yolks
2 tbsp. lemon juice
cayenne pepper, to taste
1 tsp. Dijon mustard
½ tsp. salt
2½ c. butter, melted and hot

Method

1. Combine egg yolks, lemon juice, cayenne pepper, Dijon, and salt in a stainless mixing bowl and beat thoroughly with wire whisk.
2. Place bowl on low heat, directly on the burner on the stove.
3. Whisk the egg mixture constantly until the mixture begins to set. When you can begin to see the bottom of the bowl through the mixture, the eggs are beginning to set.
4. Remove from heat immediately and begin incorporating the butter in a slow steady stream. If you notice at this point that you don't seem to have enough hands to hold the bowl, add the butter, and use the whip, I have a solution. Dampen a kitchen towel, form it into a small circle, and set the mixing bowl on it. This procedure will stabilize the bowl.
5. Continue adding butter until a smooth, sauce-like consistency is achieved. Egg yolks vary somewhat in their ability to absorb fats. The Platonic ideal here is a balance between the egg and butter flavors. The eggs *will* absorb the 20 ounces of butter.

ADDITIONAL AND DERIVATIVE SAUCES

If you are able to make the five mother sauces and this handful of derivatives and incidentals, you could most likely work for me as a professional cook.

Béarnaise Sauce

Many think this sauce derives its name from Bearn in the Pyrenees. Most likely not. There is strong evidence it was called after Henry IV, who was known as "The Great Béarnaise." The Basques do not use a great deal of butter in their cookery, rendering any claim Bearn might have to this sauce feeble. Those ingesting a well-made béarnaise are not likely to be terribly concerned with its origins anyway.

INGREDIENTS

1 tbsp. minced shallots
2 tbsp. red wine vinegar
½ tsp. coarsely ground black pepper
1 tbsp. tarragon
1 tbsp. lemon juice
4 egg yolks
2½ c. butter, melted and warm
salt, to taste

Method

1. Combine shallots, vinegar, pepper, tarragon, and lemon juice in a nonreactive glass, stainless, enamel, or anodized aluminum sauté or saucepan.
2. Place on high heat and reduce until about 1 tablespoon of liquid remains. If you have used a thick-bottomed pan, you might want to remove it from the heat a little early since the heat retained by the pan will continue the reduction process.
3. Some chefs will strain the sauce at this point, having captured the essence of the flavors in a liquid form. I prefer to leave the shallots and tarragon in the sauce.
4. Cool the reduction slightly and, using a wire whip, thoroughly combine it with the egg yolks in a stainless mixing bowl.
5. Place the bowl over low heat and whisk constantly with a wire whip until the mixture begins to thicken and the bottom of the bowl becomes visible through the mixture.
6. Remove from heat and, using a ladle, immediately begin incorporating the butter with a wire whip—slowly at first and more rapidly as you go on.
7. Taste for salt and add as needed.

Beurre Blanc

This is a sauce you will not find in many cookbooks. Yet it is a basic tool in the repertoire of any chef who prepares French cuisine or seafood. This sauce is so lush as to approach decadence. It's also quick and simple. I know of no better sauce with fish.

INGREDIENTS

½ c. white wine vinegar
½ c. dry white wine
1 tbsp. lemon juice
1 tbsp. finely minced shallots
½ tsp. salt
¼ tsp. white pepper
2 c. butter, very cold

Method

1. Place the vinegar, wine, lemon juice, shallots, salt, and pepper in a nonreactive (glass, stainless, enamel, etc.) sauté or fry pan.
2. Place pan on high heat and reduce until only 1 or 2 tablespoons of the liquid are left. Reduce the heat to low.
3. Cut the butter into tablespoon-size pieces and begin adding to the pan gradually. Incorporate with a wire whip, agitating constantly. The trick here: Don't permit the mixture to boil. If you place your butter in the freezer for an hour or two before you make the sauce, it will help you control the temperature. You may also control the temperature by moving the pan on and off the heat as needed.
4. When all the butter has been added, check the seasoning and hold in a warm place until service.

What You Need to Know

There is a neat "cheat" for this recipe. Once you have the reduction in place, add a little heavy cream before the butter to stabilize the sauce. This is the kind of cheat I don't mind at all since the dish actually becomes a little richer.

Creole Sauce

My creole sauce is a little quicker and lighter than the traditional sauce associated with New Orleans cookery. Both this and the marchand de vin sauce (below) are made with a cornstarch "slurry."

INGREDIENTS

4 tbsp. clarified butter
1 yellow onion, julienned
2 bell peppers, julienned
2 ribs celery, thinly sliced on the bias
1 tbsp. minced garlic
½ tbsp. whole thyme
1 tsp. crushed red pepper
2 c. peeled, seeded, and chopped tomatoes
½ c. tomato purée
1 pt. shrimp or chicken stock
salt, to taste
black pepper, to taste
3 tbsp. cornstarch or arrowroot
sugar, pinch

Method

1. Heat the clarified butter in a saucepan.
2. Sweat the onion, bell pepper, and celery until soft.
3. Add garlic, thyme, and crushed red pepper and continue cooking over medium heat.
4. Add tomatoes, purée, and all stock except ½ cup and simmer for 5 minutes.
5. Add salt and pepper.
6. Thoroughly combine remaining stock (cold!) and cornstarch or arrowroot.
7. Add starch mixture to the sauce and cook until translucent.
8. Taste.

Marchand de Vin Sauce

This is the "sauce of the wine merchant."

INGREDIENTS

4 tbsp. butter
8 oz. sliced mushrooms
1 bunch green onions, minced

1 tbsp. minced garlic
2 c. beef or chicken stock
2 c. dry red wine
¼ c. tomato purée
3 tbsp. cornstarch
Tabasco, to taste
salt, to taste
black pepper, to taste

Method

1. Melt butter in saucepan on medium heat.
2. Add mushrooms and sweat briefly.
3. Add green onions. Again sweat briefly.
4. Add all other solids.
5. Add stock.
6. Add 1 cup of the wine, purée, and the Tabasco.
7. Thoroughly combine cornstarch with remaining wine and add.
8. Add salt and pepper.

Sugo di Pomodoro e Panna

This tomato-cream sauce comes from Emilia-Romagna and is often served with tortellini. This one is definitely not in the Mediterranean diet!

INGREDIENTS
½ c. clarified butter
1 c. mirepoix
6 c. canned tomatoes, with juice
2 tsp. salt
½ tsp. sugar
1½ c. heavy cream

Method

1. Briefly sweat mirepoix in the clarified butter for 2 or 3 minutes.
2. Add tomatoes, salt, and sugar.
3. Simmer for about an hour.
4. Put mixture through the food mill.
5. Return to heat and add cream. Simmer for 2 or 3 minutes.

SOUPS

From the casting of the first pots in the Bronze Age to the popularity of the "Soup Nazi" on American television, soup has played an important role in our survival as a species. An American food writer recently decided that it is even nutritious food and has a place in diets! I must admit American culture just boggles my mind on occasion.

The word "soup" itself is quite ancient, probably deriving from German root. Our modern English usage came to us through the French word "sope," which meant literally a piece of bread soaked in broth. In the Middle Ages, the evening meal was the lighter meal of the day and often consisted only of a "sop"—a piece of bread soaked in a liquid. Our word "supper" also derives from this. Still today, modern European cultures feature breads in soups, and we Americans use croutons and additives like "oyster crackers" in ours.

All soups fall into just a few basic groups:

1. *Clear soups* are soups whose base is an unadulterated stock that may or may not be clarified (page 302). The lightest of all soups are the consommés, which are a clear, clarified stock with a vegetable and/or meat or seafood garnish.
2. *Purées* are thickened naturally by either blending or processing the ingredients (or some of the ingredients) or putting the soup through a food mill.
3. *Thickened soups* may be thickened with a roux or heavy cream, eggs, or a partial purée.

Nearly all my soup recipes call for 2½ to 3 quarts of liquid (usually stock), 80 to 96 ounces. When you look at any soup recipe and want to get some idea how many people it will feed, just look at the liquid quantity. Soup is liquid food, folks. This quantity will feed eight very hungry people (12 ounces each) or a dozen temperate folk (8 ounces each).

Soups are probably the most *valuable* aspect of the extraction technique. As long as a little common sense is applied, soups may be served with nearly any meal. Don't serve a rich, heavy cream soup at the beginning of a rich, heavy meal. Among the most nutritious of foods, they seem to satisfy more than the appetite. There is something very comforting about soups. If you have a large soup repertoire, you can serve soup any time as a meal or as an adjunct to a meal. A jug of wine, a loaf of bread, and soup—no offense to *thou*—will tide you through a sea of life's tsunamis.

Consommé Clarification

Consommés are not as popular as they were at one time. Should you choose to make one, though, you will need to know how to clarify your stock, for they must be crystal clear. Common consommé garnishes are quenelles, custards, and fresh vegetables:

1. Skim all fat from the stock. This is most easily accomplished if one makes the stock the day before and refrigerates it overnight. The fat will lift right off the top when cold and congealed.
2. For every 5 cups of stock to be clarified, you will need two egg whites and ½ pound of very lean ground beef. Omit the ground beef when clarifying fish or vegetable stock.
3. Beat the egg whites and add them with the ground beef to the cold stock.
4. Bring the mixture to a boil and immediately reduce to the lowest possible simmer.
5. Simmer for 45 minutes.
6. Carefully pour the stock through a sieve lined with 5 or 6 layers of cheese-cloth into another pot.
7. Bring the stock to a boil again, reduce to a simmer, and, using paper towels, skim off any particles of fat that rise to the surface. You will notice a dramatic change in the appearance of the stock.
8. If you wish to make a double consommé, boil the stock until you have reduced its volume by half.

Four-Pepper Soup

This is a soup I devised while executive chef at Mudd's Restaurant in San Ramon in the early 1980s. I got the inspiration for many soups just wandering around the 10-acre organic garden and seeing what was coming to fruition. On this particular day, four varieties of chiles were fruiting.

Yield: 8 to 10 portions

INGREDIENTS

2 lb. various peppers (chiles), Anaheim, Poblano, bell, jalapeño, serrano, wax, yellow, red, etc.
3 qt. chicken stock
1 tbsp. chopped garlic
1 c. mirepoix
1 tbsp. fresh ginger
½ tsp. whole thyme

1 tsp. fresh minced cilantro
1 tbsp. turmeric
1 pt. heavy cream
½ c. flour
6 tbsp. clarified butter
salt, to taste
white pepper, to taste

(**Method**)

1. Roast and peel peppers. Mince.
2. Add all ingredients except cream, flour, and clarified butter to chicken stock in pot; bring to boil; reduce heat; and simmer for 30 minutes.
3. Purée soup with food processor or put it through a food mill.
4. Return soup to pot.
5. Make a blond roux with the flour and butter.
6. Add the roux to the soup and thoroughly incorporate with a wire whip.
7. Add cream to soup and check for salt and pepper.

Spicy Pumpkin Soup

Try this soup for Thanksgiving. There should be some pumpkins still hanging around.

Yield: 8 to 10 portions

INGREDIENTS

1 pumpkin, 5–6 lb.
boiling water, to cover above pumpkin
6–8 pumpkins, 1½ lb. (about 6 in. across)
2½ qt. turkey or chicken stock
1 tsp. fresh minced ginger
3 tbsp. light brown sugar
½ tsp. cinnamon
½ tsp. nutmeg
1 tsp. lemon zest
1 tsp. orange zest
1 tsp. black pepper
salt, to taste
1 c. heavy cream
¼ c. flour
3 tbsp. butter

Method

1. Wash larger pumpkin and boil for about 60 minutes.
2. Drain, cut in pieces, and scrape out seeds and fibrous material and discard.
3. Scoop out pulp and purée with a food mill or food processor.
4. Place stock, sugar, and all spices in a saucepan and bring to a simmer. Simmer for 30 minutes. Add cream.
5. While the soup is simmering, make a light blend with the flour and butter.
6. Also while the soup is simmering, cut the small pumpkins in half horizontally. Cut them a little above the equator. Scrape out the seeds and fiber and neatly trim the pumpkin.
7. Check the seasoning in the soup and correct if necessary. Ladle the soup into the pumpkin halves, return the pumpkin top, and place on a sheet pan.
8. Place in a 400° oven and heat for 15 minutes.

Potage Parmentier

Antoine-Auguste Parmentier was an 18th-century French agronomist and an economist who wrote extensively on food and was responsible for popularizing the potato in France. Today there are many dishes containing potatoes that carry the appellation "Parmentier." This is the classic leek and potato soup. The soup was probably originally a Lenten soup made with water instead of stock. This soup is also the basis of the once-popular American soup vichyssoise. To turn this magically into vichyssoise, add 1 cup of heavy cream and chill the soup. Serve with minced chives as a garnish.

Yield: 8 to 10 portions

INGREDIENTS

3 qt. chicken stock
1½ lb. potatoes, peeled and thinly sliced
1½ lb. leeks, thoroughly washed and sliced thinly
1 tbsp. salt
white pepper, to taste
1 c. heavy cream
2 tbsp. butter, softened
2 tbsp. minced parsley

Method

1. Place potatoes, leeks, salt, and pepper in a pot with the chicken stock and simmer for about 45 minutes.

2. Process in a food processor or put mixture through a food mill.
3. Heat to a simmer and incorporate cream, butter, and parsley just before serving.
4. Check for salt before serving.

Zuppe di Cozze

Serve this classic Italian mussel soup with bruschetta (page 52).
Yield: 8 to 10 portions

INGREDIENTS

4 tbsp. butter
½ tsp. minced garlic
2 tbsp. pesto
4 oz. dry white wine
3 dozen mussels, scrubbed and debearded
8 c. fish or chicken stock or clam juice
3 c. heavy cream
6 oz. angel hair or vermicelli pasta, cooked
1 c. diced tomatoes
salt, to taste
black pepper, to taste
½ tsp. lemon zest
3 tbsp. minced parsley
3 tbsp. parmesan

What You Need to Know

Debearding the mussels is no big deal. For those of you who just have to know stuff, the "beards" are actually *byssal threads*, which the mussel secretes so that it may attach itself to something. Just grab the beard between your thumb and forefinger and pull it off. It will feel like steel wool. As with oysters and clams, you will need to scrub the mussels, too.

Method

1. Sweat garlic and pesto briefly in a sauté pan in the butter.
2. Add wine, mussels, and stock and cover pan.
3. Simmer until all mussels have opened. Remove mussels.
4. Add heavy cream.
5. Cook pasta approximately 30 seconds in boiling salted water. Drain.

6. Leave the pan on low heat and add tomatoes, the remainder of butter, lemon zest, salt, pepper, and parsley.
7. Add pasta to cream mixture and thoroughly incorporate.
8. Place mussels in soup bowl and pour pasta with sauce over them.
9. Serve with freshly grated parmesan cheese.

Avgolemono
(Egg-Lemon Soup)

This Greek soup is basically chicken soup with avgolemono sauce added to it. There is another soup, served traditionally at Easter, *mageritsa*, which is also finished with the avgolemono. It is made with various and sundry internal parts of a lamb. Feel free to add the avgolemono to any broth or soup you feel would be enriched by it. The Greeks sometimes incorporate small pasta, *kritharaki*, in place of the rice. Orzo, or a thin vermicelli broken into small pieces, would work quite well. This soup is so good that even my boys ate it while growing up— and they wouldn't eat *anything*! You may add more or less lemon to the soup depending on your taste. I like it lemony.

Yield: 8 to 10 portions

INGREDIENTS

2½ qt. chicken stock
1–1½ c. long-grain rice or small pasta
cayenne pepper, pinch
1 tsp. fresh thyme
salt, to taste
white pepper, to taste
6 eggs
6 tbsp. lemon juice
2 tbsp. butter
2 tbsp. flour
1 c. heavy cream

Method

1. Bring chicken stock to a boil and add the rice or pasta.
2. Add cayenne pepper, thyme, salt, and pepper. Simmer for 20 minutes.
3. While the soup in simmering, break the eggs into a bowl and beat together with the lemon juice.
4. Make a light blond roux with the flour and butter.

5. Using a ladle, add, a little at a time, about 2 cups of the soup to the egg and lemon mixture, beating vigorously all the while. You are "tempering" the eggs here so they will not scramble when you add them to the soup.

6. Add the contents of the bowl to the soup all at once and stir vigorously. Reduce heat to a *very* low simmer.

7. With a whisk, incorporate the roux in the soup. Add cream. Do not bring to a boil!

Crawfish Bisque

This is a fairly elaborate preparation. Read the recipe through completely before you attempt it. If you are a fan of the Creole cooking of southern Louisiana, you will love this soup.

Yield: 8 to 10 portions

INGREDIENTS

12–16 whole live crawfish
3 qt. court-bouillon
1 lb. crawfish tails, cooked and cleaned
1 c. minced onion
1½ c. minced celery
2 tbsp. minced garlic
1 tsp. thyme
4 bay leaves
½ tsp. cumin
cayenne pepper, to taste
1 tsp. paprika
salt, to taste
black pepper, to taste
1 c. clarified butter
2 c. peeled, seeded, and diced tomatoes
½ c. flour
¼ c. minced parsley
1 c. bread crumbs
1 egg

Method

1. Boil crawfish in the court-bouillon. Remove and cool immediately so you don't over cook them.

2. Clean the crawfish by disjointing them at the juncture of the tail and head. Wash out the contents of the head under running water in the sink.

Remove the tail meat from the shell and devein. Add to the pound of cooked tail meat. Set aside and reserve the court-bouillon.

3. Sauté onion, celery, garlic, thyme, bay leaves, cumin, cayenne pepper, and paprika in 2 ounces of the clarified butter until all vegetables are soft and beginning to brown. Add salt and pepper.

4. Add tomatoes and continue to sauté.

5. Make a light brown roux with the remaining butter and the flour.

6. Mince the crawfish tails and the shrimp.

7. Add minced crawfish and shrimp to the vegetable mixture.

8. Thoroughly incorporate.

9. Set aside approximately 1 cup of the mixture. Cool. Add the remaining mixture to the court-bouillon in a stock pot.

10. In a mixing bowl, combine and thoroughly incorporate the bread crumbs and egg with the 1 cup of the mixture you have set aside. Stuff the crawfish heads with this mixture.

11. Using a wire whisk, incorporate the roux into the court-bouillon.

12. Bring the bisque to a simmer. Heat the heads for about 5 minutes in the bisque. Garnish the bisque with the heads and parsley in the individual soup bowls.

German Cabbage Soup

I call this German cabbage soup. The person I learned to make it from called it "cabbage soup." He was German.

Yield: 8 to 10 portions

INGREDIENTS

1 head cabbage, shredded or very thinly sliced
¼ c. clarified butter
½ lb. bacon, cut into lardons
2 c. diced onions
1 tbsp. minced garlic
2 c. peeled, seeded, and diced tomatoes
½ c. tomato purée
2 bay leaves
1 tsp. thyme
salt, to taste
black pepper, to taste
3 qt. beef or chicken stock
¼ c. minced parsley

Method

1. In a stockpot, sauté the cabbage in the butter until it wilts.
2. In a sauté pan, cook the bacon until done. Strain the fat from the bacon.
3. Add the onions and garlic to the cabbage and continue to sauté.
4. When the onions have softened, add the tomatoes, purée, bay leaves, thyme, salt, and pepper to the pot. Continue cooking for an additional 5 minutes.
5. Add the stock to the pot. Add the bacon. Check the seasoning.
6. Add the parsley to the pot, cover, and simmer for 30 to 45 minutes.

What You Need to Know

The lardon is a piece of bacon cut across the grain into a piece about ½ inch by the width of a piece of bacon.

Corn Chowder with Green Chiles

I like to use either Peaches and Cream or Silver Queen corn for this recipe. As to the chiles, I like both the Anaheims and the poblanos.

Yield: 8 to 10 portions

INGREDIENTS

10 ears corn on the cob
1½ c. minced yellow onion
1 tbsp. minced garlic
1 c. clarified butter
6–8 green Anaheim chiles, roasted and peeled
3 qt. chicken stock
salt, to taste
white pepper, to taste
½ c. flour
1½ c. heavy cream

Method

1. Shuck the corn and remove the silk. Using a chef's knife, remove the corn from the ears. Use the back of the knife to scrape the cob to remove the "milk."
2. In a stockpot, sweat the corn, onion, and garlic in 4 ounces of the clarified butter for 4 to 5 minutes.

3. Dice the roasted and peeled chiles and add them to the corn mixture. Sweat an additional 2 to 3 minutes.
4. Add stock to the pot along with the salt and pepper.
5. While the soup simmers for about 15 minutes, make a light blond roux with the flour and remaining butter.
6. Thoroughly incorporate the roux using a wire whip.
7. Add cream and check the seasoning.

Note: If you desire spicier chowder, add one or two roasted, peeled, seeded, and diced jalapeño or serrano chiles.

Purée of Mushrooms and Green Chiles

I took a trip one fine fall day down to Pigeon Point south of San Francisco. The manager of an oyster farm there had invited me to look over the operation. After we ate a bunch of raw oysters, I asked him if there was a good place for lunch nearby. He told me to drive into Pescadero and look for Duarte's. I drove through artichoke fields, and there it was right in the middle of town. I had a soup very much like this one that day.

Yield: 8 to 10 portions

INGREDIENTS
2 lb. mushrooms
2 lemons
8–10 green chiles, roasted, peeled, and diced
1 c. minced yellow onion
1 tbsp. minced garlic
1 tsp. minced fresh ginger
1 c. clarified butter
1 tsp. thyme
2 bay leaves
1 tbsp. turmeric
salt, to taste
white pepper, to taste
3 qt. chicken stock
½ c. flour
2 c. heavy cream

Method

1. Slice mushrooms thinly to extract the maximum flavor and squeeze the juice of the two lemons over them. Toss to coat evenly.
2. In a stockpot, sweat the mushrooms, chiles, onion, garlic, and ginger in ½ cup of the clarified butter until the mushrooms exude their juices.
3. Add thyme, bay leaves, turmeric, salt, and white pepper and continue to sweat for another 4 to 5 minutes.
4. Add chicken stock and simmer for 15 minutes.
5. Purée the mushroom mixture in a food processor. Return to the pot.
6. Make a light blond roux with the remaining butter and the flour. Thoroughly incorporate the roux in the soup.
7. Add the heavy cream and simmer for 15 minutes.

Soupe a l'Oignon, Gratinée

This is the soup most Americans know as French onion soup. Of course, it is not the only French onion soup. There are many. This is the one with the cheese, folks. I prefer to slice the cheese for the soup because I like the rustic look of it draped over the sides of the bowl. This may be the best-known soup that features the "sop" of bread from which we derive the word "soup."

Yield: 10 to 12 portions

INGREDIENTS

3 lb. yellow onions, thinly sliced
¾ c. clarified butter
1 tbsp. sugar
⅓ c. flour
3 qt. brown stock
salt, to taste
black pepper, to taste
1 c. dry white wine
¼ c. brandy
6–8 garlic croutons
6–12 oz. Swiss cheese, Jarlsburg or Emmenthaler, grated or
    thinly sliced

Method

1. In a stockpot, sweat the onions gently in the butter for 10 to 15 minutes.
2. Add the sugar to aid in the caramelization; raise the heat to high and brown the onions.
3. Add the flour and cook until it is light brown.
4. Add the brown stock, salt, pepper, wine, and brandy. Check for seasoning. Simmer for 45 minutes to an hour.
5. Ladle the soup into ovenproof bowls, float a crouton on the top of each, place however much cheese you like on top of the crouton, and bake in a hot oven, near the top, until the cheese melts and begins to brown.

What You Need to Know

Croutons come in all shapes and sizes. These are not the little cubes Americans sprinkle on their salads. In classical cookery, the crouton, probably originating in 17th-century France, is most often a round of toasted or grilled bread. I like to cut croutons round to fit my soup bowls. Brush them with garlic oil and toast them in the oven until they are golden brown.

French Fisherman's Soup

This is similar to a soup I first made when I was night chef at the original Scott's Seafood Grill & Bar in San Francisco.

Yield: 8 to 10 portions

INGREDIENTS

1 c. diced onion
1 c. diced carrots
1 tbsp. minced garlic
4 oz. extra virgin olive oil
4 c. peeled, seeded, and diced tomatoes
2 bay leaves
1 tbsp. thyme
2 tsp. tarragon
2 tbsp. minced parsley
salt, to taste
black pepper, to taste
1 c. dry white wine

3 qt. fish, shellfish, or chicken stock
2–3 tbsp. Dijon mustard
12–16 oz. fish filets, firm-fleshed (rockfish, swordfish, snapper, etc.),
    cut into 1-in. cubes

(**Method**)

1. Sweat the onions, carrots, and garlic in the butter or oil until just soft.
2. Add the tomatoes, bay leaves, thyme, tarragon, parsley, salt, and pepper and continue to sweat for 4 to 5 minutes over medium heat.
3. Deglaze the pan with the white wine, raise the heat, and boil the alcohol away.
4. Add the stock and Dijon mustard, bring to a boil, reduce to a simmer, cover, and simmer for about 20 minutes.
5. Add fish pieces and poach until they are cooked through.

Note: You may also add shrimp, scallops, or crab to the soup.

Scotch Broth

This is a *really* hearty soup. I use the sirloin I reserve from a leg of lamb when I bone it.

Yield: 8 to 10 portions

INGREDIENTS

1 c. barley
3 qt. brown stock
2 c. mirepoix
¾ c. peeled and diced turnips
1 tbsp. minced garlic
salt, to taste
black pepper, to taste
½ c. clarified butter
2 c. roasted, diced lamb
3 bay leaves
1 tsp. thyme
2 tbsp. minced parsley

Method

1. In a stockpot, bring the barley to a boil in the brown stock. Boil for 3 to 5 minutes, place a lid on the pot, and turn the heat off. Allow the pot to rest for 1 hour.
2. While the barley is softening, in a sauté pan, sauté the mirepoix and turnips over high heat until they are beginning to brown.
3. Add the garlic, salt, pepper, lamb, bay leaves, and thyme to the sauté pan and continue to cook, stirring the mixture, for 5 to 6 minutes.
4. After the hour has elapsed, add the contents of the sauté pan to the stock and barley. Bring the pot to a simmer and simmer, covered, for 1 hour.
5. Add the minced parsley. Check the seasoning. Add more stock if necessary.

New England Clam Chowder

Not often will you find me recommending a canned product. But for the following soup, if you are unable to obtain fresh clams, the canned baby clams make an excellent soup.

Yield: 8 to 10 portions

INGREDIENTS
4 c. littleneck clams, fresh or canned
2 c. liquid from the clams or clam broth
½ lb. bacon, lardons, blanched
3 c. mirepoix
½ c. clarified butter
1 tbsp. minced garlic
3 c. diced potatoes
2 qt. fish, shellfish, or chicken stock
2 bay leaves
2 tsp. thyme
2 tsp. tarragon
salt, to taste
black pepper, to taste
2 c. milk
¾ c. flour
2 c. heavy cream

> **Method**

1. If you are using fresh clams, scrub them well and place them in a stockpot with 1 quart of water. Place a lid on the pot and place it on high heat. Steam the clams until they are all open. Reserve the liquid. Remove the clams from the shells. Dice.
2. Sauté the bacon until it is cooked. Strain the fat away, reserving a couple of tablespoons.
3. Sweat the mirepoix in 1 ounce of the clarified butter and the bacon fat until the vegetables are just soft. Add the garlic and sweat 2 to 3 more minutes.
4. Blanch the potatoes in boiling water for 10 to 12 minutes. Drain.
5. Place the stock, broth, bay leaves, thyme, tarragon, salt, and pepper in a stockpot and bring to a boil. Reduce to a simmer.
6. Add clams, bacon, mirepoix, potatoes, and milk to the pot. Simmer for 15 minutes.
7. Make light blond roux with the flour and remaining butter. Thoroughly incorporate this roux into the chowder with a wire whip. Continue to simmer. Add cream and parsley.

Split Pea Soup

The split pea, along with the lentil, is the quickest of the legumes to rehydrate. Notice the use of the roux, in this instance to "bind" the soup and prevent stratification.

Yield: 8 to 10 portions

INGREDIENTS

1 lb. split peas, washed
3 qt. water
½ lb. bacon, lardons, blanched and sautéed
3 c. mirepoix
3 bay leaves
1 tbsp. thyme
salt, to taste
black pepper, to taste
½ c. clarified butter
2 c. shredded romaine lettuce
¼ c. flour
½ lb. spicy sausage (chaurice, Italian, chorizo, etc.)
¼ c. minced parsley

Method

1. Place the split peas and water in a stockpot with the bacon. Bring the pot to a boil; boil for 5 minutes. Place a lid on the pot and allow it to sit undisturbed for 1 hour.
2. While you are waiting for the peas, sweat the mirepoix, with the bay leaves, thyme, salt, and pepper, in 2 ounces of the clarified butter.
3. After the waiting period has elapsed, add the mirepoix and the romaine to the pot and simmer for about 45 minutes to an hour.
4. Make a light blond roux with the remaining butter and the flour.
5. Slice the sausages thinly.
6. With a wire whip, incorporate the roux in the soup.
7. Add the sausage and check the seasoning.
8. Garnish with the minced parsley.

Purée of White Bean and Claret Soup

Here is the opposite end of the "hardness scale" for dried legumes. If you use the Great Northern bean for this soup, the difference will not be so great. The "small white bean," which I prefer, has the longest rehydration time of any of the dried legumes.

Yield: 8 to 10 portions

INGREDIENTS

1 lb. white beans, washed, boiled, and soaked
3 c. dry red wine
2½ qt. water
3 c. mirepoix
1 c. diced ham
1 tbsp. minced garlic
1 tbsp. thyme
4 bay leaves
salt, to taste
black pepper, to taste
½ c. clarified butter
2 c. peeled, seeded, and diced tomatoes
½ c. tomato purée
¼ c. flour

Method

1. Place beans and water in a stockpot.
2. In a sauté pan, sweat mirepoix, ham, and garlic along with thyme, bay leaves, salt, and pepper in 2 ounces of the clarified butter until the vegetables are just soft.
3. Add tomatoes and purée and continue to sweat for an additional 4 to 5 minutes.
4. Add all ingredients in sauté pan to stockpot and simmer for about 45 minutes. Add wine.
5. Purée all in a food processor.
6. Make a light blond roux with the remaining butter and the flour. Incorporate roux.

Soupe au Pistou

This is a soup from Provence, which, of course, is right next to northern Italy, hence the "pistou" or pesto.

Yield: 8 to 10 portions

INGREDIENTS

3 qt. brown or white stock
2–3 c. white beans, soaked and cooked
4 c. mirepoix
2 c. peeled, diced potatoes
1 c. diced green beans
½ c. pistou (pesto; page 39)
1½ c. peeled, seeded, and diced tomatoes
2 tsp. whole thyme
2–3 bay leaves
salt, to taste
black pepper, to taste
saffron, pinch
4 oz. pasta, small noodles

Method

1. Simmer mirepoix, beans, and potatoes in stock for about 20 minutes.
2. Add beans, pistou, tomatoes, thyme, bay leaves, salt, pepper, and saffron and simmer for an additional 20 minutes.
3. Add pasta and simmer until done.

Cream of Tomato with Fresh Basil

I like to serve this soup in a footed French soup bowl, ovenproof of course, with a square of puff pastry draped over the top. I had soup much like this one at a luncheon at Domaine Chandon many years ago.

Yield: 8 to 10 portions

INGREDIENTS

2 c. mirepoix
3 tbsp. clarified butter
1 tbsp. minced garlic
3 bay leaves
1 tbsp. fresh thyme
2–3 tbsp. fresh basil
6 c. peeled, seeded, and chopped tomatoes
3 qt. chicken stock
2 c. tomato juice
salt, to taste
black pepper, to taste
2 c. heavy cream
1 c. julienned leeks
2–3 sheets puff pastry (10- by 15-in.)

Method

1. Sweat mirepoix, garlic, and herbs in the clarified butter for 3 to 4 minutes.
2. Add tomatoes and continue to sweat for an additional 2 to 3 minutes.
3. Add chicken stock and tomato juice and simmer for 25 to 30 minutes.
4. Add salt and pepper. Use the salt with discretion, as tomato juice is most often quite salty.
5. Purée the soup in the food processor or put it through the food mill.
6. Add heavy cream and taste for balance. Add leeks to soup.
7. Cut squares of puff pastry large enough to cover your bowls and drape over the bowl. Bake for about 10 to 12 minutes or until the pastry has puffed and is golden brown.

Note: You may substitute pesto for the basil.

Cream of Mushroom Soup

This deceptively simple soup is one of my favorites. It can be different every time you make it; just change your mushroom variety. I have made it with button mushrooms, oyster mushrooms, shiitakes, and even dried wild mushroom mixes.

Yield: 8 to 10 portions

INGREDIENTS

2 lb. mushrooms, thinly sliced
½ c. butter
1 tsp. thyme
1 tbsp. minced garlic
salt, to taste
white pepper, to taste
1½ qt. chicken stock
1½ qt. milk
3 or 4 bay leaves
¼ c. lemon juice
6 oz. blond roux
1 c. heavy cream

Method

1. Sweat mushrooms in butter until they exude their juices.
2. Add thyme, garlic, salt, and pepper. Sweat for another minute or two.
3. Add stock, milk, and bay leaves and simmer for about 20 minutes.
4. Add and thoroughly incorporate roux.
5. Add heavy cream and check the seasoning.

Chilled Avocado Soup with Salsa Fresca

Here is a cold soup. I have cut back on portion quantities here. You will notice I do not have the usual 3 quarts of liquid I mentioned at the beginning of the soup section. This soup is so rich that you must serve a smaller portion if you expect your diners to be able to eat anything else.

Yield: 8 to 10 portions

INGREDIENTS

6 avocados, preferably Hass, peeled and pitted
2 tbsp. lemon juice
2 tbsp. lime juice
3 c. chicken stock
3 c. half-and-half
salt, to taste
black pepper, to taste

Method

1. Purée avocados with lemon and lime juices in processor.
2. Add stock, half-and-half, salt, and pepper to processor and continue to process.
3. Chill for at least 1 hour.
4. Garnish with a swirl of the salsa fresca.

Salsa Fresca

INGREDIENTS

12 Roma tomatoes, finely chopped
2 bell peppers (red, green, and/or yellow), minced
1–2 jalapeños, finely sliced
6 green onions, minced
1 tbsp. minced garlic
1 tbsp. fresh minced cilantro
1 tsp. cumin
salt, to taste
black pepper, to taste

If you desire the salsa hotter, you may add some crushed red pepper, serrano chiles, or more jalapeños.

Sopa de Albóndigas

This is a traditional southwestern soup. *Albóndigas* are meatballs.
Yield: 8 to 10 portions

INGREDIENTS

8 oz. ground chuck
8 oz. ground pork shoulder
¾ c. finely ground bread crumbs
½ c. minced onion
1 tbsp. minced garlic
1 tbsp. finely minced cilantro
½ c. finely minced green chiles
¼ c. heavy cream
1 egg, lightly beaten
salt, to taste
black pepper, to taste

1 c. zucchini, 2-in. julienne
1 c. carrots, 2-in. julienne
3 qt. beef or chicken stock

Method

1. In a mixing bowl, combine chuck, pork, bread crumbs, onion, garlic, cilantro, chiles, cream, egg, salt, and pepper.
2. Lightly form into meatballs approximately 1 inch across.
3. Bring stock to simmer. Add meatballs and poach about 10 minutes.
4. Add zucchini and carrots and poach an additional 10 minutes.
5. Serve garnished with chopped cilantro or parsley.

Minestrone

There are no strict requirements for the ingredients in minestrone. This is vegetable soup with pasta or, occasionally, in Milan, rice. You may logically substitute pesto for the basil since both the purée and this soup had their origins in Genoa.

Yield: 10 to 12 portions

INGREDIENTS

1 c. cranberry or pinto beans, soaked and cooked
2 onions, diced
4 ribs celery, diced
1 c. diced carrots
2 c. finely shredded cabbage
½ c. extra virgin olive oil
12–16 Roma tomatoes, peeled, seeded, and diced
3 bay leaves
1 tbsp. oregano
1 tbsp. fresh minced basil
1 tbsp. thyme
salt, to taste
black pepper, to taste
½ lb. pancetta, blanched, diced, and sautéed
1½ c. peeled, diced potatoes
2½ qt. brown, white, chicken, or veal stock
1 c. fresh pasta, cut into 1-in. pieces
¼ c. parmesan

Method

1. Drain beans.
2. Sauté onions, celery, carrots, and cabbage in olive oil until all wilt.
3. Add tomatoes, bay leaves, oregano, basil, thyme, salt, and pepper and continue to sauté.
4. Add pancetta, potatoes, stock, and beans to pot; bring to boil; reduce to a simmer; and cook for 30 minutes.
5. Add pasta and cook for 7 to 8 minutes.
6. Serve with grated parmesan and minced parsley.

Lentil Soup

This very nutritious legume is making major inroads into American cuisine. I see it more and more being served as a vegetable in quality restaurants—very often with braised dishes.

Yield: 8 to 10 portions

INGREDIENTS

1 lb. lentils, rinsed, boiled, and soaked
3 qt. beef or chicken stock
2 c. mirepoix
¼ c. olive oil
1 tbsp. minced garlic
1 c. diced leeks
1 c. sliced spicy sausage (such as andouille)
1 c. peeled, diced potatoes
1 tbsp. whole oregano
3 bay leaves
1 tsp. thyme
2 c. peeled, seeded, and chopped tomatoes
salt, to taste
black pepper, to taste
¼ c. chopped parsley

Method

1. Place lentils in stock and bring to a simmer.
2. In a sauté pan, sweat mirepoix in olive oil over medium heat until vegetables are soft.
3. Add garlic to mirepoix.

4. Add sausage, potatoes, oregano, bay leaves, and thyme and continue to sauté.
5. Add tomatoes to sauté pan. Add salt and pepper.
6. Add all vegetables and spices to pot with lentils and simmer, covered, for about 45 minutes.
7. Add parsley and serve.

Hot and Sour Soup

When I eat in a Chinese restaurant, I usually look for this soup first. If this is not on the menu, I look for "sizzling rice soup."

Yield: 8 to 10 portions

INGREDIENTS

3 qt. beef or chicken stock
½ lb. pork, shredded or ground, cooked or raw
½ c. shredded bamboo shoots
1 c. sliced Asian mushrooms
½ c. sliced water chestnuts
1 c. julienned snow peas
1 c. sliced green onion
2 eggs, lightly beaten
1 c. cold stock
2½ tbsp. cornstarch
2 tbsp. soy sauce
½ tsp. Tabasco
½ tsp. hot sesame oil or chile paste
salt, to taste
black pepper, to taste
½ c. rice vinegar
½ lb. tofu, diced into 1-in. cubes

Method

1. Bring stock to a boil.
2. Add pork to stock and simmer until cooked (if raw).
3. Add vegetables to stock.
4. Mix cold stock with cornstarch and soy sauce. Add to soup and thoroughly incorporate.
5. Slowly add egg, stirring constantly.
6. Remove from heat and add hot oil, salt, pepper, vinegar, and tofu and warm through.

Gazpacho Toledano

"Gazpacho" does not mean a cold tomato soup/salad with a bunch of vegetables chopped up in it. Nor is the word Spanish. It is from Arabic and means "soaked bread." You add the croutons to the soup, and they become "soaked." Toledo was an area where the Moors held sway in Spain. It also has a pretty good view.

Yield: 8 to 10 portions

INGREDIENTS

10 c. peeled and seeded tomatoes
4 cucumbers, peeled, seeded, and diced
4 red bell peppers
4 green bell peppers
2 c. diced yellow onion
1 tbsp. cumin
3 tbsp. paprika
1 tbsp. fresh cilantro
4 jalapeños, minced
1 qt. tomato juice
½ c. red wine vinegar
¾ c. extra virgin olive oil
2 tbsp. minced garlic
salt, to taste
black pepper, to taste
2 c. croutons

Method

1. In a food processor, purée 7 cups of the tomatoes, 2 cups of the cucumbers, and two each of each of the peppers.
2. Add all spices and herbs.
3. Add tomato juice.
4. Add vinegar and olive oil.
5. Set out individual bowls of the remaining vegetables and the croutons. These are used to garnish the soup.

Mulligatawny

This "Indian" soup comes from a city named Goa on the west coast of India. I placed Indian in quotes because it was probably made by an Indian cook for the British soldiers in Goa during the Raj period.

Yield: 8 to 10 portions

INGREDIENTS

2½ qt. chicken or beef stock
4 c. mirepoix
1 c. sliced mushrooms
1 tbsp. minced garlic
1 tsp. sea salt
1 tsp. black pepper
1 c. finely minced onions
¼ c. clarified butter (*usli ghee*)
⅜ c. flour
2 tbsp. curry powder
1 c. heavy cream
1–2 tbsp. fresh chopped cilantro

(**Method**)

1. Place the stock in a pot and bring to a boil.
2. Add mirepoix, mushrooms, garlic, salt, and pepper and simmer about 30 minutes.
3. Sauté the onions in the clarified butter until they caramelize. Add the flour and make a light blond roux.
4. Vigorously whisk this roux into the soup. Incorporate the cream. Garnish with the chopped cilantro.

Note: You may add diced chicken meat to the soup if you choose or spice it up with a little crushed red pepper.

Chili con Frijoles

This is not a purist's chili, nor is it meant to be. A purist would *never* put beans in his or her chili. This is the chili with beans many Americans grew up with. It is meant to be a comfort food for a cold winter day. It is not too spicy hot. The kids should enjoy this one. You may, of course, zing it up for an adult version by adding serranos, jalapeños, and/or additional crushed red chiles.

I've been dreading this, but I did tell you I would talk more about *chili* and *chile*.

The words "chile" and "chili" both come from an Aztec word for pepper. In temperate climes, there are two types of chile: *Capsicum frutescens* and *Capsicum annum*. The former are usually the hotter varieties.

The amount of heat in a chile is graded on the Scoville Scale. This method of measurement was devised in 1912 by a pharmacist named Wilbur Scoville.

The heat in a chile is carried by the capsaicin, a compound in all chiles. The scale runs from 0 units for the green bell pepper to 350,000 for the habañero.

Yield: 10 to 12 portions

INGREDIENTS

4 c. dried kidney beans
3 qt. cold water
2 lb. beef chuck, coarsely chopped, no sinew
½ c. clarified butter
2 c. diced yellow onion
1 tbsp. minced garlic
2 tbsp. chili powder
1 tbsp. whole oregano
2 tbsp. paprika
2 tbsp. cumin
1 tsp. crushed red chiles
2 c. canned Italian tomatoes
1 tbsp. salt
2 tsp. black pepper

Method

1. Wash the beans well. Place them in a large pot with the water. Bring to a rolling boil, cover, and boil for 5 minutes. Turn the fire off and permit the pot to stand undisturbed for an hour.
2. While the beans are soaking, brown the meat in 2 ounces of the clarified butter. Remove the meat from the pan, add 2 more ounces of the butter, and lightly brown the onions. Add the garlic about a minute before you are finished with the onions.
3. Add meat, onions and garlic, all spices, and the tomatoes to the pot with the beans. Simmer for about 1 hour.
4. Taste for seasoning and adjust accordingly.

Cream of Asparagus

Make sure you strain this soup. The strings in the stalks are not palatable!

Yield: 8 to 10 portions

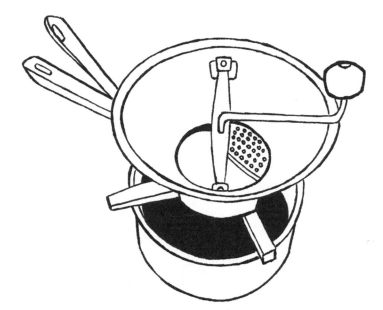

INGREDIENTS

2 lb. asparagus spears
½ c. butter
1 tbsp. thyme
1 tbsp. minced garlic
salt, to taste
white pepper, to taste
2½ qt. chicken stock
2½ qt. milk
3 or 4 bay leaves
¼ c. lemon juice
6 oz. blond roux
1 c. heavy cream

Method

1. Wash asparagus and break off tough bottom ends. Blanch the spears in boiling, salted water for about 6 or 7 minutes. Cut off the tips (1½–2 inches). Sweat the stalks in a little unsalted butter for 2 to 3 minutes. Purée in food processor.
2. Place purée in stockpot with thyme, garlic, salt, pepper, and stock.
3. Add milk and bay leaves and simmer for about 20 minutes. Push the puree through a sieve.

4. Add and thoroughly incorporate roux.
5. Add heavy cream and check the seasoning.
6. Place asparagus tips back in soup and heat through.

Black Bean Soup

Many cultures in Central and South America prefer the black bean to the pinto. I spent some time in Oaxaca in Mexico, and I don't think I ever saw a pinto bean.
    Yield: 8 to 10 portions

INGREDIENTS
1 lb. black beans
3 qt. beef stock
½ lb. ham, julienned
½ lb. smoked sausage, thinly sliced
2 c. mirepoix
1 tbsp. minced garlic
4 bay leaves
2 tsp. whole thyme
2 tsp. crushed red pepper
1 tbsp. salt
black pepper, to taste
½ c. brandy

Method

1. Reconstitute beans by boiling for 5 minutes and soaking, covered, for 1 hour.
2. Drain water from beans.
3. Place beans, stock, and all other ingredients, except brandy, in stock pot and simmer until done, about one hour.
4. Add brandy and check seasoning before serving. May be garnished with croutons or some fresh chopped cilantro.

Weisse Bohnensuppe

Here is a hearty German white bean soup.
    Yield: 8 to 10 portions

Ingredients

1 lb. white or navy beans
water, to cover
½ lb. smoked ham hock or ends
2½ qt. beef or chicken stock
1½ c. diced onions
1 tsp. whole thyme
2 bay leaves
2 tbsp. minced parsley
2 cloves garlic, minced
2 c. diced celery
1 c. diced carrots
salt, to taste
black pepper, to taste

Method

1. Cover beans with water, bring to boil for 5 minutes, cover, and allow to stand for 1 hour. Drain.
2. Return to pot with ham, thyme, bay leaves, salt, pepper, and stock. Simmer for 1 hour.
3. Add remaining ingredients and simmer for an additional 30 minutes.
4. If a ham hock was used, remove the meat from the bone and return to the soup.

Beer and Cheddar Soup

This is another German soup, but it is much lighter than you might think given the cheese as an ingredient.

Yield: 8 to 10 portions

Ingredients

¼ c. clarified butter
1½ c. diced yellow onion
1 tbsp. minced garlic
1½ qt. beef or chicken stock
12 oz. beer
salt, to taste
black pepper, to taste

1½ c. grated sharp cheddar cheese
1 c. bread crumbs
¼ c. minced parsley
1 tsp. paprika
1½ c. croutons
1 c. blond roux

Method

1. Place clarified butter in a stockpot.
2. Add onions and garlic and sweat until translucent.
3. Add stock, beer, salt, and pepper. Bring to a simmer.
4. Add cheese and melt.
5. Add bread crumbs, parsley, and paprika. Add roux.
6. Garnish with croutons and a little paprika and parsley.

Note: You may add some cheese to the top of the soup and gratinee it under a salamander or overhead broiler.

Potato Soup with Gorgonzola and Bacon

This would probably have to be in my top 10 soups. The strong flavors of the Gorgonzola and bacon seem to complement each other and make a very mellow blend.

Yield: 8 to 10 portions

Ingredients

½ lb. bacon, lardons
2 c. diced onion
2 c. diced celery
3 or 4 carrots, peeled and diced
2½ qt. chicken stock
4 potatoes, 80-count, diced
2 c. milk
1 c. heavy cream
8 oz. Gorgonzola, crumbled
blond roux, as needed
salt, to taste
white pepper, to taste
¼ c. minced parsley

Method

1. Cook bacon in heavy large pot over medium heat until brown and crisp. Remove from pot.
2. Pour off all but ¼ cup of bacon fat.
3. Sweat onions, carrots, and celery.
4. Add stock, potatoes, and milk.
5. Simmer until all vegetables are tender.
6. Add heavy cream.
7. Place cheese in processor and add 3 or 4 cups of soup. Purée.
8. Return purée to pot.
9. Add roux as needed.
10. Add bacon and parsley.

Pasta e Fagioli (faj-ee-oh-lee)

This is a true Italian classic.
Yield: 8 to 10 portions

INGREDIENTS

½ lb. bacon, lardons (or pancetta)
2 yellow onions, finely chopped
2 tbsp. minced garlic
4 ribs celery, diced
2 carrots, thinly sliced
3 qt. chicken stock
3 c. white beans, soaked and boiled
3 c. canned Roma tomatoes
1½ c. tubetti or other small tubular pasta
½ c. minced parsley
parmesan, to taste

Method

1. In a heavy saucepan, cook the bacon (or pancetta) over moderate heat, stirring, until it is crisp. Pour off all but 3 tablespoons of the fat, and in the remaining fat cook the onion and the garlic, stirring, until the onion is softened.
2. Add the celery, the carrot, and the stock and simmer the mixture, covered, for 5 minutes.

3. In a bowl, mash ⅓ cup of the beans, stir them into the bacon mixture with the remaining whole beans and the tomatoes, and simmer the mixture, covered, stirring occasionally, for 5 minutes.

4. Stir in the tubetti and simmer the soup, covered, for 10 minutes or until the pasta is al dente.

5. Let the soup stand off the heat, covered, for 5 minutes; stir in the parsley; and serve the soup in bowls sprinkled with the parmesan.

Gombo aux Crabes et Chevrettes
(Seafood Gumbo)

The word "gumbo," or *gombo*, comes from Africa and originally meant "okra." In the strictest sense, a dish without okra cannot be a gumbo. In reality, today, there are two basic types of gumbo: gumbo containing okra as a thickening and flavor ingredient and gumbo containing "filé" powder, which formerly was the ground root of sassafras but now often takes the form of sassafras and thyme ground together. No real Louisiana cook would use both okra and filé in the same dish. The Choctaw Indians introduced filé to the New Orleans market.

Gumbo is a dish that may be described as either soup, if it is kept thin and meant to be served as a course early in the meal, or a stew, if thick and ingredient laden, meant to be served as a main course. I usually elect the latter. It is served with steamed or boiled rice.

The only "trick" involved here is the stock. If you use a stock in the gumbo, you do not need to cook the seafoods and vegetables until they become an ambiguous culinary bayou.

Yield: 10 to 12 portions

INGREDIENTS

1 lb. fresh okra, sliced into ¾-in. disks
1 c. clarified butter
2 c. thinly sliced yellow onion
4–6 ribs celery, sliced ½-in. thick on a 45° angle
2 tbsp. finely minced garlic
3 or 4 bay leaves
1 tbsp. whole thyme
cayenne pepper, to taste
white pepper, to taste
black pepper, to taste
1 tsp. salt
3 c. peeled, seeded, and chopped tomatoes

1 tsp. finely minced cilantro
2 tbsp. finely minced parsley
2–12 crabs, blue or Dungeness
2 lb. large shrimp, boiled in court-bouillon
1 gal. court-bouillon
½ c. flour
Tabasco, to taste
Worcestershire sauce, to taste

Method

1. Sweat the okra in half of the hot clarified butter until it exudes the shiny mucilaginous substance inside. One of the secrets to making good gumbo is cooking this "slime."
2. Add onions and celery and continue cooking until the onion is translucent.
3. Add garlic, thyme, peppers, and salt and continue to sauté for 2 or 3 minutes.
4. Add tomatoes, cilantro, and parsley. Sauté 1 minute.
5. Add crabs and shrimp. Sauté briefly.
6. Add stock. Bring to boil. Reduce to simmer and simmer, covered, for about 10 minutes.
7. While the gumbo is simmering, make a light brown roux with the remaining butter and the flour.
8. Using a wire whisk, thoroughly incorporate the roux in the gumbo.
9. Taste for the spice balance.
10. Add Tabasco and Worcestershire sauce to taste.
11. Simmer for an additional 10 minutes.
12. Serve over plain boiled or steamed rice.

EXTRACTION: A GANDER AT SAUCE AND SOUP ON THE LOOSE

What I hope you take away from this chapter is the fact that you proceed entirely differently for liquid foods than you do for solids. The salient points are these: Begin foods in cold water without salt to extract flavor and nutrition from solids into a liquid. Remember that sauces should be thought of as more than just accoutrements. They, too, should be as nutritional as possible. Use water in which you have cooked vegetables or poached seafoods or meats whenever possible. Lighten up! Once you have a handle on the basic soup-making techniques, you should be able to devise many soups without ever taking a gander at a recipe.

THE FIVE TECHNIQUES: NO EXCUSES!

Now you are ready to cook like a chef!

In these chapters, I have shared the five techniques with you. Now you have all the ammunition you need confidently to set your sights on any savory dish on the planet—and a few desserts as well. Once you feel that you have comfortably grasped the essence of each technique, the *entire* world of cookbooks and recipes is open to you.

Recipe Index by Course

Soups and Stocks

About the Author

Chef **Joseph Carey** was born in New Orleans. He worked in restaurants while attending college at Louisiana State University and Indiana University. He has a degree in English literature from the latter. Carey worked as an executive chef in San Francisco for sixteen years, where he opened five restaurants. He then left to establish the Memphis Culinary Academy, and in Memphis he opened three distinguished restaurants. He was Memphis' first Certified Executive Chef.

Four times a year, he teaches his ten-week Professional Class to students who wish to become professional chefs. The local chapter of the American Culinary Federation elected Chef Carey to be president of the association twice. In addition to his cooking talents, he is sought after for other culinary expertise: Chef Carey designed the kitchen for the restaurant in the Brooks Museum of Art in Memphis.

He has done three local television series. The local ABC affiliate, WHBQ, hired him for an evening news spot called A Taste of Memphis; for three years, he was a regular with his cooking tips on the noon news on the local CBS affiliate, WREG; and for many years, Chef Carey did a half hour show on local Cablevision called *The American Epicure*. He has been interviewed on television in singular appearances, as well.

When national celebrities such as Tom Cruise and Debbie Rose come to Memphis, Chef Carey is consulted on a regular basis for recommendations for personal chefs and has provided chefs trained by himself to such well-known people as Dixie Carter, Annie Potts, and Hal Holbrook. He has trained cooks to cater for the artist formerly known as Prince and to George Thoroughgood. He has cooked for the Egyptian and Irish ambassadors to the United States.